THE GENIUS OF JUDAISM

THE
GENIUS
OF
JUDAISM

Bernard-Henri
Lévy

Translated by
Steven B. Kennedy

RANDOM HOUSE
NEW YORK

363 0011

Published in the United States by Random House,
an imprint and division of
Penguin Random House LLC, New York.

RANDOM HOUSE and the HOUSE colophon are
registered trademarks of
Penguin Random House LLC.

Translation by Steven B. Kennedy

LIBRARY OF CONGRESS CATALOGING-IN-PUBLICATION DATA
NAMES: Lévy, Bernard-Henri, author. | Kennedy, Steven, translator.
TITLE: The genius of Judaism / Bernard-Henri Lévy; translated by Steven B. Kennedy.
Other titles: *L'esprit du Judaïsme*. English
DESCRIPTION: New York: Random House, [2017] | Includes index.
IDENTIFIERS: LCCN 2016037490 | ISBN 9780812992724 | ISBN 9780679643791 (ebook)
SUBJECTS: LCSH: Judaism—Philosophy. | Judaism—Customs and practices.
CLASSIFICATION: LCC BM565 .L4613 2017 | DDC 296—dc23 LC record available
at https://lccn.loc.gov/2016037490

Printed in the United States of America on acid-free paper

randomhousebooks.com

2 4 6 8 9 7 5 3 1

FIRST EDITION

Book design by Carole Lowenstein

CONTENTS

PROLOGUE

It was 1979.

I was thirty years old.

The revolutionary era had sighed its last in the killing fields of Cambodia.

A scent of dry powder hung in the air over the great capitals, mingling with an insouciant sense that it was a good time to be alive.

We were sure that we were at the apogee of the age in which God had died.

It had been beautiful.

It had been huge.

Rarely had humanity seemed so radiant as in this century of doubt and skepticism, during which we had burned all of our idols, all of our religions, in the joyful fire of atheism.

Or, rather, no. The temples, the devourers of men and destinies, were the pyre. From Giordano Bruno to Nietzsche, and then from the death of God to that of Divine Man, there had been intrepid liberators who faced the blaze, some burning, some wielding torches—and we felt we were their heirs.

A moment of rejoicing.

An unparalleled triumph of freedom.

That triumph cost countless dead and wounded. It had required unprecedented acts of heroism. But God's fire had gone out. The ashes had been scattered. And we found ourselves alone, finally alone, in a world more suited to our wishes because (we thought) we had disenchanted it and could now savor the pure pleasure of being ourselves without fearing the slings and arrows of the censors.

Anything was possible.

Everything seemed to be permitted.

I recall that time as a long and languorous Sabbath of the spirit.

. . .

But doubt gripped the less credulous among us.

What if this was a deception?

A trap?

What if the coin had another side?

What if a shadow of doubt, a new kind of doubt, forced us to doubt our previous doubt?

What if, behind the funeral pyre of subjugating religion, behind the celebration of the universal federation in which the tree of life was to have triumphed over the vultures of the moral order, a worried eye could discern the silhouettes of other, more-ancient gods that one had given up for dead but that were creeping back into the world?

It was during this time that I met Emmanuel Levinas.

And then, in the United States, the Catholic philosopher René Girard.

A little later, I encountered Franz Rosenzweig's great work, which had finally been translated into French.

This was the time when I began to wonder, with these thinkers, in their footsteps, whether humanity could do without gods, if it could topple the supreme god without risking the return of the others, all the others, all those gods of ancient Indo-European paganism and the even more pernicious modern, political gods—Thor, Wotan, Prometheus unchained, hydras and dragons, the gods of race and history, of scourging nature and of science without limits, the damming of whose bloody invasiveness had required the full strength of the One God but of which nothing now blocked the return.

Above all it was the time when a growing number of texts and signs began to suggest that we should not rule out the possibility that yesterday's Judeo-Christian inquisitors might once have been, and might once again become, the inventors, the liberators, the saviors of a fragile and constantly imperiled idea, an idea that was again being surrounded by the dark tide of neo-pagan bestiality: man, man alone, that Adam who new Jewish intellectuals insisted (but who was listening?) was tenable only if conceived simultaneously as *adama* (born of the earth and its dust) and as *bria, sekkhel,* or *yech me-aïn* (created anew as an emanation of an unknowable and immeasurable intelligence).

This is the time when, seized by a part of me of which I was unaware, grasped by a force that was instantly familiar but to which I had never before been exposed in the course of my career as a speaking being, I turned to the subject of Judaism and wrote a book called *Le Testament de Dieu* (*The Testament of God*).

It turned my intellectual life upside down.

Had I not discovered, with such wonder, the Torah and then the Talmud, I might not have been able to continue writing.

It's hard to express the shock I felt at realizing that I had before me books that my hands had never held, my eyes had never beheld, but in which my name, that most intimate of intimacies, found not the accident of an origin or an occupation (Smith the smith; Miller the miller . . .) but the necessity of a place that followed in turn from a long chain of meaning divided into verses, other proper names, acts to be accomplished, arguments to make or refute: a book of life in which a place had been made for me, springing—yes—from my name.

Another thing about which I have not said enough is the feeling of indescribable glory that coursed through me, like a ray of light from within an opaque shell, when I understood that those pages contained not only the entire mental apparatus needed by someone seeking to close the parentheses of philosophical and political atheism without yielding to the murky appeal of a return to magic, occultism, and, at bottom, religion but also the resolution of most of the impasses into which my young self had strayed, the answer to so many questions that my theoretical work had left hanging. They also contained provisions for the human and political adventure that I had begun in Bangladesh and that I sensed was gathering force.

I spoke that glory in French.

I would utter the words *la gloire des juifs* without provocation or vanity, steeping myself in that beautiful word *gloire,* one of the loveliest in the French language—that word of Bossuet's, favored by Racine for moments of grace and by Corneille for moments of strength, that word of Bach and Vivaldi, which I was listening to in those years, that word used by Chateaubriand, whom I have never tired of reading and rereading.

I would repeat *la gloire des juifs,* delighting in that red word, or orange-red, loving the feel of its guttural attack, with the hardest of our French consonants followed by the lightening and brightening of that "L," which sparkled with so many poetic memories, then flaring through the "OI," where French forgives itself for being nearly unaccented, and ending with the rugged "R," as if to contain, after all, that effusion of light.

But even though I was not yet speaking the phrase in Jewish terms, I had begun thinking it that way: awkwardly; painstakingly; putting the full resources of my soul into my first readings of Rashi and Maimonides and soon of Rabbi Chaim of Volozhin, Franz Rosenzweig, Nachman of Breslov, and many others.

The *hod* of Jewish splendor.

The *karnei hod,* the rays of light and glory, that flooded Moses's face upon his descent from Mount Sinai.

And the *kavod,* derived from *kaved* and also signifying glory, weight, and price—of a Jewish life not entirely unfulfilled.

And the *me'haïl el 'haïl,* literally "from strength into strength," that propels and accompanies the beauty, the brilliance, and (once again) the glory that emanate from destiny.

And the blue of the sky and of the kings of Israel, with its lighter but more volatile tint, the color of quivering air.

And the imperceptible white of their crown.

And the pale gold of the seraphim, or the purer, invisible gold of the cherubim on the cover of the holy ark.

The glory of the Jews, like the light gleaming in lines of rain falling to the ground, like shafts of sun over a misty land, like the trail of sparks left by the masters whose wisdom I was absorbing.

I knew that that sense of glory would never leave me.

I understood that I was experiencing a source of knowledge that would accompany me to the end of my days.

. . .

Indeed, it did not stop.

I remained faithful to the work of Levinas.

I resumed my conversation with a young master, Benny Lévy, a sort of Jewish imam who concealed himself for a generation.

And then, in the company of several wise men who guided my first steps into the jungle of the text, I studied as much as I could, but not enough, never enough, with the handicap of not mastering the language, a language I still have not mastered.

Nevertheless, the Talmud was mine.

The Bible was mine—as jealous, demanding, and insatiable as she is for every man.

When writing about Sartre or art, about *The Iliad* or *The Odyssey* of a novelistic hero in a race with the devil, about the decapitation of an American journalist in Karachi, about the United States, about Baudelaire, about France, or about Europe; when pursuing, from Bangladesh to Iraq and Afghanistan, from the Libyan desert to the mountains of Kurdistan, the dialogue with Islam that has been one of the most persistent themes of my life; or when embarking, in response to Frantz Fanon, in search of those wars that are forgotten only by those who have also forgotten the messianic music of the time, the Jewish thread was always there.

And the truth is that almost nothing of what I said and did during those decades seems completely intelligible to me unless I include the inner work on Judaism that I was pursuing in parallel—although not necessarily in secret.

Is it the feeling of having "advanced," as Benny Lévy was saying to me in the last conversation of ours that I can recall?

Is it the erosion of the Jewish exception, which I see wavering everywhere—not only, alas, among anti-Semites?

Is it, in fact, the return of anti-Semitism?

Is it the deepening of our misunderstanding with Muslims, my brothers in Adam?

Is it fear in the face of creeping nihilism and the prospect of new waves of destruction?

Or is it the feeling of having entered into one of those dark ages during which it becomes necessary to separate what must be separated and to reconcile what can be reconciled?

Whatever the answer, I wanted to come back to this.

I wanted to provoke a new encounter between my two tongues: the French of my mother and father and the Jewish language, which was theirs, as well, and which they spoke even more rarely than I.

I decided, in other words, to return to the questions that had first taken hold of me almost forty years ago and never left.

In these pages one will find reflections on the criminal fury of anti-Semitism that is brewing, on its new forms, and on the not inconsiderable fear that it inspires in me.

As well as others on the State of Israel, on the reasons for defending it, and on why, having existed for a human lifetime, it is a litmus test for Jews and non-Jews alike.

And, still more, I will try to untangle why I, a Jew, put my head and body, not once but many times, into certain countries where no being is under greater threat than the Jew and where hostility to the Jew is like a second religion.

But I will devote the essence of this book to the search for, and defense of, a certain idea of man and God, of history and time, of power, voice, light, sovereignty, revolt, memory, and nature—an idea that contains what I call, in homage to one of the few really great writers to have understood some of its mystery, the genius of Judaism.

PART ONE

THE GLORY OF THE JEWS

CHAPTER ONE

THE NEW GUISE
OF THE OLDEST FORM
OF HATE

There are persuasive reasons for a Jew of my stripe to try to ignore the mental leprosy of anti-Semitism.

One is that its adherents include too many mediocre minds whose feeble arguments gain credence simply in being refuted.

Another is that there is so much beauty in living Judaism, so many thoughts with the power to elevate the soul and give it reason to hope, that one yearns to focus on those and to share them.

Still another, as expressed by most of the rabbis, sages, and thought leaders who inhabit this book (if they did not actually voice it, they were thinking it so strongly that it did not need to be articulated), is that the last thing for which a Jew is made is to engage in a quarrel that is, in the final analysis, a quarrel of anti-Semites with themselves.

And this last reason: New explosions of hatred have erupted everywhere, explosions of which the Jews are not the specific targets. These developments appear designed to put entire countries, and even the world, in a state of siege and emergency response.

The fact remains that anti-Semitism exists.

Some had thought it dead, obsolete, cast aside.

Wrong.

It is back.

Making new connections.

It has even begun to strike and to kill—to growing indifference—in French cities.

And, moreover, because observers of the phenomenon often seem blind to its new reality and, believing that they are confronting it, grapple only with its shadows, I see no option but to begin by describing the new guise of the oldest form of hate.

THE VIRUS AND ITS MUTATIONS

For, in the beginning, are words.

Anti-Semitism is a very special form of madness, one of the features of which has always been, at every step in its history, choosing the right words to make its madness look reasonable.

At bottom, it is a language of pure rage, of brute violence without logic, which knows that it is never more convincing, never so strong or blessed with such a bright future, as when it succeeds in dressing up its resentment in legitimate-looking clothes.

And the anti-Semite is someone who, at the end of the day, has always managed to make it appear as if the hate that he feels for some is no more than the effect or reflection of the love he claims to feel for others.

There was the time when the anti-Semite said, "I don't hate the Jews so much as I adore the Lord Jesus Christ, whom the Jews so viciously abused." That was the Christian argument against a deicidal people.

There was the time, epitomized by the Enlightenment and its methodical nonbelief, when the anti-Semite corrected the first proposition, going so far as to reverse it: "These people must be detested not because they killed Christ but because they invented him." That was the agnostic if not atheistic anti-Semitism of those who, like Voltaire, faulted the Jews not for being deicidal but for having invented monotheism.

Toward the end of the nineteenth century, when the capitalist mode of production was firmly established, there arrived a third form of hate, which consisted of saying, "We don't care if the Jews invented or killed Christ—we are not firm enough in our belief or unbelief to give this matter the importance that devotees on both sides gave it over the centuries. We are socialists. We care about the underdog and, filled with this concern, with our consuming love for the sacred common man, determined to find and break the chains that hold him down, we have no choice but to declare that the Jews are at the center of the most extensive system of extortion ever devised by man. And it is for this reason that we go after them." That was the anti-Semitism of French polemicist Édouard Drumont, of the segment of the workers' movement that opposed the pro-Dreyfus party, which was perceived as the incarnation of the "banker's spirit" and the "mercantilist mind." It is that of the socialists who saw Dreyfus himself as the clandestine conductor of the gang of "rapacious crows," as the "yids of finance and politics," or even as a naked pretext employed by the "Jewifying and swindling crowd" to "wash away all the stains of Israel" (from a manifesto dated January 19, 1898, and signed by most of the socialist pundits of that time, including the great Jean Jaurès). It is the socialism for imbeciles that swears not to have anything against Jews (really, nothing!) but everything (really, everything!) against "Jewish capitalism" using Dreyfus's name to "rehabilitate" itself and "prevail" in the war it is waging against "the emaciated Christian nobility" allied with the "clerical" minority of the bourgeoisie (from the same manifesto).

More recently there was a fourth strain, contemporaneous with the triumph of the life sciences, which made possible a vision of the world unknown in ancient times (and, in particular, in the Christian age, when the monogenesis of the sons of Adam was never really disputed). That fourth strain was the racist vision of the world. "Like the socialists, we are neither Christian nor anti-Christian. We really don't care whether the Jews are tied to the deadly world of money. But what is in fact worrisome is that they constitute another race, an impure, mongrel race. And we find ourselves in the regrettable position of observing the ravages that that race has caused in the healthy and beautiful Aryan races." This is a wholly separate strain of anti-Semitism, distinct in its mottoes and its consequences. Born with Renan, Vacher de Lapouge, Chamberlain, and Gobineau, it is the anti-Semitism that made possible Hitler's Final Solution.

Four forms of anti-Semitism, each distinct from the one that preceded it.

Four forms that had to differ in order to resonate with the spirit of the era, adapt themselves to the era's capacities for action and perhaps to what it wanted to hear—and so to expand their audience and propagate optimally within the social echo chamber.

Forms that are like so many faces of the same demon spirit, which take over from one another, replace one another, and are, in Hegelian parlance, successively "relieved," either because the earlier face was no longer consistent with the sensibilities or the ideological needs of the new period (What does a follower of Voltaire care about the theme of a deicidal people? What does a follower of Hitler care about eliminating oppression?) or because the mask cracks and the alibi can no longer disguise the plainly criminal foundation for which it has served as a screen (as in the moment when Jaurès, who not only signed but also wrote most of the manifesto of January 19, 1898, cautioning the proletariat against taking sides between the two "rival bourgeois factions" that were tearing each other apart over Dreyfus, understands the trap into which he has fallen and chooses Zola's side) or because the mechanism put in place proves more criminal than anticipated (as was the case with the many anti-Semitic Catholics who realized, at the end, the unsuspected scale of the crimes committed in the name of Catholicism; as with the disciples of Maurras or even of Drumont, some of whom recoiled in horror before the evidence of the gas chambers and the reality of extermination!).

BEASTS CURED OF THE PLAGUE?

That is where we stand today.

That is precisely what is happening, once again, in the early years of this century.

There are still anti-Semitic Catholics, of course, but they are an isolated minority who keep a low profile when, by chance, they score a point, as when they persuaded John Paul II to canonize one of his predecessors, Pius IX, who believed Jews were "dogs" that could be heard "barking in the streets" and "bother us wherever we go."

There are still followers of Voltaire, unreconstructed tormentors of priests, die-hard secularists, who continue to think that the religion of the One God is the mother of all dictatorships, an insult to the freedom of the mind, a disease—and that the only way to get rid of Christianity is to hit it over the head or, even better, to pull it up by the roots, which, as everyone knows, are Jewish. But this, too, is marginal; it is a rear-guard struggle. Apart from a few God-is-dead throwbacks and oddly wired Nietzscheans, as well as those who mix everything up and confuse the fundamentalist deviations of theopolitical Islam with Islam writ large, not too many people believe that the war on faith is an urgent matter.

The habit of equating Jews with money and the Pavlovian diabolization that results from that equation have not been relegated to ancient history. But on this score the words of Georges Bernanos are borne out. In an article entitled "The Jewish Question—Again," which appeared in a Brazilian newspaper on May 24, 1944, Bernanos asserted that Hitler had "dishonored" anti-Semitism. An awful thing to say, of course, because it implies that anti-Semitism could be "honorable." But it expresses the terror that gripped the heirs of Socialism for Dummies when they discovered the vast cemeteries that Nazism had strewn around Europe, for which the tale of "moneyed Jews" was partly responsible. And the same remark might explain today how neither the financial crisis nor the patent misdeeds of globalized capitalism, nor, in France, the path taken by the young minister of the economy, Emmanuel Macron, through a bank with a name (Rothschild) that was, along with that of the Foulds and Péreires, one of the targets of Drumont's La France juive, will succeed in re-inflaming, except residually, the fevers of the era of the Dreyfus affair.

As for racist anti-Semitism; as for the idea that it is genes or consistency of biological or cultural traits that make Jews a legitimate target of hate; as for the will to "free the race," that is, to relentlessly and mercilessly "destroy" the foreign "forces" that are corrupting its healthy, glowing purity; as for the charge that had been made to a "horrible little Jew" (Georges Bernanos is speaking) named Adolphe Crémieux for naturalizing "en masse" a whole "horde" of Algerian Jews who had "nothing to do" with France, shared none of its "history" or "values," and did not even have the merit, like their Arab neighbors, of having formed military units to go and shed their blood in France's wars: Well, here we are at the heart of what Hitlerism indeed rendered practically inaudible. Tiny cells—sure. Handfuls of illiterates nostalgic for the Third Reich—that, too. But crowds of Europeans dreaming, seventy years after Auschwitz, of "destroying" the "Jewish race . . . by any means"? A political force calling for the revocation of the decree that I have to thank for the fact that, like many other children of soldiers in the French African army of 1943, I today am French? A mass movement calling, as did Drumont and Bernanos (not to mention Wagner and Chamberlain), for the "excision" of the Jewish "tumor"? No, we will not see that again.

In other words, anti-Semitism can reappear as a major force only by assuming a new guise.

It can recommence firing people up and mobilizing them on a grand scale only by acquiring a new way of speaking and a new sales pitch.

And that, in fact, is what has been happening for the last two or three decades with the gradual articulation and accumulation of a set of propositions that are, I repeat, new enough not to be fatally compromised by the criminal scenes of the past and, even more importantly, appear to be in step with present-day sensibilities, emotions, and preoccupations—and even with current notions of what is just, true, and good.

THE FOUNDATIONS FOR FUTURE RAVINGS

PROPOSITION NO. 1: We have nothing against the Jews. We reject in word and deed the toxic ideology that was anti-Semitism in ages past. But we must regretfully point out that being Jewish seems, in a great many cases, to be defined by allegiance to Israel, which is (1) illegitimate, because it was planted where it did not belong, and (2) colonialist, racist, fundamentally criminal, and even fascist in its attempts to silence the voices of its opponents. And so, despite our goodwill and anti-racist vigilance, despite the sympathy that we have always had and continue to have, in principle, with this victimized people and its ageless ordeals, we do not see how we can consider those who call themselves Jews innocent of this fascism. This is the anti-Zionist argument. It goes as follows: "How nice the Jew seemed during the war the world waged for him. But then came Zionism and, with it, the conversion of victim into executioner and the tragic and ruinous dialectic by which the Jew declares war against the world. No, that is not acceptable."

PROPOSITION NO. 2: We have nothing (truly, nothing) against the Jews, they say. Their suffering over the centuries inspires universal compassion. But it strikes us that the central argument of Zionism—the argument on which the right of Israel to exist is based and justified, and which is trotted out like a "moral sledgehammer" (the phrase was used by German novelist Martin Walser during a 1999 debate over the form of the memorial planned for the center of Berlin) whenever one raises the objection of the unforgivable spoliation that lies at the source of that existence—is the chapter in their history of suffering referred to as the Holocaust. So, they continue, what about this "Holocaust"? Is it not obvious that it is a murky crime whose historical verity has yet to be fully established? A misfortune that, if not wholly imaginary, is exaggerated by survivors and the children of survivors, who have made it into a religion? And even if not imagined or exaggerated, even if the numbers are accurate and the killing procedures are as described in the abundant literature associated with the "Holocaust industry," what are six million deaths on the scale not only of world history but of the wars of the twentieth century? And what is the purpose of the insistent claim to be the survivors of an unprecedented crime, unique in the annals of history and incomparable to any other, if not to make people feel guilty and, in the name of an infinite debt, demand limitless reparations? The reader will have recognized the more or less radical facets of this strange rant, which we know as Holocaust denial, Holocaust revisionism, and negationism. And we can see how a second terrible complaint is set up: How pathetic that these unscrupulous people lay claim to a dubiously exceptional status in order to build a state the very principle of which is unjustifiable! Shame on these traffickers in cadavers, who stop short

of no lie, no moral swindle, no trick of memory, to arrive at their criminal ends! They deserve not only hate but scorn, these brazen calcula-
tors who, to quash the legitimate objections that their underhanded
actions inspire in good people, dare to manipulate something that,
since time immemorial, humanity has held sacred: the memory of
their dead.

PROPOSITION NO. 3: Whether the Holocaust is a fiction or a detail does not matter. We will not be sucked, they add, into the irrelevant debate over the exceptional nature of the crime. Let us agree to
accept the version of it fed to us by the new religion. Even so, there are
two or three things that no one can possibly deny. There have been
many other crimes in contemporary times, some of which are being
committed right now under our eyes. One, in particular, involves the
Palestinians, and, in this matter, the survivors of the Holocaust are
not innocent, to say the least. Doesn't all this noise about the Holocaust make one wonder about the absence of noise about these other
crimes? Doesn't all the light shone on those who died yesterday or the
day before yesterday have the effect of obscuring the deaths occurring
today and tomorrow? And the Jews—with their *zakhor,* their obsession
with memory, the way they have of steeping us in a drama that everyone agrees is ancient, enveloped in the fog of old crimes, exempt from
the law of forgiveness—are they not committing a third crime, a very
specific and concrete one, the daily or almost daily cost of which can
be measured, which is to muffle the voices of the tortured people of
today; to ensure that, while noisily observing yesterday's default, we
are prevented from seeing, on our own doorstep, the faces of future
victims still living and still able to be saved; to contradict the doctrine
that "we are all victims," that alchemization of suffering into pleasure
is the real credo of our postmodern times; and, worst of all, to do all
this shushing knowingly and by design, to deploy this profusion of
resources, monuments, and injunction solely for the purpose of stifling the plea of the Palestinians (for example), which Israel has condemned to abject poverty and would, if it could, reduce to the status
of second-class martyrs, eligible for a lower level of treatment, justice,
and pity? That is the third argument, that of the competition of vic-

tims or—what amounts to the same thing—competitive memory: the idea that there is not enough room for us all on the stage where we remember eruptions of evil; the idea that a human heart is too small to hold more than one sadness, more than one grief, more than one outrage; the accusation that the Jews have been profiteers in misfortune, placing such great emphasis on their duty to remember only in order to drain the aquifer of available tears and leave none for anyone else, and certainly not for their principal adversaries.

This idiotic rhetoric needs to be disassembled.

And I will explain why none of its arguments stand up to a simple commonsense analysis.

But, for the moment, those are the three pillars, the three pivots, the three engines of today's anti-Semitism.

Those arguments make up its only three chances of regaining control over hearts and minds on a mass scale.

Such is the generic form of any future wave of insanity that might claim to bring back the happy time when one could, in good conscience, march in the streets of Paris or elsewhere chanting, "Death to the Jews!"

HOW THE DISCOURSE WORKS

In fact, the machine is recycling, here and there, bits of the old themes. Here, a reminiscence of Christian anti-Semitism, which can't hurt if it allows us to saddle the Jews with a new "massacre of innocents" in Gaza, thus adding to the rap sheet against Zionism. There, a hint of Voltaire, when that tradition helps, as it does Noam Chomsky, to rally the values of tolerance, free inquiry, and methodical skepticism in defense of the ignominious Holocaust revisionism of Robert Faurisson. A twist of Socialism for Dummies is fine if that twist can, as in certain far-left circles, instill the feeling that the great separation imposed by the Zionist international (which, supposedly, distinguishes the "privileged" victims of the Holocaust from the "forgotten" victims in the Palestinian camp) suggests, however faintly, the class struggle of yore. Or even a pinch of racism might be useful, as when, in September

2000, at the time of Prime Minister Ariel Sharon's visit to what some call the Esplanade of the Mosques and others the Temple Mount, Western Islamo-leftism adopted as one the thesis of the supposed "profanation" caused by the mere presence of a Jew on this site; or when, fifteen years later, Mahmoud Abbas, president of the Palestinian Authority, took up the refrain of Jews' defiling "with their dirty feet . . . Christian and Muslim holy places" and declared as "pure" every "drop of blood" shed in reprisal by the *shahid* "out of love for Allah."

The machine also throws in, here and there, a few additional elements that are relatively new, such as the heightened tendency to perceive conspiracy, broadened into a worldview, a philosophy, almost a metaphysics. No longer just: "The Jews dominate the world and control the media" (even though *The Protocols of the Elders of Zion,* which continue to be published, cited, and treated as holy writ in many parts of the world, were exposed eighty years ago as a fake). But now: "The Jews are forgers who control the great narratives through which the history of the world is not only told but made." (From Moscow to Ramallah, Durban to Damascus, and, often enough, alas, in Madrid and Paris, aren't many people convinced that "world Jewry" fabricates accounts that suit its purposes, suppresses those that contradict its version of contemporary history and its underside, and, in short, manages for its own greater advantage the "era of the eyewitness"?) And then there is the new form of warfare of which the BDS campaign (for "boycott, disinvestment, sanctions") is fast becoming the chief weapon—as when one refuses, in the manner of Brian Eno or Vanessa Paradis, to sing in Israel; as when one contemplates, like FIFA, banning Tel Aviv's soccer team from international matches; as when the British National Union of Students comes out in favor of a boycott of "occupied Palestine"; as when a Spanish music festival censures a singer for the sole reason that he is Jewish and refuses, before his performance, to pledge allegiance to the "Palestinian cause"; and as when squads of monitors patrol supermarkets in Europe to make sure that no products bearing the seal of the new infamy have slipped in. What are we talking about here if not isolating, delegitimizing, and excluding the Jewish state and Jews in general?

But the three major drivers are those that I cited.

They are the three arguments that enable the old hate to regain its youth and permit our contemporaries to be anti-Semites without feeling awkward about it.

The problem is not how to determine, as you hear in the media, whether you have "the right" to criticize Israel or whether it is possible to be "anti-Zionist without being anti-Semitic." The truth is that one can now be anti-Semitic *only by being* anti-Zionist; anti-Zionism is the required path for any anti-Semitism that wishes to expand its recruiting pool beyond those still nostalgic for the discredited brotherhoods.

The question is no longer simply whether the Holocaust deniers are sincere or perverse, ill informed or fully aware of manipulating historical sources: The suggestion of Jewish trafficking in memory; the accusation of inventing, exaggerating, or simply exploiting the hypothetical suffering of one's own people; the idea that the Jews might be profiteers not of war but of the Holocaust, obsessively cultivating their memories for the sole aim of covering up their own crimes—all of these offer anti-Semitism a new reserve of good conscience and innocence.

Armed with that reserve, it becomes unnecessary, in the course of a demonstration of support for Gaza, to excuse, minimize, or even acknowledge the shouts of anti-Jewish hatred or the stars of David converted into swastikas. The reality is that there are only a few ways to be anti-Semitic today, only a few solutions that enable anti-Semitism to escape from the secret circles within which the defeat of Nazism confined it and to re-create something resembling the embryo of a mass movement. And one of those ways is to establish the image of an unscrupulous people using their own history to crowd out the history of others, to create a vacuum around themselves and smother the tremulous voice of its Palestinian "competitors." The coming anti-Semitism will burn the fuel of the competition of victims or it won't ignite at all. It will establish the idea of a monstrous people who suck the air from around others, preventing them not from breathing but from complaining and from having their complaints heard: It will do this or it will fail.

A LICENSE TO HATE

Each of the themes presented above is powerful in isolation.

Each has the effect of restoring the sense of legitimacy that reigned when anti-Semitic groups were expected to avenge the death of Christ, to save people from the grip of the One God, to purify healthy races of the bad Jewish seed that was corrupting them, or to come to the rescue of the small and meek crushed by Jewish banks.

But now imagine that these three themes are combined.

Suppose they are assembled and connected.

One can begin at the point of Holocaust denial and travel through Arab capitals denouncing the deceit if not the outright fraud of the Jews who have used this "phony martyrdom" as a founding myth to help shore up Israel and as a deadly weapon against today's proletarian people and states. That's the song of Roger Garaudy, the former French communist leader who became, toward the end of his life, one of the pioneers of the new red-brown trend, and who, in February 1998, at the Cairo book fair, was greeted as a hero by both Nasserites and the Muslim Brotherhood; by both Farouk Hosny, culture minister at the time, and writer Naguib Mahfouz. After surviving an Islamist assassination attempt, Mahfouz was not afraid to declare: "We are both victims of the same intolerance." How pathetic! How shameful! But hadn't this Garaudy just gained the support of Abbé Pierre? Hadn't he just been acclaimed by a brave Algerian journalist who, a few weeks earlier, was awarded the prestigious Sakharov human-rights prize by the European Parliament?

One can begin at the point of anti-Zionism, at relentless hate for Israel viewed as a neo-Nazi state "financed" by the Saudis and itself "financing" European terrorism. That is the position of Noam Chomsky, who, departing from those premises, goes on (1) to put the Palestinian people and its civilians killed in 1948 in Deir Yassin, Lydda, and Ramle in first place on the world podium of suffering, and (2) to defend, in his 1980 preface to Faurisson's *Mémoire en défense contre ceux qui m'accusent de falsifier l'Histoire,* the right of Holocaust deniers to express themselves—that is, to hush the cackling of those insufferable dead

Jews who, if they were to be allowed to continue, if their propensity for self-importance were not immediately shut down, would not hesitate to appropriate 100 percent of that scarce, invaluable capital, that much-contested resource, that is victimhood.

And finally one can begin, as Jean Genet did, at the point of selecting the ideal victim and, after "four hours in Chatila," choosing the handsome Palestinian soldiers, the fedayeen who, like the soldiers of the Wehrmacht with their "steel haunches" and "boots heavy as a pedestal" from *Notre Dame des Fleurs,* have "sexual organs carefully molded at the crotch." From this then follows (1) a degradation of Israel, whose pioneers, by renouncing their destiny as a cursed people, guardians of a fragile truth, became symbols of "white rules"—the white, Western, and racist order that repelled the author of *Les Nègres,* and (2) a revision of Bergen-Belsen, Mauthausen, and Auschwitz, which Genet was already comparing, in words written for the radio in 1948 but censored, to a "splendid rose," a "plant of marvelous beauty," before which the poet could only "doff his hat," before they became, in *Un Captif amoureux (Prisoner of Love)*, temples to "the glory" of the "great criminal" that Hitler had become—great, certainly, as measured by the enormity of his crimes, but great, too, in pure greatness, great by "the glory and the impact" of his fine demoniacal acts, and great "for having burned Jews or having them burned," because even that was no more than a hymn to the beauty of the crime.

The three names—Garaudy, Chomsky, Genet—are obviously not on the same level.

The second, I repeat, is also a great thinker, who will be remembered for his work on generative and transformational grammar long after his deplorable *Fateful Triangle,* written thirty years ago about the connections between the United States, Israel, and the Palestinians, has been forgotten.

And the third—the deserter, ingrate, traitor to every cause, and enemy of everything and of everyone, to whom we owe, in particular, the irreducible, irredeemable, and poetic *Journal du voleur*—has value not as a paradigm but as an exception.

But my point is that all combinations are, alas, possible.

Because, in all cases, what emerges is a portrait of a truly detestable people guilty of so many crimes that they have earned the reprobation that is once again raining down upon them.

The situation is akin to the construction of a new atomic bomb, this time a moral one, which may fall into the hands of crowds of people who are becoming anti-Semitic without shame or scruple—without, I daresay, even thinking about it.

Fortunately, we have not yet reached that point.

But there (and there alone) lies the danger for today's Jews.

There lies the front line on which we must fight.

It is a waste of time to track the resurgences of the Catholic, anti-Catholic, socialist, or racist strains of anti-Semitism, when the reactor vessel in which the future explosion is brewing contains a new stew of hate for Israel, obsessive Holocaust denial, and the new religion of victimhood.

I will conclude with a clarification.

That symbols linked to the drama in the Middle East are always present is of course no accident: That is how the machine is fueled. But neither should their presence be viewed as a sort of necessity, as believed by those who tell us that Islam, as a whole, is the enemy of the Jews.

Anti-Semitic attacks have been perpetrated by individuals acting in the name of the Palestinian cause, the Koran, or both—so much is clear. That there is, speaking broadly, some connection, necessarily, between terrorist, jihadist, radical Islam, and Islam writ large (and that that connection should be unraveled—nay, severed—without delay) is difficult to deny.

And, above and beyond the cause of the Jews, the way out of our civilization's current discontent depends in large part on the outcome of the struggle, within Islam, between two different Islams—of that I am certain.

That said, however, three distinctions must immediately be made.

We are speaking here of symbols and signifiers, of a process of arranging, combining, and assembling *names,* whose relation to the *subjects* that they designate, conceal, and sometimes take hostage is, as always, very obscure.

We are talking about crimes committed in the name of those names and their fatal arrangements; but, for these crimes, the community of believers cannot be held responsible—especially when they dissociate themselves from them and deny the arrangers the right to speak and act in their name.

Between the two Islams, between the Islam of the throat-slitters and enlightened Islam, which goes back at least to Averroës and which the throat-slitters have never been able to reduce entirely to silence; between the adepts of the new cult of assassins and the followers of Izetbegović and Massoud, of Sheikh Mujibur Rahman, the father of Bangladesh, and of Mustafa Barzani, the father of the nascent Kurdish nation-state; between the "students of religion" that the Taliban claim to be and the heirs of a Moroccan "Leader of the Faithful" by the name of Mohammed V, whose spiritedly disobedient rejection of Vichy's villainous laws led him, from October 1940 to 1945 (when General de Gaulle named him a partner in the liberation of France), to treat his Jewish subjects no differently from other Moroccans, to the shame of recumbent France—between these two camps, then, one must be clever indeed to predict which will gain the upper hand. But it would be irresponsible to declare the battle lost before it has even really begun to be waged.

HAS THE UNITED STATES CAUGHT THE BUG?

One last word.

If this is in fact how the machine works and if these are indeed the three components of the moral atomic bomb that is anti-Semitism when burning at full throttle, then we must acknowledge that we are faced with a phenomenon that transcends national and cultural borders, a particle accelerator of bile and violence that no nonproliferation treaty can stifle and from which no country, not even the United States, which has been so eager to lecture Europe, is exempt or immune.

Let us review, in reverse order, the three elements that make up the new license to hate.

The theme of competition of victims has found fertile ground in the complexity, the double aspect, of relations between black and Jewish minorities in recent American history.

When one reflects on that history, what comes immediately to mind (and this is a good thing) is the civil rights movement, in which Rosa Parks, Martin Luther King, Jr., and others found Jewish communities to be among their most reliable allies.

Also obvious, and also a good thing but occurring at the other end of the historical sequence, was the election of an African American president, who found some of his first and most generous backers among the Jewish community in Chicago and later across the United States.

But those observations ignore the not inconsiderable fringe of the black community that has sought not equal rights but secession.

They drop a curtain over the Black Power movement, whose founder, Malcolm X, asserted, as early as 1963, that the Holocaust was not only no worse than the one done to the blacks but also that it lay at the origin of another crime, this one inexcusable, which was to have minimized, suppressed, and, in effect, extinguished the humiliation of the blacks.

The same observations neglect the vast literature disseminated by the Nation of Islam's so-called Historical Research Department, one of the most popular products of which has been *The Secret Relationship Between Blacks and Jews*. Published in 1991, this disgraceful tract claimed to prove that the principal beneficiaries of the transatlantic slave trade were the Jews of Europe.

They leave out the ascent to power of Louis Farrakhan, the charismatic leader of the Nation of Islam, who has spent the last thirty years (with help, on the domestic front, from neo-Nazi white supremacists, and, abroad, from Colonel Gaddafi's Libya) setting the "ridiculous" six million deaths from the Holocaust off against the six thousand years of black slavery and its countless victims.

Not to mention the Farrakhan lieutenant who, on April 18, 1994, on the eve of the conference on the "black holocaust," took a ninety-minute tour of the Holocaust Museum in Washington, D.C., before emerging to declare to the American press that "the black holocaust is a hundred times worse than any other holocaust in history" and worse, in any case, than that of the Jewish "bloodsuckers," who were put in their place by Hitler.

There were the pogroms organized by black racists in Boston and, in August 1991, in Crown Heights, Brooklyn.

There were "conferences" organized together with movements linked to the Ku Klux Klan, which shared with the Nation of Islam the desire to wrest from the Jews the martyr's crown that they were thought to be using as sword and shield.

If there is one place in the world where the competition of victims as a fuel for neo-anti-Semitism has already hatched a mass movement, it is the United States.

Alas.

The second form of fuel, Holocaust denial, may not have U.S. proponents who are as prominent as are Faurisson and Rassinier in France.

And yet David Hoggan's *The Myth of the Six Million*, published in 1969, still has a following, as does *The Hoax of the Twentieth Century: The Case Against the Presumed Extermination of European Jewry*, by Arthur Butz, a professor of engineering at Northwestern University, whose "contribution" was to pull Holocaust denial out of the closed circle of neo-Nazi sects in which it had languished while helping Farrakhan's disciples to sharpen their arguments.

But, above all, the United States has the dubious privilege of hosting the Institute for Historical Review, established in 1978 and based on the West Coast. In 1992, the institute's boss, Greg Raven, declared that Hitler was "a great man . . . much greater than Churchill and FDR" and "the best thing that could have happened to Germany."

The "institute" has a network of "scholars" and a "database" that enables revisionists around the world to communicate; to exchange their ravings, grand and petty; to get together; and to organize events such as a major Holocaust denial conference in Beirut in 2001, which was eventually canceled, and another in Tehran in 2006, which did indeed take place.

In the United States, under the shelter of the First Amendment and the absolute freedom of expression that it protects, many other institutes have emerged over the years, structured as research centers that publish pseudo-academic journals. These so-called institutes lend to invented nonsense an air of seriousness or even of science or academic rigor, something that has always eluded deniers in France, despite their efforts.

The United States is the only Western country where two negationist politicians, David Duke and, to a lesser degree, Patrick Buchanan, have been candidates for the presidency, and the only one to have an elected president, Ronald Reagan, pay a solemn visit to a German military cemetery (in Bitburg) where SS troops who killed Jews are buried.

It is a country where it is possible—in the state of Illinois, for example—to withdraw one's child from school on the grounds that after reading Arthur Butz one no longer believes in this Holocaust that abusive teachers seem intent on forcing down the throats of their children.

It is a country where, in the Colorado town of Aurora, a teacher refused to teach the Holocaust, which he preferred to call the "Holohoax," and when his superiors took him to court to try to get him to obey the law, it was the teacher who prevailed, collecting damages from the school system!

And I repeat, for the record, that it is in the United States that a truly great scholar, Noam Chomsky, can place his immense intellectual authority into the service of a French "academic" who is the author of (in Chomsky's words) "in-depth and independent historical research on the question of the Holocaust."

As for anti-Zionism, it clearly operates differently in the United States than in France.

Israel is loudly diabolized on some university campuses in the United States. But beyond the campus, consider the BDS campaign. Consider these "radicals" exhorting dockworkers in Seattle and San Francisco to refuse to unload merchant ships flying the Israeli flag; then blacklisting companies whose boats are condemned to wander, like ghost ships, from port to port on the West Coast, and even up to Canada, while electronic assault units track them and let go only when, out of fuel, they agree to turn back; and then inviting the good citizens of the United States not to buy Jewish (sorry, Zionist) products and not to eat this or that for fear that suspect ingredients may have found their way into their favorite supermarkets via circuitous routes that circumvented the vigilance of the citizen watchdogs. Consider this entire campaign, whose genealogy dates back to the appeals launched in 1947 and 1948 by Arabs nostalgic for Nazism of the sort practiced by the Grand Mufti of Jerusalem and whose promoters today are Palestinian figures hostile to the two-state solution and therefore to peace, figures such as Omar Barghouti and Ali Abunimah. It is in the United States, far more than in Europe, that the campaign is causing extensive damage.

And the United States is also the site of another debate, one seemingly less charged but in fact very dangerous, over the question of whether it is really reasonable for great America, with its global power and responsibility, to spend so much energy, to lavish such great resources, and to devote so much of the brainpower available in its best think tanks and among its most seasoned diplomats—whether it is reasonable, whether it isn't a *little unusual,* for the country to run the risk of offending so many large countries, some of which are essential to American national security and prosperity, all for the sake of a *tiny little country* without any special collective importance. Could somebody please explain, just explain, why Israel enjoys such an extraordinary status in American foreign policy? *Why Israel?* Why such an emphasis on the Jews in the diplomatic affairs of the country of Jefferson and Hamilton? Indeed, this was one of the questions that I heard asked in 2003, insistently even then, in the course of my neo-Tocquevillian travels. I heard it in the heartland of Nebraska, South Dakota, and Oklahoma, as well as from anti-Zionist readers of John J. Mearsheimer (University of Chicago) or Stephen M. Walt (Harvard University). Sometimes the question was asked sincerely, at other times rhetorically, with the formulation of the question suggesting the response. That the country might have a strategic interest in defending the island of stability in the Middle East that is Israel, that it might have a political duty not to abandon the only true democracy in the region, that it is always self-defeating for a civilization to betray its roots and allow them to dry up, as the West is doing today in the case of the Christians of Mosul and Qaraqosh—such considerations hardly seem to cross these people's minds: Much more convincing seems to be the hoary explanation of an all-powerful Jewish lobby that would have America act against its own interests.

All of this spells misfortune for the name of the Jews on both sides of the Atlantic lake—while those who rail against it thrive.

If this is not yet an atomic bomb, it is already a time bomb.

And every believer in democracy on both sides of the lake, in the United States as in Europe, needs to be part of the effort to disarm it.

CHAPTER TWO

WHAT SHOULD WE DO?
WHAT CAN WE HOPE FOR?

The big question, of course, is *how* to disarm the bomb.

Anti-Semitism being what it is—a continuously mutating virus, an incurable form of madness—one has to wonder whether anything really can be done about it, whether it is not already too late, whether fighting it is a waste of time.

On bad days, I sometimes think that way.

On occasion, I see in this anti-Semitic fever the most recent effect of a very old misunderstanding, one born several millennia back at the foot of Mount Sinai, which the nations, according to the Midrash, immediately chose to understand as *sin-ah*. Yes, *sin-ah*, without the final *yod* that is also one of the letters in the name of God. *Sin-ah*, which then no longer means the mountain of the same name but hatred, solely the hatred that this moment in the history of the Jewish people evokes in other peoples. *Sin-ah*, then, is the venomous mistrust, the grim resentment mixed with envy, inspired by a people who had the bizarre idea of responding as follows to a command handed down through a break in a cloud: "We will do and we will understand; we will begin by doing; we will do without having understood exactly what it is we have been commanded to do; only later will we understand." On bad days, as I say, I tell myself that at that moment the die was cast.

I tell myself then that the nations will never forgive the Jews, those scabs, those breakers of the anti-God strike, who, instead of making common cause with the other nations to think things over, to weigh the pros and cons, to discuss, to obtain a few final concessions from the Voice, were in a hurry to close the deal, to seal their backhand alliance, to make a separate peace that they have never renounced.

I tell myself that in this case the cause, not of the Jews but of the anti-Semites, is a hopeless one and that, after one has spent thousands of years mulling the same stale jealousy, when one has spent all those centuries studying every side of the "why them and not me" question of the other mimetic rivalry (that of the "chosen people" rather than that of victimhood, although, at bottom, the two probably come to the same thing), the matter is not going to be settled in a few quick rounds of learned discussion or political negotiation.

So, chin up, stiff upper lip.

Face-to-face, power against power.

Just try to be strong enough to be sure of being the strongest for a long time and, bolstered by that strength, without going into too much detail, without returning to the origins of the divorce between the one and the others, or between *Sinai* and *Sin-ah,* continue to live, to write, to fight the fights that must be fought and that the first Jew to have my name fought, formally, at the very foot of Mount Sinai—in short, to do my work as a writer and a man.

MELANCHOLY

Such was the thinking of my father when, having passed through the season of Nazism, he exhorted the slight and dreamy child that I was to practice martial arts while also aiming for academic excellence.

Such was the thinking of my friend Claude Lanzmann when, a few years after *Shoah* (his 1985 summation of the Holocaust), he directed *Tsahal* (1994), the grave and painful film on the pressing need for the Jews to relearn the use of force, about which they had forgotten everything.

Between receiving my father's exhortations and viewing Lanzmann's film, I remember having long conversations at the home on the Avenue Krieg in Geneva of Albert Cohen, the creator of Solal, novelistic hero (*Solal of the Solals,* 1933), king of the Jews, and prince of the gentiles, who knows that, although anti-Semitism will never disappear, it is possible, by becoming stronger than the rabble, to intimidate it and thereby gain a little time, then a little more and a little more. "Time is so important," he would explain to me in that plaintive voice that always disappointed visitors. "For a long time we had only that! We had no land, no state, no army; we were the most powerless people in the universe, but at least we had time—and therein lay our wealth. It was our greatest resource." Because "they'll never like us," he insisted, fingering the rosary that always hung from his fingers. "You'll think you're one of them; they'll woo you, honor you. But never forget the Silberstein basement in Berlin! Or Rachel the dwarf and the mock rabbi's hat that she might be apt to stick on your head at any moment! And in the meantime be careful and tough; be Ulysses and Achilles; be a bigger baboon than the other baboons; have nicer teeth than they do; get their women to love you as I was loved by Amélie da Costa, by the beautiful Geneva Huguenots, and by my glorious Countess Fornszec. Live in castles as big as theirs. Try to make them feel that you're no less a lord than they are. But never, ever expect to win them to your cause, overcome their prejudice, or change them."

And is that not the underlying wisdom of the Midrash, when it evokes the figure of the Jew, a *shoter,* whom the Egyptian was going to strike when Moses killed him? A *shoter* is a sort of sergeant-at-arms or official—in any event, a notable—someone who has attained real prestige in the opulent and flourishing society governed by the tides of the Nile. But that prestige is a deception, say the sages. The *shoter* was a slave in the land of Egypt—a slave he will remain. Branded, tattooed, numbered, it seemed—never will that disappear. Yet that is the illusion that has affected many happy Jews of today and yesterday: the denial of their accursed side, the makeup covering their number, the self-incantation, the delusion.

And is that not the thinking of our sages when they say that in preparing to meet Esau, the one who would become Europe, Jacob was faced with *t'fila, milkhama,* and *doron?* First, a prayer. Second, a war (which is why, acting in the capacity of a military leader seeking to save his lineage, he divided his camp in two). And, third, gifts (which is why he sent *mal'akhim*—that is, depending on the translation, "ambassadors" or "angels"—bearing tribute to a brother who, he knew, was approaching with four hundred men to kill him). A subtle mix, in other words, of faith, strength, and skill.

Romain Gary was yet another contemporary, another great elder whom I would see during the same years that I saw Albert Cohen: We are in the Rue du Bac, Paris. My *Testament of God* has just come out. His hair is too long, his beard dyed the color of tar. He is having one of his bad days, worrying about Jean Seberg, who is talking about marrying "a lying, dealing Arab," grumbling about his son's new nanny, whom he suspects of having taken the job in order to spy on him, and convinced that Claude Gallimard, his publisher, dumped him for his nephew, Paul Pavlowitch, the worst "son of a bitch" that the world had ever seen. "I really liked your book," he tells me all the same, flipping the pages of his copy, which lies on the coffee table between us and does not look as if it had been opened too often. "God knows I had nothing to do with it," insists this funny Jew who, eighteen months later, will contrive to give himself a funeral in the chapel of Saint-Louis des Invalides, presided over by a real priest. "I don't get mixed up in that stuff, but I liked what you said about the Bible and how man without the holy is just meat. But even so, be very careful. . . ." Here he raises a finger in a familiar gesture that I suspect he borrowed from his longtime rival, André Malraux, whom he always thought, deep down, had upstaged all his best roles—great writer, great adventurer, confidant of de Gaulle. "Some will fault you for seeing anti-Semites everywhere. But if I were to fault you for anything, it would be for not seeing more of them! Even in Kufra in '41, in the Libyan desert oasis where the free French army started, there were anti-Semites. Even in Casablanca and London, among the Gaullists, you found anti-Semites. You can be crawling around in the brush with a guy, sharing the same filth and nights without sleep. You can go up in a plane with him and, when you get to the target, feel that the same France runs through his veins and yours. But there'll always come a moment when he'll make you feel that you're still the son of a Lithuanian furrier and a little Russian actress who dreamed of seeing you become an ambassador of France. But it's stronger than they are. It's in their balls. The highest you can ever hope to get is consul. And that's what you have to deal with. Scheming, pushing, lulling them, beating them up—none of that changes anything; there's nothing you can do about it."

Such was part of my thinking on the subject, and so it remains despite the years that have passed.

It is my nocturnal thinking.

The thoughts that think themselves within me on days when I'm not thinking.

The thoughts that assail me when I recall the haunting finale of Levinas's *Proper Names:* the stupefaction of those great "Israelites" who were happy being Jews in Europe, sure of themselves and of their place in that world, prosperous and surrounded by friends, covered with titles and honors, some of them powerful, before the unheralded and unexpected arrival, overnight, of "an icy wind" blowing through the rooms of their houses, "pulling down the wall hangings and tapestries," sweeping away the "petty splendors" of lives shredded into "rags" that could not mask the distant "baying of the pitiless mob."

The thoughts that occur to me when recalling the political careers that a Jewish name hindered or destroyed. Prime Minister Léon Blum, of course. Pierre Mendès France, whose latter-day beatification cannot hide the fact that, because he was Jewish—or, more precisely, because he was suspected, as a result of his Jewishness, of waging war against the France of the land and of roots—he was once the most insulted and maligned political figure in the country. Or my friend Laurent Fabius: Éliacin thrown to the wolves, overcoming them, and becoming the youngest prime minister in France's history—until the murky affair of contaminated blood (in which it is difficult not to see a pale version of the accusations of ritual killing that were one of the staples of traditional anti-Semitism) gradually brought him down. Inescapable, the "French ideology." Impossible to overcome, this form of "French exception" that appears as soon as the Jewish name comes into play. And what a difference from the lovely "non-France" that is England in this regard, the England capable of producing, a century earlier, the opposite model—the same leader but under a very different paradigm.

I am thinking, of course, of Benjamin Disraeli, that supremely insolent Jew who allowed himself to say one day that Christianity is only Judaism made accessible to the masses. And, the next, that it was the role of "little Jews" like him to bring to England the "spark of genius" that it had too often lacked. And, the day after that, in Parliament, that three thousand years ago, when his colleagues' ancestors "were living in the forests of an unknown island," his "were in Jerusalem, priests in King Solomon's temple." And none of that prevented him from serving twice as prime minister, inventing the British Empire, or conquering the hearts of London, starting with Queen Victoria!

The biography of the son of Isaac D'Israeli, the son who became the first Count of Beaconsfield, is one of the first real books, perhaps the very first, that I read as I emerged from childhood. As soon as I learned enough English, I read Disraeli's own youthful novels, notably *Tancred,* in which his glorious Marranism—his secret or hidden Judaism—is already evident. Later still I devoured everything I could find on the short-lived daily newspaper that Disraeli started when he was twenty, the utter failure of which almost put an early end to his career. Among other things, the paper urged reconciliation between the people and two aristocracies, the "British" and the "Jewish." If I ever have had a weakness for Britain, it is because it was able to take hold of this flamboyant Jew (an opportunistic convert and perhaps all the more flamboyant for it), whom the *Daily Mail* insisted on calling "Dizzy," whom the horrible Gladstone dared to say didn't have "a drop of English blood" in his veins, and whose extravagant waistcoats were mocked in the bourgeois salons, along with his "Levantine" taste for fine, shimmering fabrics, his supposedly dubious morals, and his "oriental" distaste for those grand British rites of conviviality that are hunting and racing—and because, in taking hold of him, Britain made him a national hero, a political and human paragon, a model, for example, for Winston Churchill, a myth, and a great dandy the equal of Brummell and Byron.

Such are the thoughts that preoccupy me when I consider my own roots, at once strong and fragile, solid and uncertain, in the France where I was born, a nation that crowns a Jew king for a day only to better despise him the day after and, when it can, bring him down.

Such is the Spinozan "sad passion" that invades me when I contemplate, with some apprehension, the strange genealogy of the French writer that I am. My splendid father, who ridiculed, with his own existence and bravery, those of his countrymen who were demanding that Jews of his sort lose their citizenship on the grounds that they never "shed their blood for the homeland"—and who, after that, joined the ranks of those taking charge of rebuilding liberated France. But, just before, in the generation before his and my mother's—a proximity that pleases me but in which a part of me senses danger—there was Chalom the shepherd; Joseph, the photographer from Mascara whom the disciples of Drumont permitted to photograph only Arabs; my uncles Messaoud, Hyamine, and Maklouf, who, toward the end of their lives, would send me modest letters, dictated to a neighbor except for the envelope, which they insisted on addressing themselves to "Monsieur Lévy, France," so that the letters had to be discreetly unsealed and put into another envelope. Before them and before those who came before them stretched a line of ordinary, modest Jews whose unfathomable simplicity made them the scapegoats of a world that was willing to see poverty as the precursor to paradise—except for Jews. A tenuous line, in other words, shaky, of the type that could disappear into the night of the nameless. The same night into which, from red Asia to black Africa, from Chiapas to the falls of the Sinú in the Colombian jungle, from the forgotten wars of Sri Lanka to the slums of Lagos and Karachi, I have peered like a blind man for almost four decades. Is that by chance?

But, happily, there is another set of thoughts. Those that come to me by day, or some days at any rate, those that truly dispel the night and that help me pull myself together and reject discouragement, genealogical distillations that seem alien to me, and fatalism.

There are the wonderful days when I wake up thinking of myself as a child of the Enlightenment, reasonable, rational, optimistic, energetic, ready to change the world, to defy the gravity of fate. On such days it is possible not only to fight, using both sword and strategy in the manner of Jacob facing Esau, but also to advocate, explain, oppose the unopposable, try to convince—and succeed.

Not to eradicate evil, of course—on that score, my father's lesson is immovable.

But to harry it, worry it, push it back a little—and, once it withdraws, to keep it at bay.

To wear it down, give it no ground, resist it at every step, even if—especially if—one knows that one will never overcome it; that is the goal. And that is my state of mind at these other times.

This is one of those times.

I am in a joyous moment of existence—a positive mood, not too much sad passion, a fighting spirit, full of resolution.

And that is why, in the manner of Jules Isaac, the great French historian, who tried just after World War II to take stock of the criminal folly that had carried away his own wife and daughter and to respond to that madness point by point in *Jésus et Israël,* I am going to consider one by one the major arguments (if one can properly describe as "major" such logical poverty) that feed the new anti-Semitism and try to rebut them.

WHAT WAS UNIQUE ABOUT AUSCHWITZ

First, the Holocaust.

The Holocaust does not need to be rethought. On this point, nocturnal thinking already has it right.

And nothing is to be gained by stooping to the point of presenting reasonable arguments to baboons.

But what about the others?

To Holocaust deniers who may still be open to reason?

Not those who say, "The gas chambers never existed" or (worse) "Only lice were gassed in them." No point. But what about those who say, "All right, they existed, but why this obsession with remembrance?" The wallowing in pain? And, especially, why the renewed pretense of being chosen—the dark side of being chosen, yes, but chosen all the same—which causes you Jews to pretend to have undergone a unique level of suffering, one without precedent or cure? I think it is important to try to reason with those who are making that argument.

I believe that it is crucial, when addressing such people, to refrain from adopting an oracular tone that smacks of authority. In its place should be heard calm, balanced, and specific words about the unique aspects of the Holocaust.

It is not the number of victims. The Soviets and their henchmen killed fifteen times more people.

It is not the pace or the cadence of the killing machine. The Rwandan genocide produced nearly a million deaths in ten weeks, the world speed record for crime, a gruesome but indisputable total of unmatched horror.

It is not even the cruelty and inhumanity of the assassins, all those accounts of the camps that survivors needed to tell and that, when finally heard, terrified the world. (Because, incidentally, that was the situation: We said, "The survivors won't talk," when what was really happening was that we covered our ears when they did, deeming "unspeakable" what was simply unhearable, as millions developed tinnitus to muffle voices they could not bear to hear. Much was said about the crime being "unnameable," when in fact people simply refused to name it.) So it is not that, either, not the quantity of horror that accounts for the difference, for, speaking personally, I was equally shocked when, twenty years after David Rousset wrote about the Soviet gulag, I read the accounts of Solzhenitsyn and—at almost the same moment, and equally engraved in my memory—those of Arnold J. Toynbee on the massacres of Armenian civilians: skinned or impaled alive, butchered with hatchets and saws, left in sealed boxcars, defiled when they were pulled out dead from thirst and hunger, devoured by vultures in the desert, animalized, crucified. How, confronted with such scenes, could one possibly compile a hierarchy of suffering and evil?

Nor is it the methodical, industrial nature of the savagery. Other mass murders have had their share of that. For example, the integration of the gulag's twelve (and then seventeen) "administrations" into the Stalinist production system (extraction of gold, copper and coal mining, the digging of the White Sea–Baltic Canal) rivaled the integration of Buchenwald and Dachau into the Nazi war machine.

And as for the often-invoked argument of premeditation—that is, of a criminal intent that did not have to gather steam, become radicalized, and run amok because, from the Wannsee Conference on, its aims were clear—I am not sure that it is any more convincing. The Young Turks, after all, were no less intentional, and historians of the first genocide of the twentieth century have learned to date (at February 1915, right after the Sarikamish disaster, in which the Ottoman Third Army was crushed) the moment the decision was made to completely annihilate the putative fifth column that was suspected of supporting the downfall of the Ottoman Empire. The Cambodians are another example. We now know the real meaning of subtle euphemisms like "special treatment through sociological dissolution," "gathering under the trees," and "diseased branches are cut off." And the proponents of Hutu Power: It has been established that they planned the total destruction of the Tutsi "cockroaches."

No.

What is exceptional about Auschwitz lies in three traits, just three—but they are unique.

First, the Holocaust is the only massacre designed to be *final*.

Some massacres are conducted like wars, striking at the head or targeting points of strength, as in Darfur, in which civilians were not the primary targets of Sudanese president al-Bashir and his Janjaweed cavalry, although a great many civilians died.

In others, the fate of children, for example, depends in theory on the goodwill of the killers, as in certain provinces of the Turkish Empire, where children were deported to die—although not all did—in horrifying forced marches across the Syrian desert.

Then there is the Holodomor, Stalin's slaughter by famine in Ukraine, the purpose of which was to kill Kiev's nationalistic spirit, to break its resistance, but certainly not to exterminate all Ukrainians, though that did not stop him from claiming, at a minimum, five million victims.

From this perspective, the Holocaust was unequivocal. Men, women, children, the aged, the sick, the mentally ill—they all had to go. By the end of the colossal biopolitical operation, no one capable of perpetuating the cursed race could be permitted to survive. So great was the will to annihilate that even the traces of the exterminated— their culture, language, places of worship, books—were to be wiped off the surface of the earth as if they had never existed, as if no Jewish being had ever been conceived or created.

Second, the Holocaust is the only genocide designed to be without appeal.

"Kill them all!" screamed those who swung their machetes at Rwanda's Tutsis. But if one was somehow able to get away, to hide, and then, hypothetically or miraculously, to slip into Uganda, the pack lost interest and let him go.

"Liquidate the old world," the Khmer Rouge preached, stamp out all of its fires, dispose of its last traces, to allow Democratic Kampuchea to emerge as the epiphany of the new man. But if an intellectual, a man of books, a carrier of memory and witness to beauty, should succeed in slipping the noose of the death squad and, hypothetically again, crossing the border into neighboring Vietnam, which rarely happened—the trap having been almost perfectly set and nearly impossible to avoid—rules still were rules. So that if, on occasion, someone escaped, he or she was not pursued across the border to be killed.

As for the Armenian genocide, which has the dubious distinction of having begun the bloody series and, through Raphael Lemkin, given genocide its name, it seems to me that, despite the immense hypocrisy, the deportation legislation of 1915 (referred to as the Tehcir Law) provided an infinitesimal and very near impracticable recourse, but a recourse all the same. The Turkish genociders had limited the circle of hell to the borders of the empire, and their janissaries would not pursue to Marseille or even into Russian Armenia those Armenians who had somehow managed to elude them.

The situation of the Jews under Hitler was different. No border. Nowhere to escape to. The space of the empire, as well as the space that was not yet the empire but would fall within it sooner or later, was destined, in the Nazi delirium, to be *Judenfrei*. No safe harbor, no sanctuary, no city of refuge at the gates of which the mob would stop, as it did in biblical times. Europe and, in theory, the world were traps set for Jewish game being chased on a global scale.

The third unique aspect of the Holocaust is the erasure not only of the living but also of the dead, not only of their presence but also of their memory, to the point of concealing that the crime ever occurred and preventing it from being remembered.

One might reply that every genocide of the twentieth century cast its long shadow of denial. That is true. Except that the denial generally follows the massacre. In the case of the Armenian genocide, for example, the evidence is there, all of it, in no way concealed by the culpable. On that evidence—on the official telegrams from Interior Minister Talaat Pasha, on the confidential accounts collected in real time by U.S. ambassador Morgenthau, on the innumerable photographs that immediately began to circulate, and on the eyewitness accounts that instantly became available—rested the conclusions of the commissions of inquiry and, beginning in 1918, the courts-martial that tried some of the perpetrators of the genocide and sentenced them to death.

In the case of the Holocaust, the denial was immediate and, so to speak, built into the crime.

The SS devoted considerable energy, when killing, to cover their tracks.

I know of no equivalent, for any other genocide, of the famous passage from *The Drowned and the Saved* in which Primo Levi reports what he heard from the SS upon arriving at the camp: "None of you will remain to bear witness, and, even if some of you escape, the world will not believe you. There may be suspicions, discussions, research by historians. But there will be no certainty because, while destroying you, we will also destroy the evidence."

Perfect crimes. Whitewashed crimes. Crimes without tomb or record. Crimes in which the victims are stricken not only from the rolls of the living but also from those of the dead. You saw nothing at Auschwitz. Nothing happened there. And such is the grain of truth in Heidegger's disgusting observation that "hundreds of thousands" of people, "discreetly liquidated" in "annihilation camps," did not "die" but "perished," were deprived of the "shelter of being" that can also be true death, and were automatically transformed into "spare parts in an inventory for the manufacture of cadavers." Horrible, of course. Hard to hear. But nonetheless expressive of the dark singularity of the event.

No trace . . . No recourse . . . And now no true death, no right to a singular, personal death . . . I know that one must be extremely cautious on this subject, nuanced, attentive to detail. But the devil is in the details. And these are three details that make the Holocaust a crime without parallel. That much is established, demonstrable fact.

THE COMPETITION OF VICTIMS

Competitive victimhood.

The new and very strange idea that there may not be enough room for all of the world's victims under the dark sun of mourning and remembrance.

The new and imbecilic assumption that a single head may not be spacious enough to accommodate two separate afflictions.

And the inevitable and pernicious conclusion that a good soul might have to choose between the Jews and the non-Jews; between the Holocaust and the transatlantic slave trade, the massacre of the American Indians, Timor, the forgotten wars of Africa or Asia; between the exceptional and over-memorialized suffering of yesterday and the less cataclysmic but, alas, more pressing sufferings that are the live, horrifying reality of today; or even between the dead from a synagogue or a kosher market and the "innocent French people" gunned down "indiscriminately" because they liked sports, sidewalk cafés, or music.

One could fight this prejudice philosophically by citing Rousseau's *Discourse on the Origin of Inequality,* which posits the universality and nonconditionality of human compassion.

One could, against this hazy theory that is fodder for modern anti-Semitism, set the doctrine of the "solidarity of the shaken," as did the Czech philosopher Jan Patocka, drawing his inspiration from Edmund Husserl. Patocka believed in the fellowship throughout history of all segments of humanity that have been abandoned, subjected to nihilistic violence, and devastated by nonsense.

One could—we must—wonder whether at the root of this paradigm of a victim-centered vision of the world might not lie the worst of history in general and of religion in particular: competing Adams, infinitesimal differences that have generated infinite rivalry among Edom, Jacob, and Ishmael. From Edom to Adam, says the Talmud, what is there but an additional letter, a *vav*—the red, bloody *vav* that is the matrix of a war destined to become eternal?

Not to mention the thorough indecency of the quest for victim status, an indecency that is the unacknowledged correlate of the competition—its perversity, born in the mud of Auschwitz and repackaged, banalized, metered out in small doses to allow everyone a little slice of the cake of victimhood, just enough to affirm their identity and to clear away, if possible, any singularity that might mar the purity of their martyr status. How pathetic and grotesque this reduction of human essence to a bare suffering that becomes humanity's sole definition, its sole glory, while simultaneously purging it of anything resembling intellectualism, culture, literature, philosophy, concepts, reason, truth, remembrance, and, especially, religion and prophecy: all of these useless adornments, these now-secondary qualities that appear to have been there only to obscure deprivation and to prevent people from relishing their status as victims.

Remember, too, that underpinning the competition, at its origin and at its apex, is hatred—yes, hatred once again, a pure and unadulterated hatred: Once you give in to it, you never get out. Hatred for the victim whom one intends to unseat, of course, but also for the victim whom one is endeavoring to hoist onto the pedestal to be covered in the bird droppings of the competitor's sad passion. Oh, how the iron indifference of the "pro-Palestinians" to the Palestinians of flesh and blood recalls Genet's contempt for the fedayeen whose eulogist he strove to be and for the other dispossessed, Arab and black alike, who were no more than cards in his deck!

If the foregoing objections were not enough, one could cite a little-noted aspect of the recent history of sensitivities and ideas.

This argument may be a bit shocking.

Well, I'm sorry if being reminded of it is disagreeable to some.

But it is a fact.

A fact seldom observed, but a fact all the same.

When the genocide machine began to run at full speed in the hills of Rwanda, and the world, as usual, chose the path of seeing and hearing nothing, the first to sound the alarm mentioned the specter of the Holocaust—some to ward it off, others because it seemed to them already to have been revived.

Two years before, when the former Yugoslavia burst apart and the Serbs who had inherited the federal military forces began to bomb Sarajevo and launched a campaign of ethnic cleansing throughout Bosnia, when the nations of the world—faced with the return to the heart of Europe of a racial politics that everyone believed to be unthinkable given the recent memory of Hitler—chose a policy of wait-and-see, procrastination, and even sometimes justification of the crime, the first to raise a cry and begin a campaign in favor of international military intervention were journalists, humanitarians, and intellectuals who, while not comparing apples with oranges or underestimating the singularity and uniqueness of the Nazi crime, did detect in that war the foul breath of a beast with which all of them, for their own reasons, were familiar.

The same was true fifteen years earlier for Cambodia and its self-genocide, one rendered almost invisible to the eyes of the most radical elements of that same generation because of the rhetoric that associated it (I will come back to this) with total, radical revolution, which supposedly was being carried out there. In that case, too, exposing the genocide required the weight of another loyalty that marked that generation, a loyalty not to the idea of revolution but to the memory of the Holocaust. Is it any surprise that, a short time later, it was a group of Auschwitz survivors who launched, through the Cambodia Documentation Commission, the first campaign to bring Pol Pot and his fellow Khmer Rouge leaders before the International Court of Justice in application of the 1948 convention on genocide?

The same applies to Darfur in 2007, when doctrinaire thinking made it difficult for many to conceive that a formerly colonized country could be guilty of a form of crime that they imagined was the invention and sole preserve of colonial powers. The only ones to have cried out, roared, pleaded tirelessly, the only ones to have begged the world to understand that one could wrench free of one tyranny only to foment another, were men and women whose philosophical and political education had emphasized, for reasons specific to each of them, the "never again" of the camps. There was truth in the wire story about a meeting held on March 20, 2007, at the Mutualité conference center in Paris, for the purpose of getting France's presidential candidates to make a written commitment to intervene on behalf of the persecuted Darfuris. The story emphasized that all of the participants had one thing in common: We were all Jews—and we were all so indignant about this!

This is not to be confused with another meeting two years later at the same location, where the goal was to provide intellectual arms for those trying to mobilize against denial of the Armenian genocide. Was it an accident that there, too, joining me on the dais, was the human memory of the deportation of French Jews, Serge Klarsfeld? It is significant, I think, that the entire evening occurred in an atmosphere that both distinguished and likened the Jewish and Armenian genocides to each other, tacitly acknowledging their irreducible sin-gularity as well as their similarities.

About these episodes, you can take my word. I am up to date on this part of history, which is that of my generation.

Anyone in doubt need only delve into the intellectual biographies of those who crossed paths and rubbed shoulders in any of these the-aters of misfortune.

Inquiry will prove this fact: Over the past twenty years, in the United States as in Europe, each time the killing machine has sprung back into action, the people on the front line of mobilization, emo-tion, and analysis have been not Jews necessarily but individuals who have reflected on the plight of the Jews.

Looking at it the other way around yields the same result. Where, in recent years, have I heard the agony of the Jews invoked? Not in France. Not in the United States, where, according to the new Amer-ican anti-Semites, it supposedly functions as a "moral club," to borrow Martin Walser's phrase. And not in Israel, where the high priests of the "new religion" are believed to live.

Instead, it has been in Sarajevo, where the Muslim president of Bosnia, with bombs falling around the presidential palace, gave me a message to deliver to François Mitterrand, the essence of which was this: "We are at risk of becoming the new Warsaw ghetto; please, do not allow the new Warsaw ghetto to perish."

It has been in Rwanda, after the genocide, alas, and in its twin, Burundi, where a genocide of the same sort was brewing: "Friends in the West, fellow believers in democracy, do not allow us to become the Jews of Africa, victims of a new Holocaust!"

And it has been in Darfur, where the members of the unit that escorted my team and me into the zones liberated by the resistance fighters of Abdul Wahid al-Nour kept telling us, "We are in the midst of a new genocide; you Jews, children of survivors and resisters, can-not abandon us to the same kind of executioners."

And most recently it has been around Erbil, the capital of Iraqi Kurdistan, in the sandy trenches where the Peshmerga are holding the line against the Islamic State. There, too, the sense of Jewish history is omnipresent among those who, almost single-handedly—and carrying around the memory of the countless betrayals that they, too, have suffered—await the barbarians.

And finally it has been in Europe, as I was completing this book, in some of the commentaries elicited by the drama of the migrants coming from Syria, Eritrea, and elsewhere. Bashar al-Assad is not Hitler. Aleppo and Homs are not Auschwitz. The migrants drowned in the Mediterranean or piled into the ghost trains shunting between Austria and Hungary, in the rubble of the Europe of their dreams, are *in no way comparable* to the deportees of long ago. And yet it is the memory of that incomparability, the language of that absolute collapse, its echo, still faint, in the frivolity of postmodern heads, that has, *despite the differences,* inspired some of the most commendable and (paradoxically) most measured reactions to the human tragedies that have left us all speechless.

Proof, if any was required, that remembrance of the Holocaust does not inhibit but rather disinhibits the memory and mourning of other tragedies.

Proof that, far from anesthetizing compassion, it sharpens and stimulates it, stimulating even more the spirit of resistance to today's disorders.

Proof that there is in it an experience of abandonment, a memory of dereliction and of the way that memory is constructed, and a tradition of resistance, as well (Sobibór, Warsaw . . .), one that contemporary history was slow to record but has now inscribed in indelible letters, giving today's martyrs tools to use in commemorating, comprehending, confronting, and, sometimes, convincing.

And proof, finally, that the Jewish people, far from asserting any sort of monopoly on suffering or privileged damnation, offer the world a metric of adversity and evil, a crime-detection radar, a leading indicator of trouble. Wherever massacre rages, wherever one finds a bloodbath with countless, nameless, faceless victims in unmarked graves, whenever one encounters absolute, tragic, and seemingly inexorable solitude, as in the case of the "migrants" of the early years of this century, there is in that unrecorded history a sort of standard of the scale and menace of the inhuman.

EXCEPTIONAL ISRAEL

And, finally, Israel.

It is so tiresome to have to defend Israel.

So distressing to have to present the same evidence over and over.

Not that Israel is irreproachable, of course.

Not that it is forbidden, as the frauds endlessly assert, to "criticize" Israel.

But in the face of so much bad faith, in the face of a systematic campaign of delegitimization that has no parallel on the world political scene, in the face of the role that this demonization of the Jewish state plays in the construction of the new anti-Semitic machine, how can one not respond by proclaiming the virtues of Israel?

An example of virtue: It is well known among political scholars that a democracy is not built in a day but rather is reached at the end of a long road and after severe labor pains. Hesitations, reversals, and convulsions are, alas, more frequent than progress, as evidenced, among many possible examples, by Iraq, Libya, and Hungary, the last being a great nation freed from the communist yoke but still struggling toward complete democracy.

Now, to that law (and it is a law) there is an exception. And that exception takes the form of a people of diverse origins who, one fine day, find themselves in the land of Israel. Some are Jews from Libya, some from Iraq. Some are men and women from the Soviet Union, where no one had the faintest idea of what democracy means. Some are immigrants from empires—Ottoman, Austro-Hungarian—where they may have had a vague idea of it but no real experience to validate it. And, please, let us hear no objections that the survivors who disembarked at Jaffa, Haifa, or Tel Aviv were the elite of those empires, their finest flowering, democrats by nature and culture, the crème de la crème. Many of them were as deprived, impoverished, and humiliated as one can imagine. They arrived—if they arrived—after a crossing on ships of fortune not very different from those that land on the Greek island of Kos or on Italy's Lampedusa today.

And so they land, these survivors, amid harsh surroundings. There they are, bands of exhausted immigrants, half-dead from hunger and thirst, boarded and inspected while at sea, threatened with shelling, sometimes sent as far back as Germany, parked in floating jails or in holding facilities in Cyprus monitored not by Nazis but by RAF fliers; there they are, before they get their land legs back, somehow summoning the energy to make a gesture that one finds only in books: They make a social contract! And it works! And a society emerges from that gesture, from that contract. A democracy is created, without too much hesitation, without any of the spasms that were believed to be the rule whenever one improvises a government of laws. Political science is proved wrong: A republic, the genuine article, is born overnight.

Another example: Democracies have an Achilles' heel. Even the oldest and best established among them have a terrible problem that so far remains without solution. And that problem is the impurity not of their origins but of the mix of people of which they are made. *E pluribus unum* is the American motto, drawn from Virgil, and it makes the accommodation of ethnic pluralism the most pressing of obligations. But how many obstacles are met on the way! How many decades of urban riots, standoffs between racist whites and racist blacks, the Ku Klux Klan, Black Power—the raised fist of the ghetto at the Mexico City Olympics in 1968, the Attica Prison uprising put down bloodily by a militarized police in 1971. Is there any assurance that the election of a mixed-race president, thirty-seven years later, marks the end of the story? The race riots in Ferguson and Baltimore would seem to indicate that fifty years after the epic battle for civil rights, the wound remains open and victory elusive.

A "pluralistic republic," say the French, looking back on a long history inhabited by so many different peoples, each with its own memories but bound together in an integrative project that differs from the American communitarian impulse but that has had its own moments of glory and success. But that project is clearly in crisis, with the machine designed to manufacture French citizens competing with an opposing machine that is producing ghettos and stigma. That legendary opening to the other, a form of French generosity that is, according to Descartes, the correlate of self-respect—is it not finding its limit in the lack of self-respect with which a growing number of French citizens seem to view themselves? As the lost territories of the republic expand, as acts of incivility and barbarity proliferate there, and as the children of the "Black, White, Arab" generation leave home to take up jihad, the social bond unravels.

Well, I know a country that has found a solution to the problem of multiethnicity, not a perfect solution but better than in France or the United States. I know a society composed of Americans and Europeans, Russians and Ethiopians, Jewish and Muslim Arabs, and, among the latter, citizens who embrace the great national story as well as citizens who contest it. I know a society—Israel, again—where citizens of Arab origin may openly advocate the disappearance of the very state that guarantees them a life that three-quarters of them (according to polls) would not trade at any price for a life in a neighboring Arab country. And I know that this same society is structured in such a way that the members of the minority in question enjoy, with one exception (that of obligatory military service), all of the civil rights accorded to every other Israeli citizen; that they are represented in Parliament in proportions unheard of in any Western democracy; that they speak a language that is the official second language of the country; that they produced one of the five justices on Israel's supreme court, the loftiest institution in the country; and that, when an Arab family in Baqa al-Gharbiyye decided to settle in one of the famous "colonies" in Galilee intended exclusively for Jews, the supreme court ruled four to one in its favor (Qa'adan decision of March 2000), on grounds that "equality is one of the fundamental values of the state," that "local governments must accord equal treatment to all those under their authority," and that "Jewish and non-Jewish citizens of the state of Israel have equal rights and obligations."

And, finally, a third example that, far from rendering Israel illegitimate, satanic, and fascist, should be celebrated as exemplary by serious anti-fascists.

In all of the world's democracies, there is a limit condition that, when encountered, appears to cause them to lean toward declaring a state of emergency or of exceptional circumstances in which some of the rules have to be suspended. That limit, which is well known and has been analyzed by generations of commentators, is war.

In France during the war in Algeria, it did not take long at all for the nation's leaders, its elites, its lifeblood, the leaders of the major parties, and the intellectuals to resign themselves first to torture, then to the suspension of press freedoms, and later to bloody suppression—in the center of Paris—of the right to assemble and demonstrate.

And in the United States in 2001, a single act of war—a particularly spectacular and bloody one, to be sure—was enough to usher in an era marked by the Patriot Act, by the establishment of a special prison in Guantánamo, and by the reign of intelligence agencies that quickly reverted to some of the darkest practices of a system (invented by J. Edgar Hoover) that made spying on citizens a normal and enduring function of government.

To that pattern—one that, as Hannah Arendt's "global civil war" has spread, is becoming more or less universal—there is also an exception. As in the previous two cases, the exception is Israel, a nation that had not been in a state of conflict for six weeks, as George Bush's America was when it passed its anti-terrorist legislation, or for six years, as was the France of the Fourth Republic when it lost what remained of its honor in the requisitions of the Jeanson trial and later, on October 17, 1961, in the Paris murder of a still-unknown number of Algerian demonstrators by police, but for sixty-seven years—that is, since the day when its population of immigrant ghosts, of walking skeletons, staggered out of the holds of the Exodus and decided to enter into a social contract and form a nation—and despite all that, despite a lifetime spent under a state of siege, has somehow managed to remain faithful to its democratic founding principles.

There is not a newspaper in the world that treats the Israeli government more harshly than do Tel Aviv's.

Not a hospital or a university in Israel that, in the darkest hours of the two intifadas or during the wars in Lebanon and Gaza, yielded to the apartheid temptation and ceased treating Jewish and non-Jewish Israelis equally.

Hospitals that today, in the Golan Heights and elsewhere, are treating and saving, without a hint of discrimination, hundreds of Syrian refugees in flight from the twin terrors of Bashar al-Assad and Daesh.

Courts that, when men fall short, when violations of human rights are documented, when it appears that the barrier that protects the country from terrorism encroaches on the territory of the Palestinian villages of Beit Jala and Battir or infringes on the livelihood of the inhabitants of the Cremisan Valley, or requires, as occurred near Bil'in, the uprooting of groves of hundred-year-old olive trees, accept and hear the cases, rendering independent decisions.*

Freedom of opinion and assembly scrupulously respected even in time of war—full-fledged war—as when the Arab villages of Tirah and Kafr Manda were organizing demonstrations of solidarity with the enemy—and I mean *the enemy*.

And an army about which I have often said, and repeat here, that even if it, like every army, has its rogue soldiers, even if it occasionally commits grievous errors (which usually are adjudicated by Israeli military and civil tribunals), overall it remains faithful to a military ethic based on the twin principles of protecting its own soldiers while also minimizing the number of civilian casualties on the enemy side.

I am aware of the debates on this subject that rage in the Israeli press.

I read, like everyone else, the story about the pharmacy in Gaza City that was targeted in error; I know about the café in Khan Yunis that was thought to have been an arms depot; I am aware of the many civilians who, in the confusion of combat, have been taken for terrorists.

And I am not one of those who take lightly the accounts of soldiers from the Yitzhak Rabin military academy or those affiliated with the nongovernmental organization known as Breaking the Silence, who (anonymously, by the way, which makes the accounts difficult to verify) speak of "disproportionate" use of force, "indiscriminate" firing

---

* *La Croix*, June 27, 2011, and April 2, 2015.

contrary to the military's code of ethics, and a "precautionary principle" that, applied to zones where jihadists use the civilian population as human shields, may clash with the principle of *tohar haneshek,* or purity of arms, which is the moral foundation of the Israel Defense Forces.

But that foundation exists.

The lapses, when they are known, are always investigated by the military police and, when borne out, met with appropriate sanctions.

And the best-informed observers, serious reporters who have covered Israel's wars, know that in this utterly unique army there are few strategic or even tactical decisions that are not subject to real-time review, analysis, and approval by judges specially appointed for this purpose. This "judicialization" of the battlefield, the presence of legal officers alongside soldiers and their commanders, the possibility that, in the midst of an operation, a court can assert jurisdiction over an inappropriate order, an objective deemed inconsistent with ethics, or, of course, a crime—these are not widespread phenomena. But it does explain the equally unusual initiative of the American general Martin Dempsey, then chairman of the Joint Chiefs of Staff, in sending a delegation of high-ranking officers to Jerusalem in 2014 to study what he called the "extraordinary lengths" taken by the IDF to "limit collateral damage and civilian casualties" in the war against Hamas.

None of that exonerates Israel for violations of the rules that it has set for itself, violations that are, by definition, too many.

Nor is there any question of exempting the elected authorities from their most urgent tasks, beginning with that of making peace with the Palestinians and even, if necessary, offering the "straight-up peace" based on the two-state principle and the Geneva-plan parameters that I outlined thirteen years ago, in the presence of the leading voices of the "peace camp" (a principle that I continue to believe is the only one capable of inducing each side to recognize the rights of the other while also halting the inexorable march toward a binational state that is the undisguised aim of Israel's most cynical enemies).

And it must not exempt Israel from a necessary metaphysical re-flection on Israel's place and significance in the economy of messian-ism that is the true heart of Jewish thought: Is Israel a fulfillment or a denial, a preparatory step or a ruse? Is it part of the messianic story or a sidestep?

But, for the moment, that is not the question.

The question is to know where the Jewish state dreamed by Theo-dor Herzl and realized by David Ben-Gurion fits within the grammar not of being but of nations.

And the answer is that this state was born from the love of an ob-scure advertising man for a suffering people of which he knew little; that it was baptized with the name given to that people by poets and psalmists whom he had probably never read; that it was built by dreamers who, while they were reinventing Hebrew, gave themselves new names inspired by splendid figures from the Bible and brought to this arid country the power of their lyricism, their knowledge, their spiritual and bookish competence. The answer is that these dreamers gave birth to an unprecedented phenomenon, that of a revived land, a blooming desert, a miracle of rationality and hope under the stars. The answer is that this state has not reneged on its contract and has not, despite its flaws and errors, lost all the inspiration of its pioneers.

That in a world so profoundly splenetic and disenchanted these beings have managed to survive, that they have had and retain a vital-ity and a passion both fanciful and practical—those achievements give Israel a dimension that escapes many contemporaries and makes its national epic an adventure in which, putting politics aside, a part of humanity's destiny is playing out.

CHAPTER THREE

THE STRENGTH
OF THE JEWS

But let's return to France.

France will turn out to be highly consequential for the global mind and for the course of the world-historical as it moves, at its snail's pace, along the narrow crest line that keeps us from great catastrophes on both sides.

What is the situation in France in this second decade of the twenty-first century?

Is the hate machine running at such a speed that the Jews have already lost and have no choice but to leave?

Are we living in a remake of the 1930s, when our parents saw nothing coming and waited until the last minute to open their ears—like Freud in Vienna, like Kantorowicz in Berlin (before he fled to the United States), like Léon Brunschvicg and Marc Bloch in Paris—to the rumble of the swelling Nazi mob?

I do not believe so.

I am aware of the seriousness of the threat.

I do not underestimate the dread experienced in some French neighborhoods by children wearing a yarmulke, or the discomfort of teachers trying to teach about the Holocaust in secondary schools euphemistically referred to as "difficult," or the vandalizing of Jewish shops during demonstrations in support of the "new Jews" of Gaza, or, still less, the ordeal of Ilan Halimi, who was kidnapped, held prisoner, burned, and tortured to death in the basement of an apartment building in a Paris suburb, or, several years later, the killing of a young girl in Toulouse by a Jew hater of the new stripe, who shot his victim in the head in the doorway of her school. I have not forgotten any of that or the other deaths in the middle of Paris, where it is no longer possible to do your Sabbath shopping without worrying that a pogromist will leap out and gun you down. I have not forgotten the places of worship and of everyday activity that are so heavily guarded that they have become a new sort of ghetto—something unknown even in the 1930s.

And yet I do not believe that France is on the verge of a new Kristallnacht or that the time has come for the nation's Jews to pack their bags and leave. There are differences, major differences, between the situation in the 1930s and that of today. And those differences give us reason to keep our cool and to hope.

HATE AT LOW TIDE

The anti-Semitism of the 1930s was articulated by rather strong voices.

It could count on heralds in the top ranks of literature and thought. It operated not at the margin but at the apex of French intellectual life, without anyone seeming to object. Hard to imagine, but that is how it was.

Think of Paul Morand.

Or the immensely influential Louis-Ferdinand Céline.

Or Jean Giraudoux, who, to the Surrealists' question "Why do you write?" responded blandly that he wrote because he was "neither Swiss nor Jewish."

Or Pierre Drieu La Rochelle, the respected novelist and friend of André Malraux and Louis Aragon.

But who is the Drieu La Rochelle of today? The Céline?

Can one seriously compare the minor nobility of present-day political incorrectness with the author of those despicable but talent-filled tracts, *Bagatelles pour un massacre, L'École des cadavres,* and, later, *Les Beaux Draps?*

And as for the windy diatribes devoid of talent of a skinhead philosopher (I am thinking of Alain Soral) or a former comedian now devoted to anti-Zionist agitprop (Dieudonné M'bala M'bala), are they not destined to evaporate like the foam bobbing on a polluted whirlpool?

Strength of mind counts even in the negative.

Especially when it comes to writers.

We have nothing like that today.

Nothing but bubbles of mental pus.

Not one serious voice, not one *writer*, to lend to this pestilence a fiery authority or the air of respectability required to get things done.

That is a sign—a fortunate one.

THE DIKE OF DEMOCRACY

A second sign.

And likewise a new development.

The anti-Semitism of the 1930s was not only a climate; it was also an official ideology, or nearly became one.

There were anti-Semitic deputies in the French National Assembly, anti-Semitic prefects in some departments.

There was an anti-Semitic cabinet-level minister, Jean Giraudoux again, commissioner-general for information in the third government of Édouard Daladier, which had gained the confidence of the assembly under the Popular Front.

There were orderly debates on the question of what to do with foreign Jews, whether to strip them of their citizenship, send them back to Hitler, or lock them up.

And noisier debates, too, surrounding the future commissioner-general for "Jewish questions," the powerful politician Xavier Vallat, who was shocked that "an ancient Gallo-Roman land" could have sunk so low as to be governed by a "sly Talmudist" by the name of Léon Blum and who, in a contest for the leadership of the Chamber of Deputies on June 14, 1936, received one hundred fifty votes.

Once again, there is no equivalent in today's France.

Not a shadow of sympathy, among the French ruling class, for the warhorses who miss the good old days when you could talk about having an "oven full" of Jewish artists.

Unimaginable, the case of Minister Giraudoux taking pen in hand in 1939 to rail, in *Pleins pouvoirs,* against the hordes of Jews whose "precarious physical constitution" caused them to burden "our hospitals."

Even if that were imaginable and the temptation returned, there is another decisive new factor: the prohibition etched into the stone of the law.

And when a prime minister on the left—Manuel Valls deserves to be named here—sees the popular comedian Dieudonné weaving together the three threads of militant anti-Zionism, conspiracy-based Holocaust denial, and the incitement of competition between the victims of the slave trade and the Holocaust; when he understands that, from the depths of ignorance, this arsonist is combining three molecules, any one of which is enough to inflame credulous souls but that together and heated to the melting point are the components of a moral atomic bomb; when, understanding that and realizing that France is on the brink of another nuclear threshold and that the same rule applies to the new threshold as to the old one (one more step, and it's too late; one more lapse, delay, or weakness and the explosion is unavoidable), he decides to apply the law and to prohibit gatherings at which this stew is concocted and served—when Valls does this, he encounters not one former prime minister or cabinet minister, not one big-city mayor anywhere on the political spectrum, who wishes to split hairs with him, argue fine points, or seize the opportunity to stand out in opposition.

Might one object that the nation's anger is being taken out on others? That it is the Roma, the undocumented, those stranded on Lampedusa, Bodrum, and Kos who have assumed the place of the pariah in the collective imagination? That the Christians perhaps, from Iraq to Syria, from Nigeria to Pakistan and Egypt, are in the process of becoming the most persecuted community on the planet? And that the same people who do not hesitate to take a stand against the new anti-Semitism join the chorus condemning the "invasion" of a few thousand chicken thieves, close their eyes to the criminal torching of a mosque in Auch, or close ranks against the "invaders" from Syria, Eritrea, or Iraq?

One might. And it is terrible.

For a European at the beginning of the twenty-first century, it is an admission of a terrible failure.

And the fight against racism remains vital to democracy.

But that is not what is at stake here. Here, we are dealing with two different things.

Anti-Semitism, whatever may be said of it by ideologues who want to see the Palestinians as the new Jews and their misery as the echo of that which so long dogged the Jews, is not a species of the genus racism.

Or, better: Just as it is true that one can hope to prevail only against something that one can distinguish, the twin fight against the disgraces of anti-Semitism and racism can be fought only if one begins to distinguish the differences that define the two. The racist goes after the visible differences (skin color, dress, a distinctive way of socializing and of being in the world), whereas the anti-Semite goes after the invisible difference ("the dangerous Jew, the vague Jew," in Drumont's phrase). It inflames and excites the anti-Semite all the more that the imagined Jew is discreet, indiscernible at first glance, and therefore well positioned to carry out the worst and darkest intrigues. This is the story of the persecution of the Marranos in Spain and the tragic error of all Jews who, over the centuries, have chosen to believe that by becoming invisible, by making themselves small, by appearing more genteel than the gentiles, they would ward off persecution. The opposite happened.

But my point is this: However you look at it, the situation is clear. As widespread as anti-Semitism is in France today, as insidious and potentially dangerous as the new discourse is in large segments of public opinion, as criminal as the actions based on those opinions have been, it is not accurate to say that the republic has softened its stance regarding anti-Semitism. It would be wrong to imply that the nation takes the phenomenon lightly. In the face of the evil of anti-Semitism, France's institutions are responding well, at least at the time of this writing.

Can it be that believers in democracy of all types have finally understood what binds France to its Jews and the Jews to France?

Might Renan's children be ready to understand the *Tzarfat* in France, the Hebrew in French, and the Jewish sonorities with which my country's name suddenly sounds in my ears?

Will they become aware, finally, that their country has rarely been as loved, as well understood, or as highly celebrated as by its Jewish citizens, Jews whose Judaism has been not an obstacle to building France but a cement?

It appears so.

I will return to this subject in greater detail.

To be specific, I will return to the role of the Jews in the invention and the consolidation of the French nation.

But clearly some part of this is evident.

There is, in French society today, a dim but certain knowledge of the historical and metahistorical loyalty of France's Jews to their country.

And that is another big difference between now and the 1930s.

THE NEW ALLIANCE WITH CHRISTIANS

A third sign. In the 1930s, the Jews were alone. Radically and tragically alone. To the extent they had allies, to the extent that the offenses to which they were subjected occasionally aroused indignation, it was on the condition that the targets forgot that they were Jewish and their fellow citizens forgot it, as well (generalized Marranism; Jewish shame as the basis for acceptance; a France that was simultaneously republican and Christian, Jacobin, and riven by the teaching of contempt; a France that liked its Jews only if they were sad and victimized, a negativity with no corresponding positivity); and, anyway, such allies as existed were isolated individuals not representing any movement or current of thought. There was no organized force, no segment of the body politic, to make common cause with them.

That, too, has changed.

In contrast to anti-Semitism, which has lost its champions, the battle against anti-Semitism has gained legions of partisans.

And the principal theaters of this rally are the Christian churches that for so long were the chief purveyors of hate but, on this score, have undergone an unprecedented revolution.

The case of the Protestant churches is the best known.

The rebellion of an Augustinian brother named Luther changed everything, first on the banks of the Rhine, then all across Europe.

In translating the Bible into German, he killed two birds with one stone, inventing modern German and sealing a tacit pact with the specialists in textual knowledge and exegesis, who were Jews.

After that, he could rage and rail, as in his *Table Talk*, inventing new curses for those stiff necks who, while the quintessentially Jewish feat of textualizing and intellectualizing the Word was being carried out, rejected the new religion once again.

The pact was sealed.

From it emerged a new climate in which the Hebraistic goy and the Jewish philologist would walk in step, in an alliance that, up until the 1930s, yielded so much fruit in Germany.

From it ensued, between the gesture of the Talmudist and the discourse of the pastor, between the ancient master of reading and the new exegesis, now a Christian specialty, an encounter tied to be sure to the event and in a sense contingent—an encounter that did not end, however, with Luther's sermon but left an indelible mark on Europe.

As such, it is impossible to comprehend the stunning cultural production of Austro-Hungarian Judaism at that moment in the history of the continent when the Jews for the first time overcame the barrier that Christian civilization had put in their path, unless one remembers that farther north in the Lutheran lands the Jews had acquired not only freedom of residence but also of thought.

In the case of the Catholic Church, the reversal was more recent and has a darker history.

But when the fevers have died down and the last of those nostalgic for the ancient quarrel have given up, we will be able to measure the amplitude of the earthquake that was Vatican II in the country of Charles Maurras. We will be able to measure the length of the trip that Pope John Paul II took in 1986, the longest trip of his pontificate, when he traveled the few hundred yards between the Vatican and the great synagogue of Rome.

We will recount that revolution, that leap, at the end of which the best Catholics, those deeply concerned about their relationship with the people of the Book, tipped—when the tipping point came—from the old idea that the Jews must be respected because they are the Catholics' "fathers in faith" to the new and completely different idea (completely different because it implies full equality) that they are their "older brothers."

We will celebrate those postwar intellectuals who became aware that the old story of the father and the son in faith is, under its apparently benevolent exterior, imprisoned in a logic that requires the father in faith, as in life, to die and be reborn and perfected in the son; and we will acknowledge the immense merit of their invention of the simple idea—very simple but as new as the first day—of two brothers of equal worth, contemporaries in time no less than in spirit and forming another sort of alliance, one neither old nor new since it will be an alliance of peers who explore, not individually but together, the two-lane road to being.

When that history is written, it will be necessary to understand what happened, deep down, to bring matters to that point.

It will be necessary to reconstruct in detail the spiritual itinerary of the men and women who, in the middle of the twentieth century, carried out that minuscule but decisive substitution of the brother for the father and the theology of the "alliance never broken" for the old and infamous "theology of replacement," wherein the New Testament supposedly replaced and abolished the old law.

Was the event the Holocaust?

The dawning of awareness in Christians that the old theology had played a part in the Nazi crime?

A slower, deeper maturation that would have to be dated back to pro-Dreyfus poet Charles Péguy?

A return to the starting gate—that is, to the Gospel according to Matthew and the Judeo-Christianity ("I was sent only to the lost sheep of Israel," Matthew 15:24) that was reputedly a strong strain in early Christianity but was quickly repressed?

Or the crisis of the churches?

Their loss of self-confidence?

The empty space, nearly a gulf, that appeared in the Christian conscience and (because nature abhors a vacuum) may have created a need for the Jew in the form of the missing brother?

Salvation by the brother, then?

Judaism: a life preserver bobbing on the waves in a raging storm?

A hand extended out from the origin, a hand that one has no choice but to grasp after losing oneself in overweening confidence on the long pathways of history?

The desperate gesture of one who has understood that only by moving toward a source reviled for millennia does Christianity stand a chance of revitalizing its ailing body?

Or perhaps the new persecution, unforeseen but global, of which the Christians, too, are targets, bringing them together with the Jews in an unprecedented community of destiny?

The reason does not really matter.

Because the result is beyond dispute.

Although rear-guard actions are still being fought, although a recent pope (Benedict XVI) could still argue, in a book of interviews with Peter Seewald, for the old replacement theology on the grounds that "the Jews don't much like" hearing about "older brothers" because the "older brother" in a "Jewish tradition" marked by the history of Jacob and Esau is "also the outlaw brother," the overall trend remains that of *Nostra Aetate,* the 1965 encyclical that ended official anti-Semitism in the Catholic Church.

And when, on June 13, 2014, another pope, Francis, observed in an interview with the Catalan daily *La Vanguardia* that "inside each Christian is a Jew," and when he said that though as pope he performs the Eucharist every day as a Christian, it is nevertheless as a Jew that he prays over the Psalms of David (*"mi oración es judía"*), one must admit that something huge has occurred. The Catholics have released the synagogue and removed the blindfold that they had placed over its face—the synagogue of Notre Dame de Paris with its broken scepter, its fallen crown, and its grotesque, outsized helmet positioned sideways, which forced the synagogue into a humiliating and piteous list. Or that of the Strasbourg Cathedral, sublime in its beauty, the fine veil over its eyes already suggesting an accessory of grace.

The Jews of France and of the world no doubt have other allies, as well.

Allies among the atheists, the agnostics, those of no faith, free thinkers.

They have some—but not enough!—among the adherents of the third religion of the Book, which is also, at present, the most resistant to that mode of relating to the text that the Jews call study.

But the most important alliance, the one that has come the furthest and put aside the greatest number of divisions, the one made most solid by the immensity of misunderstanding overcome, is the alliance with the Christians. Even the Nazis understood this, as evidenced by the SS parades in which "Christ, that Jewish pig" was held up to ridicule.

We must not fail to understand this and must work harder than ever to consolidate the new pact.

On the one hand, a Christianity in crisis, in its ecclesiastical form, but enduringly alive in minds and hearts; on the other hand, and I am coming to this, a Judaism that has recovered its self-confidence and pride.

On the one hand, a Christian consciousness that, having gradually retracted the concessions to paganism that it had made in an effort to eradicate that same paganism, is returning to a form that a Jewish mind would call "Noahic"; on the other hand, a Jewish consciousness that (and I am coming to this, as well) re-envisages the redemption of Nineveh and views Ninevite humanity as precious.

On that side, a God concerned with the masses and trying to deal with the Platonic "human animal" (that's not nothing!); on this side, one who prescribes only the pursuit of the exceptional.

Is this not a climate that has become more favorable to an unprecedented rapprochement, by clearing away the hypocrisies, the more-or-lesses, and the ulterior motives of yesterday's Judeo-Christianity?

Provided that we understand this twin movement correctly and do not repeat the errors of the past, and provided that we Jews consent to take the hand that after so many centuries of humiliations and torments the Christians are finally extending to us, is this not the opportunity for an unprecedented treaty with the potential to yield almost unimaginable fruit?

A ROCK CALLED ZION

There is Israel, of course.

Not just the general virtues of Israel, its value as an example, and so on, but the way in which its existence changed everything for every Jew.

We all have our own experience of this.

Mine begins with the Six-Day War and the unexpected moment when the de-Judaized Jew that I was at that time began to fear for a country that meant nothing to him and about which he knew only that it had recently attained a national form that he thought outmoded.

I was emerging from adolescence.

And I already had the taste for adventure that would soon take me to Bangladesh.

But in the impulse that led me, on that Friday, to appear at the Israeli consulate in Paris and offer to join the volunteers streaming in from all corners of the globe to lend a hand to the young nation assailed on all sides by Arab armies, in that impulse there was a spirit that, in retrospect, I believe, was not in the same category as the simple yen for adventure.

Even more inexplicable was the emotion that gripped me when, three days later (it was June 12), forty-eight hours too late to be able to take part, however symbolically, in Israel's just war against a coalition of states in league to lend the finishing touch to the unfinished genocide of the Nazis, I set foot for the first time on soil that was both utterly foreign to me and yet strangely familiar.

At the time, I knew nothing about the Zionist adventure or its meaning.

I am from a family that embraced Heine's famous saying that Judaism, Zionism included, was a source of "insults and pain" that one would not wish on one's worst enemy.

If I had been aware of the then-burgeoning literature that sang of the redemption of the Jews through work and land, if I had had the slightest idea of the meaning, from the work of Theodor Herzl and Bernard Lazare down to Max Nordau's *Degeneration,* of the ideology of the farmer-soldier arriving, out of fidelity to the religion of Moses, to plant olive trees in the dunes of the Negev, it would have seemed to me hopelessly Boy Scoutish and far less dignified than the contemporaneous ideology of the Chinese people's communes.

Clearly my Judaism, supposing I really had any at the time, and my metaphysics, supposing I was aware of the collection of reflexes and concepts that would one day come together to form my brand of metaphysics, were much closer to Moses's other big deed: the first one, when he "comes out toward his brothers," as the Bible says, becomes their leader, and urges them, after the murder of the Egyptian, never to compromise either with politics or with any of the acts taught on the world-historical stage that he left behind in Egypt or (it follows) with the *lachon hara,* the "bad language" of mudslinging and betrayal that is the language of power. Had I then had the vaguest idea of the religion of Moses, "my" Moses would have been much closer to the inspired shepherd who brings all of Israel together to say to it, "You are as the sand," echoing the announcement made to the patriarchs: "Your descendants shall be like the sand of the sea."

Not olive trees but human beings were compared to sand, which is, of all solid substances, the most mobile, the most formless, mutable, shifting effortlessly, soundlessly, without altering the ground on which it lies, without any digging, with nothing more than the caress or slap of the wind, imperceptibly.

Not the earth and the buildings raised upon it but human dwellings summoned, ordained, urged, called upon to forget, since they are only sand, the boundary markers, the pilings, the stone, the mortar, the gilding, the stucco, the distended volumes of that enormous edifice known as social life, where everything is connected, where all is substance and consistency.

Was the lightness of sand soluble in Zionism?

Was my metaphysics soluble in that swarm of signifiers that swirled around the Jewish nation?

Probably not.

But metaphysics is one thing; life, often, is another.

And can't the same individual be fluent in the two political languages, those of essence and expedience?

It is a fact that Zionism, which was, doctrinally, not my style, bowled me over when I encountered it.

It is clear that a link was forged then between that nation and me, a link that nothing could break.

I remember as if it were yesterday the customs officers at Tel Aviv's Ben Gurion International Airport, as if they were Guillaume Apollinaire's angels at the gate to paradise.

I remember the lively disorder on Dizengoff, the calm euphoria that reigned in sidewalk cafés, and an air of camaraderie and celebration that I have encountered on just one other occasion: in Paris, a year later, in May '68.

I remember Jaffa with its sinuous, climbing alleys, its blockhouses of emblazoned ochre stone, and, farther down, on the beach, a story that affected me as if its subject, a man I never knew, had been my friend: the story of the assassination, fifteen years before the birth of the state of Israel, of Haim Arlosoroff, the prince of left-wing Zionism, the only one at the time preaching true dialogue with the Arabs, a figure now forgotten, though he was in his time the most valuable, bravest Zionist leader after David Ben-Gurion.

I remember Ben-Gurion at home at the Boker kibbutz near Beersheba, recounting, in the midst of an interview designed to flesh out my very first article, his theory of redemption through the desert. There is one advantage of the desert, he explained to me in the garden of the farm to which he had retired like a modern Cincinnatus, a place reached at the end of a long drive through a landscape of rock and megaliths that appeared to have been furrowed by the very finger of God. In the desert, he continued, it is not nature that is generous with man but the other way around: Man augments nature with his prodigious intelligence. Listening to him, I had the feeling that whole new perspectives of thought were opening before me, to which I had only, one day, to give philosophical form.

I remember another kibbutz, in Degania, on the Sea of Galilee, and my insistence on going to reflect, without knowing exactly why, in the little military cemetery in which lay sixty-seven heroes of the war of independence who had fallen there under fire from Syrian invaders.

Farther north along the shore of the Sea of Galilee is the kibbutz that Jean-Paul Sartre and Simone de Beauvoir had visited three months earlier at the invitation of my friend Ely Bengal. I remember a miraculous moment there, in which I was hypnotized by a gray line that I thought was the shoreline before being informed that it was the boundary between the sky and a horizon that stretched out beyond the clouds.

I remember high deserts and seas that lay below sea level.

I remember stony landscapes in which I sensed the mysterious imprint left by eyes that had looked on them for centuries upon centuries before me.

And I remember the strange feelings that overtook me when I came in contact with the wall in Jerusalem. I had told myself it would have no particular effect on me, but then I could not resist touching it, like the soldiers who, automatic weapons slung over their shoulders, eyes closed before the stone of the wall, drank in the so-often-imagined symbol, now suddenly real, for which they had just risked their lives.

I remember all of that.

I remember a country where everything whispered to my soul in its soft native tongue.

And the truth is that, though I was then so tepidly Jewish, there I found the most unexpected of inner homelands, a rock on which I knew immediately that I would lean from that point forward.

The rock has two faces, of course. And since the existence of Israel is not the least of what fuels the new anti-Semitism, danger also emanates from the rock itself, completing a vicious circle that is central to the tragic aspect of Jewish destiny today.

It is also complex. And the unique experience of Israel, the responsibility of a certain number of Jews over a land to which they have long been tied by memory, prayer, and longing, the embrace of politics and policy that they were paradoxically spared by ostracism and by the usurping kings that kept them in exile—all that constitutes one of the hardest and ultimately riskiest trials that the Jewish people have ever had to endure. And no one today can predict what will come of it. No one can say whether the Jews, for having embarked on this path, will have to bear the blame placed by Samuel on those who submitted to Saul, or whether they will remain Moses's pupils; whether they will build a new Babel or, as the founding fathers intended, a new kind of kingdom; whether this national gestation—the longest, bumpiest, and most chaotic in all human history—will produce an ordinary state or a return to Jacob, the man who earned the nickname Israel because he had struggled (with God and men) to ensure a place under the tent for all those who chose to share his name and who, in so choosing, made that tent not only the symbol of the sad fragility of the nomad, defenseless against the winds of heaven and the arrows of enemies, but the mark of a people who, seeing themselves as "Men," preferred as protection the fine cloth of words and the flimsy parasol of commentaries to the granite walls within which bodies that are always too heavy gather to bury themselves. In short, no one can predict whether or not Israel will turn from a fascinating country into an admirable or sublime one.

But one thing was apparent to me from that first trip, some part of which I have never let go.

Hate being what it is, in its present form or a former one, the fact and the idea of Israel contain precious blessings.

The fact: If dark times, truly dark times, were to return, if the supposed "Jewish question" were to be presented again with new but just as terrifying answers, there would be, for imperiled and defenseless Jews, not a "solution" but a way out, which they so tragically lacked before. Even if vulnerable and under threat, even at the risk of pulling the front line of persecution closer to home, Israel would provide a providential fallback.

The idea: The very fact that this might be possible, the awareness, however vague, of the existence of this country of refuge, the feeling of premonition, even among those Jews most reluctant to acknowledge or discuss their Jewishness or, even worse, to have a Jewish word spoken in their name, that if the world were to become uninhabitable for the Jews there would remain this habitat here—that idea, that awareness, is, even for Jews of that stripe, a reassuring and happy thought in the back of one's mind, a bit of knowledge only dimly known that may not ever or often come to consciousness, an assurance of pride, of having a grip on life, an assurance of dignity. Oh, those self-shaming Jews! Those reluctant Jews whose mistrust regarding the subject of Israel is the correlate of the will to know nothing about outmoded Judaism, that residue of the ancient exiles, that remainder in the calculus of nations on an upward arc to victory, or that will to melt into the sort of world citizenship practiced in my family and, later, more radically, in the revolutionary circles of my youth. Well, even they prove the rule! Even for them the idea of Israel functions as the shelter I have described! I do not know of a single Jew in the world for whom the presence of Israel is not a promise—perhaps a promise deferred, but a promise nonetheless.

EMMANUEL LEVINAS, ALBERT COHEN, AND OTHERS: JUDAISM STANDING TALL

And then there is this last reason, which is related to the self-perception of the Jews of Europe, independent of Israel.

Its emblematic French figures of the 1930s are pretty well known: the Camondos; the Cahen-Salvadors; the many variants of the Rothschilds; or Alfred Dreyfus, who was still living but had not recovered from being the too-visible Jew who paid so dearly for the indecency of his visibility.

We are familiar with the axiom and the sequence of theorems about which the great German-speaking Jews of the same time agreed:

an impoverished Judaism, cut off from the Talmudic corpus and reduced to the Torah alone; a devitalized Torah, itself reduced to abstract principles that were little more than rules of conduct; a Judaism
characterized by a structural and even substantial identity between
the Law and laws, the Word of God and the rights of man, Mosaic
revelation and the Revolution of 1789, Jewish ethics and the Kantian
categorical imperative.

But what is less known is how the entire post–World War II
period—all those years, those decades, spent taking the measure of
what had just happened and of what caused the world to have been
blind to it—where the theater of a rupture with that civic but blood-
less Judaism, a rupture that began slowly, almost imperceptibly, but
then, from the 1970s, gained speed and suddenly became visible.

There was Emmanuel Levinas and his philosophical power play:
Greek, *and* Jewish; Athens, *but also* Jerusalem; Plato, Husserl, Heidegger, *Logos*, yes, but do not forget, when philosophizing, that other
rationality, that other deposit of meaning and concepts that he calls
"Biblical sense."

There was French novelist Albert Cohen and the invention of
Solal, that solar, Apollonian Jew, almost Greek. This "Solal" did not
turn his back (this was one of the themes of my conversations with
Cohen) on the anti-natural wager that is at the heart of Jewish language. He did not forgo the distance from oneself, the intimate dis-
agreement, difference, and gap without which Judaism no longer
makes sense. He certainly did not become, in other words, some Jewish version of a neo-Nietzschean superman and never lost sight (this
most of all) of the inbred pessimism (imparted to him by his creator)
about the durability of anti-Semitic hatred. But he invented and em-
bodied a type of man that the world had not seen since time immemorial, a man who can be summed up in three very simple sentences
that would, for all their simplicity, echo resoundingly in people's
minds all over the world.

First, Jews have a body. They are no longer a people of cloud,
pure spirit grafted onto a fleshless, cadaverized body as depicted in
the anti-Semitic literature of the time.

SECOND, JEWS CAN BE GOOD-LOOKING. They are no longer the unsightly beings suggestive of the ruinous split between man and world that Hegel described as their metaphysical fate. They can be appealing; they can be flamboyant; they can even—if they are Maurice de Rothschild, whom the author of *Belle du Seigneur*, a respectable functionary at the League of Nations, would sometimes observe through his window enjoying the company of a lady friend on the grounds of his estate in Pregny—court without shame or scandal the old nobility, the Ariane d'Aubles of France, Switzerland, and Navarre.

THIRD, JEWS ARE FREE. They have been free since they left Egypt, during which time the synagogues of the world have celebrated, on Passover, the unprecedented liberation of which the rest of humanity seems to be unaware, preferring to continue to relegate the Jews in word and deed to the same inevitable servitude. Well, Solal is the escape from Egypt in the flesh; he is the column of cloud and fire placed before the eyes of the unbelieving; he is the first truly free Jew of European literature.

And then there were all of those young Jews who, when they were not studying, pure and simple, went to school on Solal and Levinas and, without calling into question the republican pact made by their elders, restored the dignity of Jewish thought, which, according to Scholem, the Western world had a very hard time appreciating for its true value, despite the Holocaust. Judaism, an act of affirmation. A positive Judaism lived clearly, truthfully, and honorably. A Judaism proud of its values, of the intellectual tradition it bore, and of its memory. A Judaism that began to consider itself less in terms of what the world owed to it than of what it could offer to the world.

There were, of course, those who did not welcome that act of revolt and affirmation.

There were Jews, including prominent ones such as Raymond Aron, who continued to fear that Jewish affirmation—the renunciation of Marranism and of the unwritten rule that nothing of the inner Jew should ever come to the surface—could only exacerbate the ambient anti-Semitism and, far from protecting Jews, expose them once again to danger.

And I recall the worry, perhaps even the fear, of the last representatives of Franco-Judaism; I remember the apprehension of those eminent men, now largely forgotten, who guided my entry into the ranks of what people were once again—timidly—calling the French Jewish community. I can picture their fine, pensive faces, at once trusting and anxious, in the old black-and-white photo taken one day in September 1979 in front of the memorial to the unknown Jewish martyr in Paris. They appear trusting, of course, because they had invited me to give the annual address in honor of those who died in the Holocaust and because I had reciprocated by agreeing to speak before the sons and daughters of deportees, before the veterans' standard-bearer, in the period between Rosh Hashanah and Yom Kippur, a period that tradition describes as days of awe. But they are anxious, as well, understandably anxious or at least perplexed, as they hear me sing the praises of the affirmative Jew to the point of glorifying an obscure, nonobservant Jew by the name of Pierre Goldman, who had been murdered in Paris several days earlier.

I think they were wrong.

And I think that most of them thought so, too.

The way of Franco-Judaism, the way of their fathers—*their* way, perhaps—had proved a dead end, had it not? Did they not know better than anyone how that denial of oneself, rejection of the name and of study, had left the Jews of France defenseless when darkness set in?

And hadn't the members of their families who did not return from the camps, those who were being remembered that day, sinned through their excessive confidence in what they thought was their dual Franco-Jewish citizenship? They had sinned in the manner of the great historian Marc Bloch, who shouted, *"Vive la France!"* until the moment that he was shot, shortly before Aragon's twenty-three partisans suffered the same fate.

No.

The affirmative Judaism of which I was the awkward but fervent herald on that day full of ill omens, at a time when the great anti-Semitic beast had in fact begun to stir for the first time since the war, had at least three advantages.

In a war where the enemy was making the supposed invisibility of its victims the very reason for hating them, suddenly showing oneself to the other side, meeting the enemy face-to-face, was not a bad strategy.

In a war where it was beginning to appear that nothing would be more useful to the new killers of Jews than to forget that they had *already* killed them and that the "Final Solution" had *already* occurred, a lucid Judaism, one that spurned the advocates of letting the dead bury the dead, was obviously better equipped to confront the returning danger.

And, finally, if Judaism really is animated by the genius that I have mentioned, if it truly is the rock that I praise, then what a protection we find right there! What armor! What a shield! Had self-denial disarmed the Jews? Had it prevented them from understanding what was happening to them when they were rejected by the national fabric into which they had become so intricately woven? Then, to that same extent, would not "affirmationism," the will of France's Jews to remain fully French while also becoming once again fully Jewish, would not their unambiguous embrace of their Jewish name (no longer the name of humanity's victim or of its star pupil but the name of the secret Adam who can stimulate, in the fragile center of everyone's thinking, the spark of a question), give them the will and the wherewithal to fight?

Judaism standing tall.

A vigilant Judaism confident of its resources.

A Judaism that does not apologize when offended but that fights back.

Which suggests another contrast with the disastrous 1930s.

The Jews are strong.

I do not mean in the sense of the brute force that is usually conveyed by the word "strength."

Their strength does not derive from the treasury bonds that Drumont and his ilk, like their opposite numbers in the United States, imagined the Jews had stashed away in "Jewish banks."

Their strength lies in a force about which the Drumonts of the world never had the faintest idea, so far was it beyond their grasp.

Had they been able to grasp it, that force would have quickly eroded the meager substance upon which they built their clamorous, empty, and mediocre existences.

They are strong through study and spirit.

They are strong through their memory and through their effort to know.

Jews are strong when they mine intelligence from its matrix of gangue.

Strong in knowing that the sage is greater even than the prophet.

They are strong when, through intense effort, through unrelenting struggle with the self, through an asceticism of spirit that does not deny the body or its knowledge, they dedicate themselves to the astonishing discovery that God is a writer whose Book must never become an unclaimed inheritance.

And it is because they are full of this strength, because they are rich with this irradiating wisdom, as old as the wounds of Egypt, a wisdom that makes them bleed, groan, sigh from the effort to understand, sigh at not understanding, and exult with wonder when finally they do understand; it is because they have this wound of the soul, as old as the time when, still oozing from the whips of Pharaoh's kapos, they were ejected into the silence of the desert with a mission to escape; it is because they have an open cut that will close, scar over, and be reopened many times until an unimaginable amount of time passes—it is for that reason, at bottom, that they have nothing to fear. It is because existences consist of words recorded in one form or another and are tested not through the endurance of the human plant but through meaning sought, made, and faced that the Jews are supremely existent and called to triumph over their adversaries.

To that form of Judaism I came both very early ("I was thirty years old . . .") and very late (so many years spent without studying, without increasing my knowledge, and, above all, without wrestling with the language—and, yes, it is getting late).

But I know it is there.

I know that if I want it, it is within reach.

And that certitude is sweetly consoling.

I am not afraid.

One must not be afraid.

We are certainly not living through a return of the 1930s.

Victory belongs to those who succeed in reclaiming that which the realm of nothingness nearly swallowed up but which, fortunately, the angels remembered.

CHAPTER FOUR

JEWISH FRANCE

And then there is another reason, perhaps the most important one of all, not to lose heart.

That reason is France.

By that I mean the place of the Jews in France as it has been formed over the centuries and the role of the Jews in that process.

Not only the "Frenchness of the Jews," the sense of France that resides in their hearts and souls, which the adherents of Franco-Judaism grasped very well. (This was the good part of their vision of things.)

But also the "Jewishness of France," an essence tightly woven into the nation's adventure in a way that the disciples of Drumont did not want to understand—or perhaps one that they understood all too well when they spoke of "Jewish France." And this, while less known than the Jews' feeling of being French, is even more important.

Three stories.

Three sequences, three highly symbolic moments in the history of my country, each extraordinary in its own way.

RASHI AND THE INVENTION OF FRANCE

The founding of France.

Its first steps, its first words, on the world scene.

And the way the Jewish voice accompanied that genesis—an accompaniment that has been oddly unremarked.

But let us begin at the very beginning.

I am among those who were never bothered by the adage about France being the eldest daughter of the Church.

And it never bothered me because, France being defined, like all the world's nations, by the conjunction of time (during which a memory is built), space (more or less stable and bounded, in France's case, by the ocean), and above all a language (derived from Latin), the French nation emerged in the wake of an unprecedented power grab, or perhaps a redoubled power grab—in any event a spectacular one.

At the head of the coup is Clovis, a Frankish prince who, like all the other barbarian princes, speaks a Germanic language but who suddenly adopts the language of the vanquished—Latin.

But before that, upstream of his linguistic conversion and presiding over it, comes his conversion to a religion that is the other name for Latinity and that is coming to be called Christianity. It is his entry not into the "ancient city," in the sense that Fustel de Coulanges will eventually give to the term, but into the "city of God," as Augustine described it in the pages that are among the most inspired and most complex ever to have sprung from the Latin tongue.

And thus France is born.

It is born, whether we like it or not, from a bifurcation in the idealized primal unity of what Dumézil, going back in time in the way one struggles to paddle a canoe up a tumbling stream, called the Indo-European languages.

And it would not exist but for the prodigious event that caused a part of Europe to break off from the Frankish Empire, which would soon molt into the Saxon Empire, then the Hohenstaufen, and then the Habsburg, sloughing its successive skins before becoming the unstable Holy Roman Empire, the oxymoronic form of the name well expressing its hectic destiny, from the enduring fragmentation of the Germans to the fascinating supranational confabulation that was the Austro-Hungarian world. France would not exist without the clean break that led a warlord (and what a warlord! Among the cruelest who ever lived! One relegated by Voltaire, in canto V of *Maid of Orleans,* to the last circle of hell, alongside Anastasius II, the apostate pope!) to refashion his warriors, body and soul, in the image of the Christ he had just discovered; to adopt, in an act of astonishing and preternatural voluntarism, the religion, culture, *Weltanschauung*, and language of those whom he had just conquered; and, in so doing, to forge a first but ultimately enduring link, one that would be re-forged after his time, from reign to reign, with a population of monks, scholars, learned men, and copyists who would consolidate the language that is such a fundamental element of France's very being.

Among those men there is one who is too often overlooked.

A scholar whose name is too often eclipsed.

His name was Rashi.

He was and remains the world's greatest Talmudic scholar.

He was not merely one Jewish thinker among others but rather *the one* who tirelessly annotated and explicated the sparse, laconic words of the Torah and the Talmud; narrowed the yawning gap that had separated us from scriptures thought to be inaccessible; proved in a stroke the verse about the Torah being "not in heaven" but within man's grasp; unlocked, in other words, that pure intelligence that without him would have remained unintelligibly wound around itself. He is the one, therefore, who made and still makes Jewish thought possible for everyone.

But, living in eleventh-century Troyes in the Champagne region, where he cultivated wine grapes, Rashi was also one of the greatest geniuses in the history of France and, a few centuries after Clovis, one of the nation's most unlikely pioneers. Yet this side of him is little known. . . .

In my mind's eye I see him thriving in the Champagne country that is still two centuries away from the first expropriation and expulsion of the Jews, carried out by Philippe le Bel when he was short of cash.

I observe his *position* in the feudal world, where it is not unusual to see a Jew become a lord and where his own grandson, Rabbeinu Tam, also a Talmudist and steeped, like his grandfather, in the holy texts and versed in the language of Moses and Christ, will become a member of the king's council and take part, with his own silver-taloned hawks, in the ritual of Frenchness that is the great hunt.

I imagine his constant dialogue with the Christian priors, abbots, and theologians who consult him, who are troubled by his views, who question him on this or that point of interpretation of a verse from the "first testament," which they know only through the Vulgate of Saint Jerome.

I note that it is he and he alone whom Godefroy de Bouillon, the future Defender of the Holy Sepulcher and Christian quasi-king of Jerusalem, comes to consult about his chances for success on the eve of his departure for the First Crusade.

I listen to what he says about women, about their eminent place in creation, about the crime committed by men who repudiate a spouse who has concealed her leprosy.

I read the splendid passages in which he explains that a man must deserve his beloved, that it is usually wrong to be jealous, and that it is by being unjustly jealous that he instills in his wife the idea of betrayal: Was Rashi not laying down the foundations of what will become known as courtly love, which will loom so large in the invention of the French spirit?

But above all—and not to deviate from the question of the French language, which, as I say, is the true crucible of France and its ideas— there is an underappreciated oddity that was pointed out by Arsène Darmesteter, the very learned professor of French philology at the Sorbonne in the nineteenth century and author of the monumental *Les Gloses françaises de Raschi dans la Bible* (*French Glosses in Rashi's Commentary on the Torah*).

The men of letters of the time, essentially monastic copyists, write in Latin.

They speak French, of course.

Their vernacular, the language they use in their everyday dealings, is possibly that early French known as *langue d'oïl*.

But they do not write it.

Because most of what they are copying, up to the twelfth century, is religious text, they have no reason to write other than in Latin.

And if things had stopped with them, with their books of hours, holy scriptures, occasional exegeses, and feudal chronicles singing the praises and recounting the feats and deeds of the local duke, the emerging French language would have left no trace or memory.

There are exceptions, of course.

There are the *Serments de Strasbourg* from 842 and the *Gloses de Reichenau* dating from the end of the previous century.

There are the *Vie de saint Léger* and the *Vie de saint Alexis,* the former recounting the martyrdom of a seventh-century bishop and the latter the fifth-century legend of the son of a Roman senator who became a beggar.

Later, between the ninth and thirteenth centuries, would come *La Chanson de Roland*, the *Roman de Renart,* and the *Roman de la Rose.*

There would be the work of another native of Champagne, Chrétien de Troyes, the subject of a whole school of early twentieth-century medievalists, who asserted that he was a member of the powerful Jewish community of Troyes of which Rashi was the figurehead: there would be the idea of taking the name of a city and the first name Christian (which, of course, was common enough but, reasoned these medievalists, can here be seen as affirmation or denial), and there would be *Philomena,* his first book, as far as we know, which he actually signed "Chrétien le Goy," in other words, "Christian the convert" (the other, and opposite, explanation of "le goy" being merely an allusion to the village of Gouaix, adjacent to Troyes, where he may have been born).

But the most important exception, the one that you hear the least about but that counts the most in the history of this linguistic gestation, in the slow evolution of French from the *langue d'oïl* and Latin, is Rashi himself.

For what exactly is Rashi up to in his house of study in Troyes?

He is writing his commentaries on the Talmud in the language that was his Latin—namely, Hebrew.

But because those commentaries have the characteristic—like all Talmudic commentaries and unlike the emerging Christian gloss—of being full of allusions to daily life and the thousand and one practical problems that confront the believer in the course of that life, they necessarily require modern analogies, references, and words.

So Rashi's Hebrew text bristles with words that, although they seem to be Hebrew words because he transcribed and phonetically reproduced them in Hebrew characters, are really words that a wine producer from Troyes would use in the daily life of the modern eleventh century to settle an everyday question of business, law, family life, practical morality, ritual offering, coexistence with a Christian woman insisting that a Jewish man swear an oath on a relic, taxes, contracts to be drawn up or fulfilled, the repair of a winepress or mill, cooking, or inheritance.

With the result that there are, inserted into his gloss of the Bible and the Talmud, thousands of French words drawn from the vocabularies of the wine grower, lawyer, boilermaker, barrel maker, farmer, hunter, miller, toolmaker, weaver, man-at-arms, tanner, spice merchant, and butcher.

And these words, which by definition did not appear in the illuminated manuscripts of the monks, words that had no reason to appear in their verbatim copies of ancient texts, words that became necessary only in the writing of a holy book that is also, like the Talmud, a guide to life in which the *mal'akhim* (angels) involve themselves in the doings of everyday life—the fact is that, without Rashi, we would not be aware of their appearance, their sound, or even their existence.

Rashi's writings are a memorial to French at its beginnings.

They are not only the preserve but also the preservative, the formaldehyde, the liquid nitrogen in which Old French was captured and saved from oblivion.

But, as we know from Benveniste, Hjelmslev, and Jakobson, that is how languages really function. The preservative, the conservator, is also an actor. And, by fixing Old French, by restoring its "living sound" through his "anathematized book of spells" (words from James Darmesteter's tribute to his brother, delivered in 1888), by enabling posterity, both immediate and distant, *to see the voices* of the first French language, by conferring upon it its nobility and, through its transcription into a holy text, rescuing it from its inferior status as a popular tongue, trivial and undeserving of being written down, Rashi's work is also the starting gun for the complex process of generation and degeneration, decomposition and recomposition, creative destruction and retransformation that will become the history of the French language.

There is no need to confine Rashi's influence to the metaphorical or ideal realm.

No need to imagine a space for thought separate from that of things, an immaterial and noumenal realm, an ether of ideas that would pass through people without their noticing, a circulation of spirits that could eclipse opaque bodies.

No.

A text written in Hebrew participated concretely in the genesis and metamorphoses of early French.

At the intersection of these two worlds; at the juncture of these two languages and two ways of seeing; between, on the one hand, the French lexical work that is just beginning to emerge in the pregnant Middle Ages but that will burst forth soon enough in the extraordinary brilliance of Descartes and, on the other, the labor of this discreet Jew who, living quietly among his compatriots, works the titanic trials, strivings, and struggles of the life of the mind in order to expand the realm of the intelligible—there was a contagious, driving effect.

And that's why it can be said without the slightest risk of exaggeration, without stretching the letter or the spirit of the historical record, that Rashi is one of the inventors of France. When, the day after an anti-Semitic attack, France's highest authorities solemnly declare that "France without Jews would not be France," that is what they are saying. Even if they are not aware of it, they have Rashi in mind.

THE KINGS OF ISRAEL AND
THE REPUBLICAN CONTRACT

Another thing they have in mind, whether they know it or not, is the founding of the French republic.

That founding is the subject of an official chronicle composed, from Ernest Lavisse to Jules Isaac, by the historians of modern France, a chronicle that is the civic religion of every student in France.

Whoever utters the word "republic" invokes, according to these historians, another exceptional event no less important than the baptism of Clovis: the Revolution of 1789.

And whoever invokes the revolution also invokes those inspirational figures who were the thinkers of the Enlightenment, among them Jean-Jacques Rousseau, who was the first, it is said, to have formulated the twin theory of the general will and the social contract.

And whoever invokes Rousseau and (thus) the revolution evokes a Greco-Roman imaginarium that supposedly supplied the stock of references available for imitation by Frenchmen living during this period of history and thought. Consider Rousseau's practice in the *Second Discourse* (where he aims "to use a language suitable to all nations") of imagining himself "in an Athenian school" reciting "the lessons of his teachers" and having "Plato and Xenocrates" assess him. Consider chapter 4 of his *Social Contract,* one of the most important, in which, seeking the model for the virtuous republic of his dreams, the place in the world where, for the first time, the people were sovereign, he finds it in early Rome. Consider his disciples, the revolutionaries of the Constituent Assembly and later of the Convention, who, in new decks of cards purged of their kings, queens, and jacks, feature the philosopher's portrait along with those of Brutus, Cato, and Solon. And consider Tallien, who calls Robespierre a "Sylla"; Robespierre, who describes Tallien as "Gaius Verres"; the Valmy regiments, organized on the model of the Roman legions; the military honors inspired by the civic wreaths of Sparta and Athens; the red cap of the *sans culottes,* which is that of emancipated Romans; and even the victims, such as Madame Roland, Buzot, and Vergniaud, who mount the scaffold reciting Plutarch's *Lives.* In short, a Greco-Roman phantasmagoria that, when one rereads the works, revisits the speeches, reports, and decrees of Saint-Just, when one reviews the fiery appeals in Marat's *L'Ami du peuple* or Hébert's *Le Père Duchesne,* seems to be the major paradigm, perhaps the sole paradigm, of the republic in the course of its construction.

But let us change the focus for a moment.

Let us take a step back from these martial inspirations.

And let us adopt, toward the whole matter, a wider perspective, one less fraught, one based on a longer view of history.

Rousseau's theory did not fall from the sky.

His concept of sovereignty based on the individual's surrender of a share of his freedom for the benefit of all is the culmination of an older tradition of thought inaugurated two centuries earlier by another convulsion studied by Blandine Kriegel, a contemporary philosopher: the prolonged and noisy peasant revolt and subsequent democratic movement that occurred across the Netherlands, Belgium, and northern France, a movement to which Rousseau was heir.

Now, it turns out that in this earlier history, for the whole host of thinkers who, before Rousseau, had begun to ponder the idea of sovereignty, for the many who plowed this ground before Rousseau's work and its subsequent practical applications by the revolutionaries of 1789 eclipsed them, the major reference was not the Greeks or Romans but none other than the Hebrew kingdoms.

We will not dwell on Spinoza, who certainly was not eclipsed, but whose *Tractatus Theologico-Politicus* may be read as one of the "De Republica Hebraeorum"s that, in the seventeenth century, became almost a literary genre, and turns on a fine distinction among three concepts of sovereignty, all of which have to do with the history of the Israelites and of the Israelites alone: whether one "withholds" it, as in Egypt; "entrusts" it to Moses, as after the crossing of the Red Sea; or "divides" it between priests and kings, as in the era of Saul.

We will not dwell on Thomas Hobbes (although a Latin version of his *Leviathan* was available as early as 1668) or on his *De Cive,* which was the first important work to have made the decisive, nearly Copernican substitution of modern contractualism for the Aristotelian naturalism that had prevailed up until then. Hobbes, too, made that substitution, by relying not on the exemplary republic of the Romans but on the community of those who had fled Egypt; on Moses's sort of ministry; on the war of the Jews according to Flavius Josephus—in short, on the saga of the Hebrew people, whom Hobbes believed to be "not only the most free" but also "the most opposed to any human subjection."

But we cannot fail to evoke the lofty figure of Jean Bodin, inventor of the French version of the doctrine of sovereignty in the sixteenth century, who was a forthright Hebraist, perhaps a Jew, perhaps a Marrano, an avid scholar of Maimonides and his *Guide for the Perplexed,* and an associate of the great professor of Hebrew and Syriac at the Collège Royal, Jean Cinquarbres.

We must not overlook the fact that chapter 8 of the first of Bodin's *Six Livres de la République,* the one that deals with the question of sovereignty, opens with a discussion of the comparative meaning of the word in three languages, Latin, Greek, but also Hebrew, and that, when one must decide among them, when it comes time to make the most effective argument for limiting the *plenitudo potestatis* of papal and other priestly power, when it comes to offering his contemporaries and their descendants the ultimate weapon against the "canonist chicanery" practiced by the adherents of absolutism, it is not Plato whom Bodin cites but Moses, not Paul but Joshua, and not the Romans but the Hebrews, who, he says, "always show the appropriateness of things."

How amazing it is to dive into these old debates and dig into the record. One finds the author of this new *République* contesting the climate theory of Polybius by citing the unity of humanity proclaimed in the Old Testament; Grotius reproaching him for being insufficiently Greek—that is, too Jewish; Guillaume Du Bartas, by contrast, in one of the best scenes from his political poem, *La Magnificence,* drawing inspiration from Bodin to compare the war-like minds of his time with the example of the Israelites seeking out and swearing in a king to free them from the priestly judges; Hubert Languet entering the fray to insist that a promise is enough and is made no better by an oath; or Theodore Beza replying, no, you also need the oath, it is an essential part of the promise, because there can be no true contract in the absence of a solemn confirmation taking the form of positive laws by which the sovereign will be bound. And how amazing, indeed, to see that all of these discussions (which were, as I say, the real compost from which sprang the flower of the social contract and then the tree of liberty as understood by the French revolutionaries) are led by authors whose points of reference, most prominent examples, inspirational figures, and guides are no longer Cleopatra but the Queen of Sheba, no longer Romulus but Saul, no longer Tarquin but King Solomon, no longer the Gracchi but Judas of Galilee.

An example: the question of the abuse of royal power, of the right to rebel, and, ultimately, of regicide, a question that will become so important in 1792, when Louis XVI is deposed and tried.

All of that is there.

Everything, or nearly everything, is covered.

Between Duplessis-Mornay's *Vindiciae contra tyrannos* and the more moderate work of Jean Bodin, the terms of the discussion are laid out in their entirety, so that Barère, Robert Lindet, and Robespierre on the one hand and the defenders of Louis XVI, François-Denis Tronchet, and Raymond de Sèze on the other could have adopted them word for word.

Except that these authors speak not of Caesar and Brutus, not of Tarquin and Servius Tullius, but rather of the meaning to be given to the verses from Jeremiah concerning the respect owed to Nebuchadnezzar; of the section of Deuteronomy devoted to the duties of the king; and of the story, in Kings, of Ahab's theft of the vineyard of Naboth the Jezreelite.

Through what mysterious process was this tradition so thoroughly erased?

What accounts for the fact that nothing remains of it, neither in Rousseau's work nor in the words of the orators who, on the floor of the Assembly, read the forty-nine counts of the accusation against the king and, after the trial, attempted to put into words and then into institutions the old project of a civil power based on a contract and resistant to the abuses of a tyrant? Why the obsession, upon the flight to Varennes and then at the trial itself, to hark back to ancient times, when ready at hand and much closer in time was a vast literature that posed in eminently modern terms the set of problems associated with resistance to tyranny?

What shell game, what trick of the devil or of history, can cause such a store of knowledge, an entire continent of thought, to be submerged in so little time, so that the very name of Jean Bodin, with his collection of precious references to the Second Book of Samuel and to King David's reign, should have evaporated so completely just as the moment arrived to apply them to the task of establishing republican France?

For this malign miracle I see only one reasonable explanation—or possibly two.

The first is that the calmer, gentler Hebrew example, more inclined to compromise than was the Greco-Roman, would have frustrated the terrorist frenzy of the assassins of Louis XVI.

And the second, which is related to the first, is that that example was already present, too present, in the model of sovereignty from which they were attempting to depart—that of the monarchy.

One forgets that from the anointment of Clovis and into the coronational liturgy, the kings of France, while expropriating the Jews and chasing them from the kingdom whenever it suited them, also never ceased to affirm their kinship with David.

It is not widely enough appreciated that, despite pogroms, despite the blindfolded symbol of the eclipsed synagogue at the cathedral doors, the bishops who blessed new monarchs never failed at the decisive moment to call on "the blessing that Holy King David received from heaven as did Solomon his son."

I am not sure that many are aware—though the contemporaries of the revolutionaries of 1789 obviously knew full well—that the surname David was given to King Pepin because of his small stature, to Charlemagne because of his warrior-priest side, and to Louis VII because of his humility.

Or of the fact that, when Pope Gregory IX wanted to honor (in *Dei Filius* of 1239, a bull invoked by Pius X in 1908, upon the beatification of Joan of Arc) the country that "the Redeemer has chosen" as "the agent of his divine will," he compares it with the "tribe of Judah," which was favored over the tribes of "the other sons of Jacob," and which was (I am quoting Pius X) "the prefiguration of the Kingdom of France"; and he paints this chosen kingdom as a sort of "quiver" that the Redeemer "wears hanging about his loins" and from which he draws, in the purest biblical style, "his arrows of election."

Not to mention the thousand signs great and small that continued to stoke the will of France's kings to hold fast to the rope that tethered them to their Jewish descent.

The consecration of the Abbey of Saint-Denis, described by Suger as the foundation of a new temple.

The mantle of fleur-de-lis bestowed upon the king at the end of the coronation ceremony, which, for some, refers to the iris on the diadem of the high priests of Israel; for others, to the iris sculpted atop the capital of the temple of Solomon; and, for still others, to the iris on the coins minted by Simon bar Kokhba during his revolt against the Romans.

The history, so little known, of the great Jews ennobled by the Carolingian kings, such as Natronai ben Habibi, a descendant of the house of King David seconded to Charlemagne by the caliph in Baghdad to assist in the capture of Narbonne from the caliph's Umayyad Arab enemies, to whom Pepin grants, in addition to the hand of his sister, the title of Count of Septimania. Or Natronai's son, William of Gellone, assumed to be a descendant of the tribe of Judah and made Duke of Toulouse, Marquess of Gothia, and one of the preeminent princes of the court of Charlemagne.

The creation, in 791, by a converted deacon of Louis the Pious, of the Judaic Academy of Saint-Guilhem-le-Désert.

Or the Collège de France, that paragon of the transmission of knowledge created by King François I at the behest of the head of the royal library, Guillaume Budé, whose chief goal was to have, in addition to chairs in Latin and Greek, a suitable locus for the third language of learning, which was Hebrew.

All of that lies jumbled in the heads of the revolutionaries.

It is the collusion of the Hebrew model with the Ancien Régime that repels them so powerfully.

And here is a final proof, eloquent and delicious, that I found in a history of the Jews of Bordeaux.

It concerns a man by the name of Peixotto.

Engraved on the pediment of his house is a coat of arms topped with the crown of a count. After the revolutionaries get wind of this, a strange trial begins.

Peixotto is smeared by the anti-royalists.

Peixotto defends himself by repeating what he has already said in a similar action directed against him in 1789: He is a Levite, the descendant of a noble family, recognized and welcomed in all of the royal houses of Europe.

The local military committee of the Terror exclaims that this is even worse! This is the telling detail, the circumstance that is not mitigating but implicating! If this Peixotto is really who he says he is, if he is—and he appears to be—one of the country's most titled men, his crime is inexpiable, and it will not be sufficient to destroy this slab of stone representing the twelve tribes over which his house is supposed to preside! The place for this Levite, this epitome of the Ancien Régime, is no longer jail but the scaffold!

Peixotto succeeds in saving his life, but only by a whisker, by proving that because he has not been tightfisted in the acquisition of national assets he has the wherewithal to pay a colossal fine as well as a subsidy for the *sans culottes* of the Gironde.

In short, the revolutionaries knew what they were doing.

The periods were too close in time; they could not have just "forgotten" that living spring—or, to adopt the voice of Bodin in the first book of his *République* series, that "sacred fountain" whose first spouting dates back to the ancient Hebrews.

Even if they had managed to forget it, other voices would have been there to remind them. Mirabeau's *Sur Moses Mendelssohn, sur la réforme politique des Juifs* (*On Moses Mendelssohn and the Political Reform of the Jews*) is dated 1787. The *Essai sur la régénération physique, morale et politique des Juifs* (*Essay on the Physical, Moral, and Political Regeneration of the Jews*) of Abbot Gregory appeared in 1788. An ideologist by the name of Volney, who, after the revolution, wrote *Histoire de Samuel, inventeur du sacre des rois* (*History of Samuel, Inventor of the Coronation of Kings*), was already mocking, in a book that emerged from his history course at the École

Normale Supérieure in year III of the republic, the "superstitious adoration of the Romans and Greeks." No one knew, he said, by what sleight of hand that worship had accomplished the double tour de force of burying recent ancestors who "swore by Jerusalem and the Bible" and elevating to the "sanctuary of all liberty" societies in which, by night, citizens hunted enslaved people for sport (as the Spartans did the Helots) and, by day, behaved as if ruled by Attila or Genghis Khan (Athens); societies in which, generally, people lived under a system of "eternal war, executions of prisoners by cutting their throats, and massacres of women and children" (Rome).

But there you have it.

Robespierre, Saint-Just, and the others were determined to make a clean slate of this past.

That Hebraic spring bubbling in the depths of their memory, a memory that was in the process of becoming that of the nation, had at all costs to be dried up, plugged, *driven back*.

And the same applies to Napoleon, who put the last touches on the occultation.

The time is shortly after his coronation, the Roman fanfare of which was immortalized by David. Not the king, but the other David, the skillful but rather despicable painter, who went so far as to paint into his picture, just behind the new emperor, a look-alike of Julius Caesar.

Four years have passed since the grotesque ceremony in which he decided, amid a great profusion of eagles and Roman laurels, to sign, once and for all, the contract offered to the centuries to come by a revolution of which he believes (like Hegel, whom he did not know but who recognized in him the spirit of the world approaching the end of its odyssey) he will write the last act. And he has the nerve to ask the seventy-one rabbis and Jewish notables gathered together as a Sanhedrin if the law of the republic is compatible with theirs, when it was the latter that in large part made possible and even engendered the former!

The deceit continues with every one of the protectors and developers of the republican idea who never, over the course of two centuries, dreamed of questioning the legend of a French republic born

immaculately from our ancestors, the Romans. Whether we are talking about the Second Republic, the Third, the Fourth, or the Fifth,
whether it wears the face of Lamartine, Gambetta, Pierre Mendès
France, Charles de Gaulle, or François Mitterrand, there is a taboo
that will not be broken, one that has become a state secret and a secret
thought, which is recognition of the contribution made from the beginning through the most seminal works by the children of Jerusalem
to an achievement that, to this day, continues to be presented to us
exclusively as the daughter of Athens and Rome.

Is it necessary to point out that neither France nor the world
gained in the exchange?

And that between the self-assured, dominant, and martial republic of the Romans and the diffident and shaky kingdom of the Hebrews, between the pomp, splendor, rolling drums, and platoons of
lictors of the former and the Jewish republic whose leaders were so
reluctant to be leaders that they had to be pursued and cornered in
the depths of a barn or under a pile of baggage and who ended up accepting the job only because of the condition imposed by the judges
and by the people of moderate, limited, discounted, pained sovereignty, sovereignty based more on what separates men than on what
they have in common—between those two models, the comparison
frankly does not favor the Roman.

Fortunately, ideas never disappear forever.

There is a time—of this I am certain—for ideas that are born but
have not yet been permitted to thrive.

And I like to believe that, just as the language of ancient France
lives in the limbo of Rashi's work, the memory of the Hebrew kingdom resides in other limbic regions—those that Baudelaire said were
the temporary home of children who died before being baptized.

May another Baudelaire come one day to rescue them.

May there be Baudelaireans political enough to come baptize
them *as French.*

And who knows whether here might not lie one tool among others
for the re-founding of the imperiled French republic?

For the time being, this reminder.

For the time being, I am pulling on the thread of Judaism that lies in the weave of words and thoughts that have enabled the ideas of law, human rights, separation of powers, and democracy to be thought in France.

And I am happy to have been able to identify, to name, and, in a modest way, to celebrate that other phantom Jew without whom France would no longer be France.

JEWISH LIKE MARCEL PROUST

I turn now to a third moment, one that occurred much later.

That moment was the crisis and rebuilding of French literature at the dawn of modernity.

A crisis of poetry, says Mallarmé, while he is busy blowing it up from within in a terrorist act not unlike the acts of the real terrorists, or at least the accused terrorists, whom he defends before the court.

Magnificent language, but mineral, dried from the inside out, standing on the edge of silence and resting there for twenty years with Paul Valéry, the survivor of the Mallarméan shipwreck.

Dada came along soon after, followed by the Surrealists, dancing on the ruins and destroying the last pillars of what was once, of all the languages of Europe, the most suave and measured, the most virtuoso and velvety, the best suited to the metaphysics of love and the love of metaphysics: a play of mirrors and cut-glass flasks, rigor, and waltzing, the adventure of clarity and of sentences without end, a fantastical, fatal swirling that was suddenly frozen in place.

Here is Lautréamont and his farces, his clever parodies, his love of exaggeration and collage, his dislocated, frazzled writing, sabotaged from within, rhetoric destroyed by rhetoric, literature by literature, the pirate and vandal in his personality.

And Rimbaud, who fell silent.

And Baudelaire, who, in another way, fell silent, as well.

Raymond Roussel and his vertigo.

Elsewhere, as the mighty tire, so many self-important little writers and big novels in the manner of Paul Bourget.

In music, in painting, the sublime but equally vertiginous moment of impressionism. For what were its practitioners doing except making light from nothing? Color from the nothingness of light? Form, matter, and even life from the insubstantial scent of lilacs, opacity as flimsy as fog, reflections from an impression that has already disappeared?

And then a clap of thunder, a shock wave that shook the depths of that dying language. From an impressionist, in fact, a literary contemporary of the insubstantiality that was haunting the festivals of light in poetry, music, and painting. Except this other impressionist genius, this Pissarro with a pen, this literary painter who placed his lily pads in the ponds formed by the Vivonne, this brother of Debussy who transformed into a symphonic and aquatic poem the empty gulf that had opened under the feet of his era, turned out to be Jewish. He would use his Jewish being as a powerful lever with which to raise the French language.

I know that Proustians do not like to hear the author referred to, bluntly, as "Marcel Proust, the Jew."

I am aware of the many works that have disputed, from the outset, that the revolution in the novel that bears Proust's name had anything at all to do with his being Jewish.

And I am not unaware of the writings in which Proust himself heavily emphasized the (relative) complexity of his genealogy (Jewish mother but Catholic father and brother, as he notes drolly in a letter to Montesquiou dated May 19, 1896) and complained, in a letter to Robert Dreyfus, that Drumont's *La Libre Parole* was wrong to include him among the "young Jews" who "despise Barrès" (although he goes on immediately to say: "to correct the story, I would have had to say that I was not Jewish and did not want to be"—in other words, in substance, I refused to call for a correction, preferring instead to be called a Jew, and chose not to deny my Jewish side).

Except that *In Search of Lost Time* is strewn with countless Jewish clues and slips.

There are the Saturday luncheons in Combray that bring Françoise to "tears of merriment" when a "nonplussed visitor" arrives "who was not acquainted with Saturday's special customs" in the narrator's family.

And another sequence in which Françoise demonstrates that she possesses "for things which might or might not be done . . . a code at once imperious, abundant, subtle, and uncompromising on points themselves imperceptible or irrelevant," but recalling "those ancient laws" that forbid " 'seething the kid in his mother's milk' or 'eating of the sinew which is upon the hollow of the thigh.' "

And the many explicit references to the "racial eczema" of Gilberte's father and his consumption of "gingerbread" because he suffered from "the constipation of the prophets."

And the appearance, as the narrator's grandmother is dying, of the cousin who was referred to "by another set" as "no flowers or wreaths by request," a thinly veiled reference to the sobriety of Jewish grieving rituals.

And the quasi-Talmudic dissection of the name of Swann and that of Madame de Marsantes, where *The Guermantes Way* insists on "Mater Semita" instead of the simpler and more obvious "Mater Sancta."

On the border between the work and the life stands the formidable person of Madame Proust, Marcel's mother, whose maiden name was Weil and whose great-great-grandfather was a rabbi. At his mother's funeral, as we know from the archives of the Consistory, Marcel insisted on the recitation before the high society of Paris: the Montesquious, the Albuferas, the Grouchys, and the Abel Hermants.

There is that "charge of fuel and anger," described in a 1908 letter to Madame Straus, that makes him want to pen a vengeful article denouncing the historian and Byzantine scholar Gustave Schlumberger, who was anti-Dreyfus and violently anti-Semitic, a sort of "prehistoric buffalo, with his patriotic mustaches, shy and blushing in front of all the converts of the Haber and Heine families." As for the vengeful article, the ratio of forces in the literary society of the time was such that he decided not to write it. Instead, he recycled the "fuel" behind it into *In Search of Lost Time*. But that cold anger, that frustrated rage: Who can doubt that they were those of a Jew genuinely offended by the spectacle of a triumphal villain evading punishment, at least for the time being?

Beyond the clues in the work and in the life, we know that he was a reader of the Zohar: "See the Zohar," he records in one of the notebooks that are the diary of his creation; "see the Zohar," he writes, to learn how to "break the spell that holds things prisoner," to "haul them close to us," and "keep them from falling back forever into nothingness." One thinks—he is thinking, he cannot not be thinking, when writing that—of the Kabbalah of Isaac Luria, of his theory of the sparks bottled up in the earth's crust and of their rise and redemption in the messianic light of intelligence, which is the only thing that can check the enchanted nothingness that is evil.

No less important is Proust's manner of being; his way of viewing the world; his distance from the social and from himself; his essential non-adaptation, of which I have always thought inwardness, illness, and suffocation to be merely phenomenal manifestations.

There is the evidence of Proust's inner exile, the sense of being outside the world, that struck all of his contemporaries and that I cannot but believe were part of the adventure of body and soul that Judaism was for him.

How, then, can we avoid forming the hypothesis that this Proustian exteriority, Proust's recognition in himself of the element of foreignness and uncenteredness, this incapacity, as Sartre would say, to occupy a condition that is a hallmark of Judaism (including that of "being a Jew"); how can we avoid forming the hypothesis that this description of man unbound from the order of time that is the great Proustian hypothesis but that is also, word for word, the description of man living the life of the "world to come," which one finds throughout classic Jewish thought and in the idea, central to that tradition, of the possibility of transcending time and space; how can we avoid the conclusion that all this will become, through *In Search of Lost Time,* the miraculous tool that will permit the French language to free itself from itself, to shed the weight of nothingness that was silencing its best writers, and to become again the cutting-edge laboratory of intelligence that it had been for so long?

Every nation, especially the oldest one in Christian Europe, is secretly undermined by the dark nature of its beginnings.

All are gnawed by the gaping void in the dead body of the hallowed ground under their feet, ground seemingly solid but forming, in fact, a delta of shadows.

Like the others, perhaps more than any other, France was and remains menaced by the dark, morbid, and occasionally bloody passion of its champions, whether nasty pieces of work, like Barrès, or good men, such as Péguy, overtaken by the effects of that primitive language that they attribute to the soil and of which they become the bards.

I like to think that the power to steer clear of those shadows depended on the rejuvenating bath of exile, the proclivity toward self-alienation and gradual withdrawal, the love of words conceived as an unending adventure of the spirit that Proust practiced, as prescribed by the Talmudic sages, up to the last day of his life. That power and that practice draw on both angel and pariah, the man yearning for the angelic as well as the pariah status that are the two faces of Jewish being and also the two faces of the author of *In Search of Lost Time*.

Céline, whose character in *Journey to the End of Night* sees in Proust's long story no more than a "diluent futility" of "rituals and motions that wrap themselves around worldly people," empty beings, "ghosts of desires, irresolute smut-fingering seekers always awaiting their Watteau," comes finally to understand (as expressed in a letter to Lucien Combelle in 1943) that *In Search of Lost Time*, with its "jumbled mosaic," its "tortuous" and "arabescoid" phrasing, and the "drape of tulle and impeccable iridescent polish" that creates its "poetry," is "designed" and "built" like a Talmud.

The same goes for Paul Morand, another notorious anti-Semite who also recognized, almost immediately, the astonishing genius of writing that was (pay close attention; these are words that he used much later in *Le Visiteur du soir*) "singing, precise to a fault, reasonable, responsive to objections that one had not yet thought to make, honest in raising unforeseen difficulties, subtle in its insights and twists, stunning in the asides that hold it up like air in a balloon, dizzying in its length, surprising in its assurance couched as deference, and well constructed despite its rambles," writing that "sheathed you in a web of incidents so enmeshed that one would be lulled by its music if one were not suddenly arrested by an expression of unprecedented depth or comic brilliance."

And the same, too, for his models (the Sagans, Polignacs, Montesquious, the countesses of Chevigné and Caraman-Chimay, Henry de Breteuil, and General de Galliffet): I am not at all persuaded that they "underestimated," as it is always said, this droll character with the fly's gaze and the disturbingly exquisite manners whom they found haunting their parties and conversations. And, even when they did underestimate him, when they were slow to see in him anything but a snob, a sponger, an eccentric fascinated with the Jockey Club, prone to spying on duchesses through the keyhole of their salons, they were quick to discover, upon reading him, not pain but pleasure!

Because in the end here is a little Jew who offers them the incredible gift of giving flesh and blood to their family names; to their escutcheons and coats of arms; to their graceless mansions; to their churches in Normandy, about which all that they have heard lately is that their neglect is a "great pity" (Barrès, again); to their deep, flat lands no longer fit (according to the Charles Péguy of *Présentation de la Beauce à Notre-Dame de Chartres*) for anything more than burying beneath their "heavy sheet" those who have died or are going to die; to the great families of France's history who no longer believe in themselves and their prestige; to the steeples of Martinville, to the slopes of Méséglise and Roussainville: in short, to these "place names" that he has just cloaked in a splendor of which the aristocrats of recent vintage have lost even the memory.

Here, as Levinas would say, is a "Sunday Talmudist." Though there is certainly no indication that he was familiar with the Talmud (unlike with the Zohar), Proust was haunted by the existence, the principle, and the construction of his own Talmudic book, a book whose essence Levinas described, in surprisingly Proustian terms, as being not so much "analysis of the Word" but the "association of one biblical 'landscape' with another so as to release through the pairing the secret scent of the first." And he wound up creating a Talmud out of landscapes dear to his characters, out of their scents and their clandestine rites, out of Roussainville imagined as Sodom, out of Illiers transmuted into a fragile Combray, or (and these are Levinas's words) out of the "nobility without Versailles" that was henceforth the nobles' lot and for whom he was the Hebraic Saint-Simon.

That Proust's feat has another, hidden dimension—that his aristocratic figures are often, and as if by chance, born Rothschild, Halévy, Lippmann, Singer, or Wiener, that Robert de Montesquiou, one of the keys to Charlus, may have been the lover of Charles Haas; that the models for the Guermantes are all half-Jewish in the mind of author and narrator, socially or romantically linked to some of the most prominent Jewish figures in Paris at the time; that they make up what Proust's biographer George Painter calls a "semi-Gotha" that always finds that "Israel" (the last word is Proust's in a letter to Lionel Hauser) is "the source" of its "fortunes"; in short that the names from *In Search of Lost Time* are stand-ins for Jewish names, just as Jacques du Rozier conceals Albert Bloch—is also true and can only confirm, even to the most skeptical eye, the Jewish (and even Kabbalistic) subconsciousness of the great work of Marcel Proust. As always with Marrano gestures, the obviousness escaped Proust's contemporaries, who saw only the flash and marveled at the strange and fabulous mirror that *Search* offered France.

A Gemara of place names.

A Mishnah of a Faubourg Saint-Germain completing its passage, prefigured by Chateaubriand, from the age of "superiorities" through that of "privileges" to that of "vanities."

The equivalent of Rashi's book but in which—in a gesture symmetrical to that of the Prince de Ligne, who, in his *Mémoires sur les Juifs*, elevated the great Israelites to the highest ranks of the aristocracy, or to that of Chateaubriand, who made them, in his *Itinéraire de Paris à Jérusalem,* the spiritual brothers of the dispossessed, decimated nobility that littered the routes of Europe and of which he was a survivor—the seigneury of the Villeparisis and Montmorencys, the Saint-Euvertes and Cambremers, would be substituted for that of the Hillels and Shammai, Simeon ben Gamliel and Johanan ben Zakai, Rabbi Eliezer ben Hyrcanos and Rabbi Jose the Galilean.

Here is a captive Jew but a Jew all the same, who, in *The Guermantes Way,* pens an extraordinary sentence that could have been pulled straight out of the Kabbalah of Chaim of Volozhin, to the effect that the world "was not created once and for all, but is created afresh as often as an original artist is born."

Here is a secret but lucid Jew who, at a time when Paul Valéry, then so quintessentially French, is writing that "the Jews have no art," reinvents, in the language of classical clarity and simplicity in which France had known its glory but that had dried up, another way, a new sinuousness, an associational and analytical liberty suddenly multiplied tenfold, an art of splitting hairs that boosted and revived the intelligence of which that language is so eminently capable but was in the process of forgetting.

Modern American English has Faulkner.

British English has James Joyce.

German has Musil, Mann, and, soon, Kafka.

Italian has had Dante and Spanish Cervantes.

And French has Marcel Proust.

To free it from a fate exemplified by the dry destiny of André Gide, it has a reader of the Zohar, the descendant of an Alsatian rabbi.

And for French to be reborn from the fine ash that falls over every language the nation needed an oddball whom the other great twentieth-century reinventor of the language, Louis-Ferdinand Céline, found to write in a "convoluted Franco-Yiddish," though he could not refrain from noting, in the same letter, that to find French to match it one had to "go back to the Merovingians," a tribute all the more resounding for being involuntary!

Twentieth-century France will have other great authors, of course.

And I am not saying that the history of French can be reduced to this confrontation between a tacit Jew and an impenitent anti-Semite.

What I am doing is exploring the mechanics of words.

Of interest to me are the physics, chemistry, and hydraulics that make it possible for a language whose wellspring appeared to be on the point of drying up to reemerge as the great rushing river, the Nile, the Niagara that is every living language.

I am saying that it took those two, Céline and Proust—but first and foremost Marcel Proust—to get it done.

I am watching him, too.

He moves about, and travels, in his real country and his real landscapes.

He avenges the censure of Baudelaire through his *Contre Sainte-Beuve*.

He venerates Mallarmé and his manner of "solemnizing life"—his letters to Reynaldo Hahn attest to this admiration.

He observes from a distance the curious Mr. Valéry, who, like himself, sees psychology as a geometry of time.

He does not mention Rimbaud but remembers, in his Combray walks, the "lake that goes up" and the "cathedral that goes down" from Rimbaud's "Childhood."

He greets Raymond Roussel and asks about Lautréamont.

He does not participate in the Dada-Surrealist fracas that, to judge from the letter to Gaston Gallimard in which he upbraids "the charming dada" who "revised the proofs" of *The Guermantes Way* and substituted "Bergson" wherever he had written "Bergotte" (his name escapes me, he wrote, "out of momentary amnesia"—but it was certainly André Breton), succeeds in penetrating the hermetically sealed windows of his room on the Rue Hamelin.

He forgets nothing but reinvents everything.

While in no way repudiating the deserts through which his language has passed, he rehydrates them, irrigates them—one wants to say that he lays down new nerves and blood vessels.

And that is why I assert that if there are still French poets, novelists, and rhetoricians—and even, amid the ambient noise, an audience for them—we owe that to a phantom Jew, a Jew so profoundly Jewish that he did not even have to identify, like Pascal, with the carnal Jew or, like the Racine of *Esther* and *Athalie,* whom he so admired, to create choruses in imitation of the Psalms of David, to give a great boost to the language handed down to him from the seventeenth century, to resuscitate the art of the novel that Flaubert had condemned in reaching his conclusion about the irremediable stupidity of humanity in general and the French in particular—and to bring about the greatest revolution in the French language since the invention of classicism.

CHAPTER FIVE

HOW MODERN JUDAISM ABOLISHED THE IDEA OF REVOLUTION

One last sequence. Being nearly contemporary, it might seem minor to some.

They would be wrong.

First, because on the scale of the phenomenology of the French mind, it is of capital importance.

Second, as noted at the outset of chapter 3, because it, and France, will turn out to be highly consequential for the course of the world-historical.

And, finally, because there are few circumstances in which we can so clearly discern the effect of the genius of Judaism on the history of our country and on the ideas that it still exports to the rest of the world.

THE CAMBODIAN MOMENT

The scene is Paris in the late 1960s.

One might even say that it takes place in large part in a very specific place: the École Normale Supérieure on the Rue d'Ulm, for some time the bastion of the aristocracy of the revolutionary movement known as Maoism.

We students are reading Jacques Lacan, Louis Althusser, Michel Foucault.

And to a lesser extent Jacques Derrida, Georges Canguilhem, Roland Barthes, the linguists of the Prague School, and the disciples of Ferdinand de Saussure.

It is the site of a French moment of reflection that we believe to be scarcely less intense than the Greek moment in the fifth century B.C. or the German moment of Kant, Schelling, and Hegel.

And the news arrives (true or false, it hardly matters, for in matters such as this, the way one receives it counts as much as its basis in fact) that there is an area of the world (China, and then, in its wake, Cambodia) where revolutionary leaders have read these thinkers and drawn from them a new idea of revolution and what it takes for that idea to succeed.

How and why does this fascinating news reach us?

It reaches us because—and this is a fact—some of the future leaders of the Khmer Rouge studied at the Sorbonne.

But, even more, it reaches us and registers because of the intellectual approach that is playing out in the rice paddies of "Democratic Kampuchea," no less than in Tiananmen Square in Beijing.

All past revolutions have failed, they acknowledge.

All have turned into their opposite and spawned new forms of tyranny.

Well, that is because they were only superficial, because they overturned the old regimes but without taking into account the iron law formulated by French thinker Louis Althusser when he conveyed that an overthrow is always just a way of preserving upside down something that people were satisfied to turn on its head.

That is because, in Moscow, in Cuba, in the Africa of the wretched of the earth, in Korea, revolutions modified property systems, transformed the relations of production, and changed the beneficiaries of state revenues, but they left intact the unbreakable core that, underlying these infra- or super-structures, in the depths of language and its order, in the folds of desire and attraction, in the chasms of the real and of the resistance that it offers to symbolic and imaginary blows, was, according to the French philosophers, the beating heart of human subjugation.

That is what, from their far remove, the Chinese and later the Cambodian revolutionaries seem to be thinking.

For there they are—with everything occurring as if they had read what our professors and mentors had been thinking twenty years before we did; as if they had heard one of them murmuring that "language is fascist"; as if they had seen another sketching out his analysis of the history of sexuality, which was less "what power fears" than "the means by which it exerts itself"; as if they had taken into account a third thundering that "the real" is the other name for the thing against which liberating utopias "collide" and "are brought up short." They seem to take literally a body of thought that later, outside France, will be described as "deconstructionist," the full flowering of which will occur well after the time these future revolutionaries spent in Paris.

There they are reinventing, from A to Z, a new Khmer language not tainted by the inner "fascism" of the old one; regulating marriages and, beyond marriages, the ensemble of sexual practices of the Red Guards and those whom they terrorize, ending by emptying cities in order to break the resistance of that epitome of the real that is living in the world; putting thought and action together to implement the first radical and total operation of emancipation in the history of humanity.

Try to imagine the scene.

Try to imagine the heated discussions about the matter that raged around the basin in the courtyard of the École Normale, in which swim descendants of the goldfish that swam there at the time of the debates between Péguy and Lucien Herr, between Sartre and Nizan.

Try to picture the young men and women crazy about literature but avoiding it; drugged on politics but perceiving in it the very archive of evil; nostalgic for a pure greatness of which the last incarnation was the French resistance to Nazism—the real version, not the one about which they chanted, "CRS, SS," in the streets of Paris (equating France's regional security police to the Nazi SS)—but at the same time forcing themselves to see in the meek and humble, in the poor in fact and in spirit, the precious essence of the human.

Try to imagine them at that moment when, considering themselves the witnesses to an unprecedented turmoil the stakes of which were no less than "breaking the history of the world into two parts" in order to "change man at the deepest level," they read each morning in

New China, the voice of the Cultural Revolution, about a revolution so inaptly named when one thinks of the number of books that it burned but so aptly named when one considers that it was the first to claim to yank the roots of the old world out of people's heads, out of their souls, and even out of their flesh.

It is the moment of truth, we think.

If the new man emerges, it will be there and only there.

And if he does not emerge, he will emerge nowhere; he will have been a chimera.

We know what happened: Not only did the new man not come forth—what came was worse than the ossified systems that usually follow failed revolutions.

Less well known is how that disillusion would ramify through our minds and spirits. Horror, of course. Shame at having believed in it, even a little. And repulsion at the mass graves. But, also, a decisive lesson: Because the Chinese and Cambodian revolutions had relied on extreme radicality, because they had gone to the limit of what was humanly thinkable about changing humanity, and because they had left no possibility of explaining their possible failure as being the result of having spared the old world at any point, thereby allowing it to reemerge, it was revolution as such, the very idea of radical change, that had been, to our way of thinking, run through the heart.

Even less well known is how this came about. Let's admit that this generation did experience this moment as a moment of demystification as radical as the devil's bargain that, for a very short time, seemed within reach before disappearing into the shrouded night. Imagine a generation understanding deeply and unshakably that, in China and Cambodia, it has observed at work the pure chemical formula of a perfect and pitiless revolution and realizing abruptly that, precisely because it was perfect and pitiless, that revolution led necessarily to the very worst, to bestiality untempered by mercy or recourse and responsible for destruction and genocide. And remember, too, that this new knowledge suddenly took form in a new crop of well-founded and well-reasoned books. How did all this come about? It is due to another facet of Judaism and another version of its genius. Behind this generation's deliverance lay the decoupling of history from messianism—or, better, the rediscovery of a messianism that revealed in stark detail the dark and criminal foundation of the "religion of history."

JEWISH FACES OF MAOISM

For if an observer carefully reviews, frame by frame, the film of the years and even of the months and weeks that followed the revelation of the crimes of the Cultural Revolution and the "reeducation" of all the Khmer representatives of the old world, what does he or she see?

The observer makes out two familiar figures gathered around the basin at the École Normale, Christian Jambet and Guy Lardreau, one of whom in our eyes is wearing the halo of the unmatched prestige of representing the proletarian left in Beijing at the apogee of the Cultural Revolution and there being noticed by Lin Biao. They are the first to grasp the depth of the disaster. They turn it into a book entitled *L'Ange* (*The Angel*), which touts the virtues of the Christianity of the fathers of the Church, the last wave of Christianity to have reflected the Jewish spirit.

With them is their editor, the author of these pages, who, with André Glucksmann and others, proposed a "New Philosophy," the real target of which was not Marxism, as is widely claimed, but rather historical progressivism (the belief that history was heading toward an inevitable end point) and, even more than that, the will to purity, whose hideous face was revealed by these last two revolutions of the century. Their attacks rely on the Jewish narrative—at first discreetly but then, in my own case, directly.

That same observer will notice a Polish Jew born in France, Pierre Goldman, whose name tends to fade from the Wikipediated glossary that serves as our history of ideas, which is a shame. And may these lines encourage readers to make a side trip into the two fine books that he left us, which he liked to say that he had written with his blood. Pierre Goldman, activist and gangster, returning from Latin America in 1969 to offer to help the Maoist organizations obtain the weapons that they would need when the time came for the great insurrection, was one of the exemplars, probably the most inflammatory, of that will to break history in two. But he was also one of those Jewish names for whom the problem (vague at first but then nagging) of the memory of Auschwitz—and then that scent of Auschwitz that could be detected wafting above Phnom Penh and Beijing—eventually caused horror to win out over fascination. That this born rebel, this indomitable person who continued to his last breath to believe in the liberation of humanity, came to understand in his way the lesson of China and Cambodia and, through that understanding, also understood that a revolution is horrible to the extent that it is radical, that it becomes a nightmare to the extent that it succeeds—of these things I can attest for having had several conversations with him in the months preceding his assassination by the extreme-right terrorist group Honneur de la Police. But that the "never again" of Auschwitz and fidelity to his own name were then his compass, that fidelity to his Jewish memory had served ultimately as a fire alarm in the sense intended by Walter Benjamin, that his extreme political lucidity in those years had had a direct effect on the return of his Judaism, any reader of *Souvenirs obscurs d'un Juif polonais né en France,* his first novel, will readily discern.

That observer will take note of another Jew, Benny Lévy, for the concrete role he is recognized to have played in ensuring that French leftism resisted the temptation of terrorism to which its Italian and German counterparts succumbed at the same moment. He himself has made it clear that—though he indeed played that role, and though he indeed experienced that recoil of horror, though he indeed dissolved the political organization he led—he recoiled in 1972, after the Palestinians massacred Israel's athletes at the Olympic Games in Munich. What we did not know at the time (something that he would confide much later, in the preface to his 2002 book, *Le Meurtre du Pasteur*) was that he had already begun, in secret, to move toward "the gates of messianism"; that it was through that reflection on messianism that he, too, was wondering "how to go beyond the political vision of the world"; and that, if the decreasingly obscure memory of his Jewish name caused his break with politics, it also determined, at the same time, the much longer and deeper break with *the political* as such and with the very idea of revolution that had been its guiding star.

Our observer, in other words, will detect two of the peaks of what Jean-Claude Milner, in a communication both precise and credible, called "the dark triangle": a triangle composed of the Polish Jew born in France who was Pierre Goldman, the Egyptian Jew born outside France who was Benny Lévy, and a third, Robert Linhart, who very quickly opted for silence. And, within that triangle, the observer will see programmed and concentrated first the repression of the Jewish element; then its emergence, an event all the more insistent for having been denied; and, finally, its shattering return at the moment when the veil was lifted on the genocidal nightmare that was the indirect consequence of the vertigo of absolute knowledge and absolutist politics.

The observer will see Jacques-Alain Miller, another young Maoist, another exemplar of this moment in French thought, who would devote part of his life to reading and editing Jacques Lacan: Miller became aware, in the process, of Lacan's close connection with Judaism and its method of reading.

And then, in reviewing the film—in reconstructing the detailed chronicle of that moment in thought when radical politics, inebriation at the blank page of history beginning anew, and the fight to the death between the old and the new all peaked and then, almost immediately, lost their power of attraction and ebbed—one encounters the colossal and nearly inconceivable matter of the Jewish turn taken by Jean-Paul Sartre.

THE "CONVERSION" OF SARTRE

I have given this account of Sartre elsewhere.

But I cannot avoid returning to it here, in the context of this history.

For here we have the most celebrated fellow traveler of that rebellious youth, one who nearly found the formula, the Rosetta Stone, the code key for revolution.

Here is the godfather of the Maoists, their friend and backup, the man who agreed to lend his name to their newspapers and who, in one of them, at the time of the massacre of the Israeli athletes in Munich, contributed an article in which he described that form of terrorism as an understandable and, alas, defensible "weapon of the powerless."

And then the astonished world watches as this fanatic renounces his former doctrines, turns his back on the revolutionary ideal born in the close fraternity of POW camps in Germany, an ideal tempered into the still-brittle metal of the revolutions of the twentieth century to which he, with the rest of us, believed the Maoist forge would give pure and refined form. Like his young comrades, he becomes aware of the dark, potentially criminal, and even genocidal dimension that was the ultimate truth of the "fraternity of terror," the necessity and nobility of which he had spent half his life theorizing about. And why? Because he encounters one of the points of the Milnerian triangle: He dialogues with Benny Lévy, who has already embarked on his journey from Paris to Jerusalem. Benny introduces Sartre to the work of Emmanuel Levinas, a contemporary whom Sartre had spent his life avoiding. And through Levinas, with Benny Lévy setting it all down in black and white, Sartre discovers the glory of Jewish being.

What a stroke of the genius of Judaism, this moment when the old Sartre, blind but reading through the eyes of his young secretary, murmurs that, against the intense joy derived from the idea of bodily resurrection that he finds in the Talmud, the doctrine of "nausea," which held the self to be insubstantial, "no longer holds."

What a stroke of the genius of Judaism, the sudden appearance of the ethic that was his great design as well as his great regret, as he had spent his life announcing without delivering it: Well, here it comes, that ethic, announcing itself, filling itself in, revealing itself like heat-sensitive ink, except that in this case it is the heat of the concept, drawn from Levinas, of a subject obligated to the Other, shaped by others, one whose subjectivity takes on and retains its form only through contact with the face of the other man.

What a stroke of the genius of Judaism, the last stage of the hand-to-hand struggle with Hegel that had been the great contest of Sartre's existence and that he thought he had lost after the *Critique of Dialectical Reason*. "Now prepare for combat!" he seems to say. Not all of the chips were down after all; not all the bets had been placed. It proved to be enough (while still dialoguing with Benny Lévy, as Benny shuttled between Sartre and Levinas) to raise the case of a people whose inevitable disappearance Hegelianism had announced and programmed. Enough to evoke that people's puzzling survival through forms that were not those prescribed by the Hegelian canon. And, behold, the very persistence of this stateless, landless nation of people who gather around a table or a book (the table of a house of study, the book of the Talmud) changes everything. Far from being condemned by Hegelianism, this people, by its existence, by its obstinacy in being, its endurance, its trial, condemns Hegelianism.

What a stroke of the genius of Judaism, finally, is the concept of messianism that bubbles up in the dialogue and eventually makes up its framework. Because it signifies an adventure that plays out daily; because that adventure is inspired by moral rather than economic or political concerns; because, contrary to common perception, it involves a messiah who, as Levinas says in one of the Talmudic essays that Sartre and Benny Lévy read and discuss together, will appear only at the end of history—or even, go figure, the day after, the day before, or never. Because the messiah in question is, of course, neither Jesus Christ nor Hegel's world spirit nor Marx's proletariat nor any other guardian on a similar scale, but just an everyman, or a beggar, or you, or him, or anyone else among us. For all these reasons, a political miracle occurs, producing a Sartre different from the one who had, unprompted, made so many pledges to terror in word and deed, a new Sartre who refrains from making one last pledge, who, more accurately, *withdraws* his pledge, rescinds his belief in History writ large, in the process of which one kills as if one were merely clearing a field, a process in which "revolutionary desire" had been the terrifying engine.

This is certainly not the first time in French history that the idea of revolution has fallen into disrepute.

Consider only a few very great cases. Recall Baudelaire's likening of revolution to destruction, expiation, punishment, and death; Chateaubriand's observation in *The Genius of Christianity* that the hosanna of the French Revolution "had changed into a cry of long live death!"; and the wave of counterrevolutionary thought that certainly did not depend on the genius of Judaism for its castigation of the "satanic nature" of the revolution of 1789 and of all that might draw inspiration from it in the future.

But Sartre is not Joseph de Maistre.

He is not the enemy of Baudelaire, about whom he wrote one of his best books. But he does not belong to the tradition of those who, like Baudelaire, liken democracy to syphilis and the republican spirit to smallpox.

So this reversal, this dismantling of the idea of revolution by the revolutionaries themselves (by the most prestigious among them!), this live demonstration, this proof via the extreme case that revolution always and necessarily shares a bed with barbarism and death, constitutes an intellectual event without precedent.

WHEN MODERN JEWISH THOUGHT DOES AWAY WITH THE IDEA OF REVOLUTION

Sartre's "conversion" is the equal of Chateaubriand's.

In it lies a transformation as edifying as Chateaubriand's discovery of that Providence with a hidden face that allowed Christianity to, among other things, invent the individual, assure the preeminence of the moral over the political, and offer barbarian kingdoms a way to avoid choosing between popular anarchy and despotism, which is what did Rome in.

And those who, in Sartre's case, screamed about a plot, about taking advantage of an old man, about abuse of power, about a metaphysical burglary—those who deplored the grip of a "little Egyptian rabbi" over the quintessential symbol of France (second only to de Gaulle) and the idea of France—do not look any better than the editors, the pawns, who, like Sainte-Beuve, tried mightily to prove by the calendar that *The Genius of Christianity* was a fake and that one could believe neither in the veracity of the accounts it contained nor in the sincerity of its author.

The Genius of Christianity was subtitled *The Spirit and Beauty of the Christian Religion.*

It was an apologia—a militant, hortatory one, from the vantage of today—written to remind the author's contemporaries (who were just then hearing again the bells of Notre Dame, which had fallen silent in the previous decade as vandals resembling those of today's Islamic State had sacked the altars, pillaged hallowed spaces, and decapitated statues of France's kings) that, "of all the religions that have ever existed," Catholicism was, first, "the most poetic" and "the most hospitable to arts and letters," and, second, a "human" body of thought that, while it "refines taste," also invigorates morality and freedom.

Poetry and liberty . . . aesthetics and morality (or, what amounts to the same thing, politics) . . . That is exactly what is at work, symmetrically, in Judaism. And that is exactly what happens after the Jewish takeover brought out by what Benny Lévy, during and after his Sartrean period, refers to variously as "the generation" or "the New Philosophy."

Poetry?

I say that Judaism, too, contrary to the widespread nonsense about Jewish iconoclasm and the putative inability of Judaism to appreciate form and its metamorphoses, is one of the most conducive of all bodies of thought that ever existed to the production of beauty and arts. Witness the synagogue of Dura-Europos in Syria and its painted decorations, its frescoes, its plaster rosettes, the vines resembling those that Flavius Josephus describes adorning the great gate of the temple, the sculpted lions, the marquetry and ceramics, the silks. Witness the Leipzig Mahzor or the gilt Haggadahs of Barcelona and Sarajevo. Witness Maimonides urging us, in the commentary to the treatise "Fathers," to sculpt our existence so as to turn it (I am paraphrasing him here) toward the aesthetic peak that is pure intelligence and to offer to our souls the beautiful music and paintings that will cure it of its torments. Witness, too, the Mekhilta recommending solid-gold cherubim for the holy ark—indeed cherubim, the highest sphere of angels, those half-human half-divine figures that are paragons of holiness and about which the text repeatedly emphasizes, as if to be certain of being understood, that it is when the faithful make them from silver after gold has been "prescribed" that they become "idols." Witness, finally, the story of "Bezalel, son of Uri, son of Hur, of the tribe of Judah," of whom God says to Moses, in Exodus, that he filled him with a divine spirit so that he might "conceive the work in gold, silver, and copper." For this I would gladly recognize Bezalel as the Jewish counterpart of Luke, patron saint of artists.

I say that Judaism, too, has been a powerful force in the genius of French, European, and world literature. Consider Proust again, who conceived *In Search of Lost Time* (Midrash means "search" in Hebrew) according to the layout of a cathedral, which itself is an open Bible (see his translation, a work to which he devoted many years, of Ruskin's *Bible of Amiens,* as well as the definition, in *Search,* of the cathedral as the face of the Book before there were books). Consider Spinoza, whose Latin, whatever else might be said about it, is infused with the breath of Hebrew. Consider Kafka, coming late, very late, to understand—but understanding nonetheless, as attested by the very strange entry in his journal for January 16, 1922, picked up by Maurice Blanchot—what he, too, owes to the language of the Torah and why literature, in its real existence, can only be a "new Kabbalah," a "science of letters" that is itself based on a "secret doctrine" that, he adds still more strangely, "could have been developed" if "Zionism had not appeared in the meantime." Consider Joyce, who, in citing Homer's *Odyssey* as the source of his *Ulysses,* refrains from mentioning the other source, perhaps more important, of the prodigious work of fission, fusion, sealing and unsealing, crushing, and dissolution of signifiers that he had to perform to wake himself from the nightmare of history—yes, Joyce, who refrains from saying that he is working like the practitioners of Talmudic *pilpul* and that, more or less consciously, more or less secretly, he owes to them his stance in letters, his art of inducing the blankness in words to speak, to undo their silences and rearrange them into a previously unknown music. The Joyce of the magnificent phrase in *Ulysses* about "the tables of the law graven in the language of the outlaw." Consider, again, Céline, the anti-Proust, the French writer who, as I said, never in all his life ceased measuring himself against Proust, battling with Proust, believing that he had but one and only one serious competitor, Proust: Consider Céline, yes, who, in *Rigodon,* declares that "after the Bible, despite Racine, despite Sophocles, everything is sentimentality."

That is what I think—I believe in the beauty, the extreme poetic power, of Judaism.

But I also believe the inverse.

I believe, as Chateaubriand believed of Christianity, that Judaism is no less steeped in liberty than in beauty and that it contributed no less to the deepening of our political thought than to the blossoming of our poetics.

I believe that, like Christianity, to which Western civilization is in debt for rescuing it from the circles of pagan hell and for having given birth to the idea of man formed in the image of God and therefore endowed with rights, Judaism was no less emancipating than it was lavish in splendor.

And I also believe, again as an aside, that Chateaubriand knew this, as well, as attested by a text drawn from his *Martyrs,* an oratorical joust in the Senate between the advocate for the pagans, Hierocles, and that of the Christians, Eudore, performed before Emperor Diocletian and Vice-Emperor Galerius. The Christians in attendance hold their breath, terrified, because they know that the outcome of the argument will determine whether or not Rome's Christians, starting with those in the audience, will continue to be thrown to the lions. To overwhelm them, Hierocles goes back to origins—that is, to a "certain deceitful person" named Moses, whose "gross crimes and presumptions" contaminated his successors. But then Eudore, whom the reader recognizes as a stand-in for Chateaubriand, delivers a speech in praise of Moses, calling him the "legislator of the Israelites" who had the wisdom to endow his people with admirable laws that have "resisted time" and given rise to institutions so "miraculous" that they enabled that people to resist all manner of oppression and subjection and, "four thousand years later," to "still exist."

The emancipating power of Judaism.

Concretely, miraculously emancipating in France and Europe today.

And that is because, beyond the miracle that Chateaubriand saw, well after Rashi and the *République* of Jean Bodin, coming on top of everything that Judaism was able to contribute through these latter two and over the centuries to the country of Clovis and Rousseau, even without taking into account the idea of man borne by faith and the way in which that idea worked itself out in the history of nations, Judaism is at the origin of this ultimate progress toward emancipation. You read that right. I believe that we must not fear uttering the word "progress." There lies, I believe, a real and authentic advance in reason, a curtailment of human unreason. I even believe that, as highlighted by Alexandre Kojève, this progress involves "a leap forward for the spirit." And that leap forward is this: after millennia of harm in its sacred form, followed by centuries in its profane, political version, the end, finally, of the idea of revolution—its extinction, like a dead star. And the fact that, at the end of the adventure, the very word "revolution" has become unutterable, as unutterable as the insatiable, coruscant, and necessarily untenable justifications for the carnage the word has wrought.

Of course, there remain and will always remain die-hard adherents of historical progressivism and its dead star.

Carnage will continue to be defended and justified, in the teeth of the Cambodian model, by those same die-hards.

But they can be one of only two types.

Either they are survivors of those years and owe their latter-day prominence to the disappearance of the greats.

Or else they are late-arriving neos, in which case any resemblance between them (between the outraged people who, to paraphrase André Gide, become communists or revolutionaries in the same way one might become a great hairdresser) and the seekers after the absolute who operated in the "dark triangle" of the 1960s and 1970s would be purely coincidental.

And had they encountered these whiners and pounders of podiums around the courtyard basin of the École Normale, the grand dukes of the golden age of Maoism would have viewed them with sovereign disdain, as learned professors forced to listen to callow students spouting awkward sophistry.

A CONFIDENCE FROM MICHEL FOUCAULT

During this same period, I had a conversation with the other great intellectual of the era, Michel Foucault, to whom I owe in part—believing that everything is related—my passion for Chateaubriand.

Our conversation was public and appeared on March 11, 1977, in *Le Nouvel Observateur*.

We had spoken of the need to see the force and forms of power—that is, through people's minds, in its "infra-statal" forms.

Of the uses made of sex and sexual practices by modern systems of repression and control, which, far from forbidding or censoring sexual expression, forced it.

We had lingered over the tendency of the Red Guards in China to promulgate rules on the subject of masturbation.

In short, Michel Foucault was reviewing one by one, but without saying so, the principal problems raised and reconsidered by the two revolutions of the end of the century, as well as the main themes making up what was in the process of becoming "the New Philosophy."

And all of a sudden he said to me, point-blank: "You know very well that it is the very desirability of revolution that is the problem today," as if he were trying to tell me that "in the form that we desired it, it has become impossible; in the form that turned out to be possible in China and Cambodia, it is no longer desirable."

That said it all.

It was certainly not formulated explicitly in the Jewish name—or in the name of that name.

But he defended the New Philosophers at the risk of annoying his companion in thought, Gilles Deleuze.

He had become interested in Pierre Goldman's fate, declaring him, at the time of his trial, to be "Jewish and innocent."

He was, almost as much as Sartre, familiar with Benny Lévy, the two Benny Lévys, the one who had called himself Pierre Victor and whom he had accompanied during the turmoil of the time when Benny led the French Maoists, and the other, whom he had seen, along with the rest of us, return to the glory of his Jewish name and who, in the preface of his book, tells the story of how Foucault had called him one morning to say that he was "beginning research on the pastoral power" and wanted to "ask for clarifications" (like Sartre!) on the theme of the pastor in "the literature of Israel."

All of which is to say that I do not believe I am stretching the meaning of the text by making of Foucault's statement to me about the ultimate non-desirability of the revolutionary form the climax of this Jewish history, finding in it the story's last twist and the exit, for now, from its labyrinth.

The revolution, the real one, revolution in the sense that had been given to the word from the Rhineland of Marx and Engels right up to the École Normale, the project of radically changing the human species and gaining access to the absolute in this world, the hope that for centuries had seduced generations of great minds and peoples while simultaneously justifying and covering so many crimes, the legitimization of concrete evil by abstract good and of mass murder by revolt that brought tears of impotence and rage to Orwell, Koestler, Ciliga, and so many others—all that was over.

A page in the history of the modern world, and perhaps not just of the modern world, was turning right before our eyes.

At the same time, a new era was opening, which neither Sartre nor Foucault would see, one in which a generation drunk on itself would discover concern for others, in which the arrogant people we had been—the people who had wanted everything, and right away, even at the cost of multitudes of dead, mown down in joyous fury and the most abject and facile good conscience, pitched into the dustbin of history as if it were history's crucible—would now try to divine the secret of humility that the great progressive machines had taken hostage. Others would come, or the same become others who, after so many decades lost chasing a fire itself fleeing from flame to flame, would now practice patience, let time wash over them, and, after so many declarations, turn to face the question and the meaning of reparation.

And we owe that—I will say it one last time—to the insistence of the Jewish thread running through an era that had begun by not wanting to know anything about it, to a new type of political Marranism of which the chief practitioners were themselves slow to become aware, and, in the end, to the major turning point at which, in a phrase that Benny Lévy did not like but that expresses rather well the paradox of those years, some of the intellectuals and moral authorities of the day moved "from Mao to Moses."

That is where we stand.

I know that it is hard, in history, to see beyond a generation, but the demonstration was so relentless, the path so honestly cleared, that we will stand there, it seems to me, for a long time.

PART TWO

THE TEMPTATION OF NINEVEH

CHAPTER SIX

WHAT DOES IT MEAN
TO BE A CHOSEN PEOPLE?

But now the heart of the matter.

The question that I have been circling from the start of this book.

The one that comes to mind as soon as anyone mentions—today no less than yesterday, in the time of Sartre and Foucault as much as in the time of Chateaubriand—the matter of the name "Jew."

That scandalous, almost scabrous word on which, since Jews have been Jews, their misunderstanding with the nations hangs.

That word is "election," the Jews' status as a chosen people.

And that is where we must begin, provided that we can strip the idea of the load of prejudice, bad literature, and stupidity that has weighed it down over time.

THE SCENE

We have to go back to the verse.

The first.

The one where the whole story starts, with its knot of misapprehensions that will poison twenty centuries of relations with Christianity and fourteen with Islam but that has its own share of truth.

We are in Exodus.

The Israelites, having left Rephidim, are still far from the Promised Land.

They find themselves in the middle of the desert, in a spot so empty that it is almost abstract, the exact opposite of the Egypt they just left, which, to judge from the end of Genesis, is the very definition of fertility, prosperity, and culture.

They wander in anti-Egypt, where, after their bath in the goods and culture that were Pharaoh's realm, after their long sojourn near the forty-nine Gates of Impurity in which they nearly perish, they experience an inner draining, an emptying, and, at bottom, a deliverance from the pagan immanentism that was dogging their feet and minds. And in contrast to the bodily but also social needs that were second nature to them, the Hebrew says that they are *panoui*—that is, at once vacant, free from the pleasures in which they were mired, ready for intellection.

They then arrive at the foot of an ordinary mountain—to tell the truth, not even a very high one (though soon it will be said that one could, from its base, see the glory of God at its summit) and poorly identified (even today it is not known with certainty whether the mountain is in Arabia, in present-day Jordan, in the southern Negev, or elsewhere).

Just a mountain.

A mountain with no history.

A mountain that is eventually converted, thanks to epics both literary and cinematographic, to a Middle Eastern version of Fuji or Kilimanjaro, whereas in fact it is a nothing mountain, abstract, being itself a form of desert that, like a desert, allows the mind to be limited by nothing, no landscape, no features—just a little high ground to serve as the site of the prophecy.

Because God, that day, called Moses to appear.

He made Moses climb, alone, the slope of the mount. And God told him two things that caused Moses to hurry back down the mountain to tell the twelve tribes that were waiting for him in the sand of the desert.

He told Moses this: "All the earth is mine." Equally dear to my heart, without exception, are all of the peoples of the earth. I am the God of love of all the sons of Adam and thus of all the sons of Noah, who are, to this day, my equally beloved sons.

But before God told him that, there was this other thing: "You shall be for me a treasure." Among all the sons of Adam and Noah is one human population that I call a treasure (*segula,* in Hebrew) and that I have placed "on eagle's wings" so that they may be "brought to me." I am God of all peoples, and I repeat that all peoples are equal in my heart. But there is one, here, at the foot of this rock, to which I say that it shall be, if it obeys my voice, a people precious among all others, a treasure, and that is the people of Israel.

THE DIALOGUE

It will be noted, first, that at no point does the biblical text mention election or choice. Words were available in Hebrew to express that idea. There was the word *behira,* which signifies both "free will" and "choice," and that would have expressed what the stock phrase implies in the words "chosen people." But that is not the word that was selected and it does not appear, to my knowledge, in any of the verses that touch on this story.

And, second, this gift is not a gift at all, because it is accompanied by a condition: It is *because* this people is receptive that they are precious; *because* they are open to the Word of God that they are treasured; for better or for worse, this quality of being treasured is tied to the *unconditional* faith that they swear when declaring, in a nearby verse, that they would obey and they would understand, that they would begin by obeying and then, later, much later, they would come to understand what they had been asked to do and had done.

It will be observed, third, that God had offered this gift—sorry, he had proposed this pact (it is because you are unconditionally receptive to my voice that I deem you a treasured people)—to Edom, to Ishmael, and probably (Deuteronomy 14:2) to "all the peoples on the face of the earth." And it was only *after* the entire earth had refused, *after* the other peoples had, without exception, found a good reason to wriggle out of it, that, *in desperation,* he had turned to this small group of people who finally accepted him.

It will be observed, fourth, that this gift, if there had been one, would have been a poison apple. Suppose Israel does not honor its part of the agreement. Imagine that it is not up to this "alliance" that it has committed to. Suppose that it does not do what it will one day come to understand. Well, in that case, absolutely all of the texts are in agreement: The curses will be proportional to the blessing of the *segula,* and the Jews, unfaithful to their promise, the Jews, who choose God but forget him, the Jews, who are a treasure but who squander the treasure that they are, will be as the last of the last, the lowest of the low, no longer the head but now the tail, no longer the cream of humanity but its dregs. Here, in verse 3, on the very first day of this very first transaction, does not Rashi say that the terms of the contract, the words that God speaks, are "harder than tendons," that the promise is not much of a gift, being nothing but the "particulars" and "punishments" that are to accompany disloyalty?

Let's be precise. What exactly is a "treasure," anyway? What does God mean, precisely, when he says that, from now on, they are his treasure? On this point, too, the texts are clear. In his gloss of the verse, Rashi notes that the same word—*segula*—is used in Ecclesiastes (2:8) to refer to the gems and other objects of value that great kings amass over the course of their reign. This kingly treasure has a particularity that Rashi, true to those gradual shifts in the flavor of the text that are his way of commenting when he does not adhere to *peshat,* or literal commentary alone, can relate only to God. It is never entrusted to a factotum, minister, or treasurer, as are ordinary treasures. It is a treasure so special that the king guards it himself (and for himself). Not because it must be shielded from thieves or from the covetous eyes of his subjects, no. The reason is both plainer and murkier: It is in the nature of this treasure not to be manifest. By definition it is intimate, hidden, something that one keeps secret, secrecy itself, the secret being.

That is the essential point.

And we must not fail to take its measure.

These people are a treasure, but the others do not know it.

These people are a treasure, but they do not really know it themselves: That they are a treasure has been announced to them, but they do not understand the news too well.

And if neither the Jews nor the other peoples know it, it is because the truth can be revealed to all alike only at the end of time, when the procession from the many and its episodes to the One reaches its end, when the wait is over and the day has come to say, "God is One" and "his name is One." Before the seal of secrecy can be lifted, before the treasured people can be recognized and celebrated for what they are, the clamor of history must be stilled: All of time's moments, all of the world's varieties and diversities, all of the events and dissensions borne by the great river of time, all of the scattered shards of the shattered vase of creation must come back together in the messianic dream fulfilled. We are still far from that point.

THE TORAH AND WHAT PEOPLE READ INTO IT

And in the meantime, what do we do?

Until we get there, to kill time until the end of time, the representatives of the treasured people have a task to accomplish. I mean a *task*. Once again, not a right but duties. Not privileges but obligations. A swarm of obligations and duties that are the historic meaning, the small change, of their being a treasure.

There are rules for them to follow.

There are detailed instructions for them to observe.

Above all, there is the Torah, written and oral, which they are responsible for learning, studying, and passing on.

All peoples read the Torah, of course.

They read it to a greater or lesser degree, but they read it: We all know that the Christians and Muslims ratified the essence of the written Torah.

But the citizens of the treasured people have a duty to read it in a certain way: fervently, passionately, using all of their mind, all of their mental strength, and, sometimes, their life, too, in that fierce, depleting hand-to-hand combat with the text that is known as study. And, more important, hardest of all, is approaching the Torah (and this, according to the Talmud, is the most enigmatic but most essential point) as if it had "seventy faces."

Faces . . .

So many centuries before Levinas, faces . . .

And the number 70, which is no ordinary number. . . .

In this case, too, we must read very closely.

That the Torah has faces means, first, that the act of reading it brings it to life and that the reader animates it by making it his own. The same word is used for appropriation of the Torah through study (*kinyan Torah*) as for possessing a woman through love (*kinyan ishah*), and the fact that the same word is used demonstrates that we are operating within the same discourse of love, within the same logic of reinvention of the other through the love that one bears for him or her and through a form of reading that Levinas would have described as being akin to a caress.

"Caress," in turn, implies two things. That the Torah is not "taken," that one does not "appropriate" its reality, or, more precisely (and speaking in the manner of Jacques Lacan), that the Torah is not a "reality," that it is not something that one can hold (in the sense of possessing it) in the "now," that it is, instead, a "real" that resists being seized and that can only be grazed. But, most of all, the metaphor implies that the text is a living thing, full of verses that are themselves living, desired, desiring, endowed with a soul, and sometimes capricious: They are not the frozen, closed, rigid beings that fanatics take them to be.

But hold on! The idea that the Torah has faces must also be grasped in its literal sense. Those faces are the faces of the subjects who appropriate it, their actual faces, indistinct up to that point, not fully formed, but that study will help to make distinct or, perhaps, to escape from the shipwreck in which, like each of us, they might have perished. Because it takes on the face of the subject who studies it, one can say that the Torah calls the subject to an encounter with himself and reveals to him his true face. One can say that it is, as the philosophers contemporaneous with, again, Jacques Lacan would say, literally *given to* the subject. Or, better, that the adventure of study is an adventure in subjectification and that the subject of the commentary, its topic, is I—*as a subject*.

This is the opposite of the Gospels, which announce "good news" and invite the faithful to fusion and martyrdom—that is, to the consummation of existence on the fire of adoration of the One.

It is the opposite of the Koran, which means "recitation" and exhorts the faithful to regain their voice through that of God, to immerse the capacity for speech in the profuse, infinitely repeated utterance of the name of Allah, and, finally (except perhaps in Shi'ism), to dispense with commentary, which is superfluous where it is not inappropriate and illicit.

The Torah is an infinite book. The Torah is a book on a human scale, a human-like book. The Torah is a book composed, ultimately, by the people who discover themselves in it. It is a book that, as Maimonides said in the last words of his *Guide for the Perplexed,* invites me to be me, stimulates my singularity, and helps move me to the apex not of my narcissistic and phenomenologically individuated self but rather into the self-other, who discovers himself in what he has learned.

Does not the Zohar say that the messiah will come only after the reservoir of souls of Israel has been emptied? When each of the subjects to come from the Jewish people will have come to be a subject— by finding his face in the Torah? Is it not said that each man is a letter and that the book of the world will be written when no letter is missing and the entire alphabet of humanity is suitably spelled out?

But again: That those faces should be seventy in number and not, for example, twelve, as in the twelve tribes of Israel, that Rashi should choose, when giving a number to these possible faces, the number of infinity extended—that is, the number of the nations—provides us a last bit of information that, if we understand it rightly, is perhaps the most decisive.

It tells us that all subjects—absolutely all, with no exceptions— have their place in the Torah and in it will find their face.

It means, as is said in Exodus, that God did not come solely for the individuals gathered that day at the foot of Mount Sinai, to whom he announces that they will be his treasure from that day forth, but for all those who are not there with them that day but are the objects of the same redemption.

It is the full "humanism of the other" (Levinas, again . . .) that is expressed in the verse.

It is the height of Sinai, which is there, ultimately, so that all people may ascend it with their gaze.

It is the whole of man, man complete and unabridged, all of humanity, the entire human herd that God pastures in every latitude and every age; it is Adam, the already born and those still to be born; it is all of us who are offered, as a promised land is offered, to man and to intelligence.

And everything occurs as if the Jew were none other than the one who, being present from the very first moment, still and always alongside men and with them, accompanying the nations in secret and helping them to name themselves, leading them in silence to an inner encounter that they want without knowing it, that they hope for while fearing it (hence the ambivalence of the nations' desire, seeing their guide both as a scapegoat and as evidence of their possible fulfillment and redemption . . .)—it all unfolds as if the Jew were none other than this: in the best case, man unique, that man at the culmination, man who is the true subject of messianic times. Otherwise, among the most pessimistic and gloomy of us, among those who have said goodbye not to messianic hope but to its concretization, the Jew is the other name of an assuring, reassuring, confirming proof that man has substance, that there is still a singularity and unity to man—in short, that being human has meaning, even if, in everyday life, in the culture, amid the turmoil of nature and the world, one has sometimes the feeling that it all adds up to nothing or, in any event, that nothing proves this "humanity."

There is no Jew absent from that relationship with the nations: That is what the number 70 for the faces of the Torah expresses.

Far from being a separate being who, as implied by the well-known (and so poorly interpreted) passage in Numbers, would turn his back on the nations, the Jew exists only as a function of the nations, in his relationship with them and for them.

He could be sufficient unto himself; he could enclose himself in his houses of study, in what is sometimes called "Jewish life." But that would be a terrible mistake! Being a Jew has its whole and proper meaning when it exposes me to something outside myself, when it implies a passage through time and a peregrination within what is still called, for the time being, History.

The truth is that there is no purely Jewish being. And there is neither plenitude nor profundity of Jewish being without exposition of who and what one is, without responsibility for the world, without constant awareness of the gentile, who is to be met and recognized as an inestimable part of oneself. And, conversely, the nations, the true nations, daughters of Edom and Ishmael, the nations faithful to their angels and, beyond their angels, faithful to the memory that must be shared if one wishes also to be faithful to the legacy of Noah—in short, the nations that adhere to some simple rules that unify the human species: These nations put themselves in great peril when they refuse to expose themselves to that which is exposed to them—that is, when they sever and cast away the Jew in them. Examples include the France of Philippe le Bel, those Arab countries that expelled their Jews, and, of course, the German tragedy that was Nazism.

That is what the verse says.

That is what must be gleaned from the emphasis placed on the number 70 in so many commentaries, from Rashi to the Kabbalah.

Reading the Jewish text, reading it as it should be read, is to generate a universal that is obviously not the extensive one of the Catholics or, upon reflection, the intensive or radiant one of Levinas, of which I, too, have often made use in my work.

This other universal that escorts human beings on the path of their history and to the center of their substance I propose to call by a new name: the "secret universal." Because that is, ultimately, what the story of the treasured people is really about.

THE THREE VERSIONS OF THE SECRET

Let's dig deeper.

How, concretely, might a secret universal operate?

How might it work, if it is neither apostolic nor prophetic? (The prophetic age came around after the era of Esther, as humanity entered into the age of intelligence—*hokhmah*—marked by a wisdom that the Talmud always described not as a lesser good, a step backward, or a freezing of the spirit, but, quite the contrary, as a *step toward* the return and full realization of the prophecy.)

How does this secret Jew get anything done if he does not preach, testify, or proselytize and is obviously not the type to intercede, in the manner of a Mormon, in favor of lost souls?

How do his prayers and words have the effects that I described, such as helping nations know and introduce themselves, guiding people secretly on their path of redemption, and so on?

That is another question.

A very difficult one, and murky. A question to which it is possible to respond only through imagination or dreaming.

I see a torpedo effect, first. A stimulus. Tied to the way Talmudic disputes have of suspending the obvious and, with each verse, cracking the shell of what has already been seen, understood, appropriated, or rejected. Tied to their war on the mechanical. To their utility as a lever for anyone wanting to upset petrified thought, dogmatism, or simple laziness. The struggle against prefabricated words and phrases. The twilight of all the idols, including, of course, the profane. And the element of truth to the cliché that there is a Jewish philosophy, a Jewish literature, a distinctly Jewish mind given to doubt (Marx, Freud), deconstruction (Derrida, the "last of the Jews"), or to encouragement of skeptics and defectors from groupthink in religion and politics (the great Jewish literature from Austria-Hungary at the beginning of the twentieth century).

An example: Imagine a Muslim Talmud. Imagine the great intelligence of Islam launching an assault on itself and the Koran, as the Jews do with the Torah. Imagine imams, scholars, and sages of Islam subjecting the verses devoted, say, to jihad, sharia, and the Umma to the work of commentary, soul-searching, stimulation, and suspension of accepted meaning that the Jews have practiced, which goes by the name of study.

Such work is done, of course. I have encountered imams who do it, holy in spirit and deed, in Kurdistan and Bosnia, in Moroccan and, occasionally, Egyptian universities, once in Pakistan, other times in Panjshir. But what if they became the rule instead of the exception? Imagine that the fruit of, or even the original documents from, the intense theological work that must have accompanied the drafting in Rabat of the new family code, with its recognition of women's rights, were to circulate through the rest of the Arab-Muslim world and suddenly gain wide acceptance. Imagine that an Abdelwahab Meddeb, the great Arab poet and author of *The Malady of Islam,* who remained faithful to the Sufi tradition of Ibn Arabi, whose call for a rereading of Islam, for its contextualization, and even for the elimination of certain tenets, were to sound a real echo in the world of real Muslims.

It is not hard to picture the stupefaction of the backward fundamentalists: their hatred of thinking, their deep-seated misology exploding instantly into shards. But for all the sons and daughters of Ishmael, for all those who are bound to a text still held to be flawless by a majority of its guardians, a text that it would be sinful to alter and may even be sinful to read, what freedom! What joy!

Next, I see an effect of structure. I see the theorem, familiar to logicians, according to which a whole is formed only with support from that which is outside the whole and that a being independent of any other, an inside without an outside, an entity that is its own cause, the product of its own workings, without otherness, cannot exist.

But hold on! There is other, and there is other. And in the history of nations, more than anywhere else, one must make careful distinctions between the different modes, the various possible systems or registers, of otherness.

There is the other who appears to us as a foreigner, no more, no less, loyal to his own nation, residing among us or on our border, friend or enemy depending on circumstances and the vagaries of a world correctly described, when all is said and done, by Carl Schmitt. That situation is well known, and we need not dwell on it.

There is the other considered as barbarian, forever and necessarily barbarian, as in the ancient Greek conception; that vision is the poison of nations, the demon of human plurality; the source of intolerance, racism, and hatred of one's neighbor; the root of nationalism in its more or less closed forms. From this second form of otherness we also form amalgams, but bad ones, amalgams that smell of rot, of death, of war, of all against all. Kant's cosmopolitan idea remains the best response to this shrinking of politics, as well as the best palliative.

And then there are the Hebrews, whose otherness, as I have said, can be summed up by their resemblance to a body of sand. As a metaphor, sand can stand for the multitude but also, remember, for silence, light and tacit mobility, flexibility, and the capacity to change shape and form. To shift sand from one place to another changes nothing, has no sound, can hardly be seen. The Jews have done just that so many times! So often have they experienced that quite bearable lightness, not of being but of individuality, by virtue of no longer being confined within the turgid volumes that make up the edifice of society. For them, all that shifts easily. All that's required is the time to pack a suitcase, open a door, take off, and, sometimes, learn a new language. So let us imagine that the nations—by which I mean the peoples who have accepted the servitude and the grandeur of inhabiting a nation-state—did not hold that sand-like quality against the Jews. Let us imagine that they were to cease committing the error (the very error that should not be committed!) of transforming them into foreigners or barbarians.

Here, too, what a fresh breeze of freedom! What a cool, rejuvenating stream! Sand against earth. Grains of sand strewn over the compacted soil of nations. Matter, still (sand, too, is matter), but one that seems to float into space and to reconnect with time, only to provide a measure of its passing. It is Kafka. It is Proust. It is Rashi in the court of the counts of Champagne, ennobling the French language and making possible, a century later, the *Perceval* and *Lancelot* of an author whose first name was "Christian" but who was probably Jewish. In the economy of being, it is an outside-time and outside-space from which the actual spaces and times of being are ordered or disordered. It is these Jews (and it matters little whether they are rare, whether they are only the remainder of humanity and of themselves) who are not entirely of a certain place or time but who enable that place, at that time, to live fully in the present without sinking into the despair of an infinite and immutable present.

Nations have to choose. Either Spinoza, who, starting from a rejection of transcendence, produces a *Deus sive Natura,* in which humanity is submerged. Or Moses, who, because he established a people of sand (and because, well before that, he buried the Egyptian in sand), is able to offer to nations that agree to mix a little sand with their soil the following provisions: a share of the delicacy found only in the sand, a delicacy that will be the best remedy for their darkness and pride.

And, finally, this hypothesis—or reverie.

I imagine, for Jewish words spoken since the night of time, another time, a secret time, which would not belong to history or its dim self-awareness.

I imagine another space, likewise secret, withdrawn from the phenomenal realm and its manifestations but no more invisible, ultimately, than was the infinite space of Pascal and no more or less inconceivable than that noumenal space that Kant said was impossible to represent but had to be assumed in order to take in those of our representations that appear to us to be inconsistent with our everyday phenomenal space.

I imagine, then, that in the circles of that space-time are stored, preserved, and backed up the moments of truth, redemptive acts, fragments of prophecy and wisdom, and flashes of brilliance that human intelligence has produced whenever it has followed the model of Moses. These moments, acts, fragments, and flashes, precisely because they are opaque to those who produced them as well as to those who merely witnessed them, have to migrate somewhere! So I imagine them as flecks of light, sparks, coming together. Or as gold dust forming a nugget and then becoming treasure. I see a point of incandescence, a dense flickering, and eventually, upon the convergence of the multifaceted reflections of human beings and their cultures, a single, definitive ball of fire.

It is Hölderlin's "Now come, fire!"

It is the blinding beauty that Proust has in mind when he says, in the passage from his *Carnets* in which he describes his reading of the Zohar, that "only what has appeared in the depths deserves to be expressed" and that a "church tower," even if "unseen for days, has more value than a complete theory of the world."

It is the *keter,* the crown, the ball of flame that the Kabbalists place at the peak of the edifice of knowledge.

It is the intuition of Baudelaire in the fragment of *My Heart Laid Bare* where he envisions—is it to applaud, to deplore, or to dispel?—a "fine conspiracy to be organized for the extermination of the Jewish race," wherein the Jews are (this bit of the phrase is so beautiful!) "librarians and witnesses of Redemption."

Or perhaps it is a sort of cloud that can be seen as the living part of the digital cloud, within which, at last report, the world's read-only memory is being brought into alignment: sometimes as the light layer of mist that hid from Kant and hides from us, to the last moment of the last day of our lives, the starry sky that is the first half of Kant's epitaph; sometimes as the equivalent of the roof over the house of humanity, from which the poets of the next age will throw the disorder of their writings, telling themselves that they will wind up forming phrases and making some sort of sense; or sometimes as an inverted *tzimtsum,* intelligible to certain ears—not the retreat and retraction of God making space for the world, which is the proper meaning of *tzimtsum* to the Kabbalists, but rather an emanation, a condensation at the expense of the world, a spouting of sparks, an expansion of lightning and knowledge.

DON JUAN IN THE SINAI

But, for now, that is not the essential point.

What is essential is to grasp that no pride is attached to the unconscious knowledge of being a "treasure."

No national or tribal vanity.

No sort of exclusivity, communitarianism, or sectarianism.

Nothing resembling scorn for others or diminution of their merits. (From *Baba Metzia*, 59a: "To publicly shame one's neighbor is, in a way, to kill him.")

And the very idea of a privilege, of greater dignity, the very idea of an added increment of sacredness derived from the simple fact of being Jewish (by mother or by name), is completely foreign to the profound genius of Judaism.

The temptation exists, of course.

It is even present in the texts of the tradition.

And it is the story, recounted in Exodus, of Korah, a great Jew of prominent lineage, the first cousin of Moses by dint of being the grandson of Kohath, son of Levi, who gives it a shot.

On the surface, it looks like a political coup.

Profiting from one of Moses's repeated absences to go up the mountain and negotiate with God, Korah hatches a political-military conspiracy, recruiting two confederates, Dathan and Abiram, and mobilizing two hundred fifty men of standing, whom he inveigles by making them believe that by following him they are going to increase their prosperity; with them, he attempts to rouse the people against the damned family of Amram, Moses, and his brother, Aaron, who were not satisfied with royalty but wanted to lay claim to the priesthood, as well.

But the heart of the Korah conspiracy—the great claim that will enable him, above and beyond the two hundred fifty, to rally around him those disappointed in Moses's leadership; the seemingly anodyne argument of which Moses, upon his return, immediately detects the fearsome metaphysical scope and which pushes him into direct physical confrontation with his rebellious cousin, hand to hand, censer against censer—goes far beyond mere populist manipulation. Korah is competing less with Moses than with Aaron. He covets not the royalty of the former but the priesthood of the latter. If he has a political vision, it is a political vision not of this world but of God and the relation of man to God. His real argument consists of saying that the tribes are already—here and now, camped in the Sinai—the holy nation that they are called to become (but only at the end of time). "The whole community is holy," says Korah to Moses, "every one of them; why then do you set yourselves above the Lord's assembly?"

We know how the story ends.

The next day, Moses prevails.

And he does so first by seeing the two hundred fifty fools who had thought that Korah was offering them a shortcut to heaven in fact rise in that direction, but in the form of human torches, and then by asking God to arrange, for Korah's edification, a *bria chadasha,* a creation, an event, something that has never happened before and that will mark not only his victory but the enormity of the crime that he had to prevent. And the event occurs. The earth opens its mouth and swallows Korah alive and whole.

The great medieval commentator Rabbeinu Behaye began to wonder.

Why did Moses not ask his cousin to pull himself together?

Given that Moses spent so much time negotiating, interceding, and trying to outrun catastrophe, why, in this case, was he unmoved, icily promising the offender the most grievous of punishments?

And why would a man who was typically so cautious take the risk of calling for a miracle, formulating a wish that, if it were not granted, would appear, according to biblical logic, as a profaning of the Name?

Because the situation was dire.

Because Korah's crime, his way of asking casually, with the air of a Jewish Tartuffe stroking the egos of the people and their leaders, "Don't you know that the whole assembly is holy," the fact that he, who all the commentators agree was a wise man, believed or wanted to believe in the story of "election," but as ignorant people construed it—*that* is the worst crime conceivable, one tantamount to destruction of the world.

So to punish that crime, to discourage the sanctification of the nation, which the Kabbalists say bears similarities to the projects of the inhabitants of Sodom or Babel; to punish this sorcerer's apprentice who was in the process of plunging his people, as a mad scientist

might do, into a supposedly magical but in fact diabolical precipi-
tate; to atone for the sin of this man who, like the Sodomites and the
Babelites, like those representatives of the dregs of humanity, was
ready to form a group whose aim was to turn their back on the divine and undo all of the liberating work undertaken by Moses since
the Israelites left Egypt, there was no other *tikkun,* no other reparation, than a new day of creation, a recommencement of the world, a
bereishit, an "In the beginning" in reverse: the earth's mouth opening
and closing on Korah as if he had never existed, as if he had never
come into the world, as if the world were not his world and needed
to be remade.

The truth is that there is no hypostasis of the holy nation.

The holy nation is holy, it is *segula,* by vocation and destination, but
certainly not by situation.

It is holy but in the perspective of the "world of truth" (*olam haemet*)
that is to be attained, but obviously not in this world (*olam hazeh*), despite what theocrats of Korah's ilk would have us believe.

As we have just seen, there is no "social" identity to this nation
with a closed core defined and delimited once and for all. Jewish
thought detests, above all else, the idea of legions of the faithful
"clothing themselves in the garments" that others "have worn before
them"—that is, to speak plainly, and the Kabbalah sometimes speaks
very plainly, legions mechanically repeating verses chanted in the
same form by others before them.

We also know that there is no full "political identity" marked by
immanent grace or definitive examplariness and nobility. Great moments, yes, as well as exceptional peaks when the Jewish nation was
illuminating for itself and for others. But otherwise the link is fragile.
And the rule is the demon of division and the de facto division of its
kingdoms; the mediocrity of most of its sovereigns; their persistence
in sin, including David and Solomon, who were great kings, towering
figures, but with their share of accursedness. David's adultery with
Bathsheba and his guilty defiance of God in the famous incident of

the counting of the people of Israel . . . Solomon's excessive pride, his many wives and concubines, his speaking to animals, his worship of the idols Ashtoreth, Molech, and Chemosh . . . What a contrast with the spotless helmet of the Achaean kings, with the bronze virtues attributed to the kings of Rome! Is it by chance that the *haftarah* selection (the selection from the Bible always read in tandem with the Torah portion) that is always associated with Korah is the first book of Samuel, chapter 11, which expresses the unworthiness of the kings of Israel and the infamy of those who believe that one can establish a monarchy the way one puts up a tent? And is it by chance that modern Israel, a country that, as I have said, does not yet know whether it will evolve from a fascinating country into an admirable and sublime one, continues to produce in such great number scholars, writers, sages of all kinds, engineers, and artists but still has not been able to cultivate a political class of commensurate stature?

I have met most of the prime ministers of Israel. From Begin to Rabin, from Shamir to Netanyahu, from Shimon Peres and the other grand dukes of Zionism to Ariel Sharon and others, I have had many occasions to observe the mistakes they make, their inexplicable failures to communicate, their missteps and acts of naïveté, their tendency, once in power, to forget the great generals, professors, or eagle-eyed geostrategists that they had sometimes been.

And I sometimes tell myself that this is the curse of Saul. Or the earlier curse of Gideon, the great soldier and mediocre king, an invincible warrior who, once crowned, became so much less than himself. I tell myself that this is a great misfortune.

But at other times I say, no, it is a good thing, an antidote to the idolatry of the political and the deathly glacier with which it is smothering humanity. And I dream that there is, in Jewish culture's painful experience with sovereignty, a form of virtue, grandeur, and, yet again, genius: a blessed lack of credulousness and the good fortune, though seemingly as often for the worse as for the better, that Israel is still not a state like the others; that it has not forgotten the shifting nature of the sand of its beginnings; that there remains this group of people defined by their removal from the space occupied by all the other groups undermined by the bad language that Moses rejected—and that there exists this unique experiment in transcending politics or of breaking, *within politics,* with the political vision of the world.

With regard to the land, finally, the land to which the Hebrews are called and that is, in a certain sense, theirs, is it not said, "The land shall not be sold in perpetuity, for the land is mine. For you are strangers and sojourners with me." Is it not clear that to be a Jew is to be a stranger, not only among others, in the manner of any other "minority," but even at home, living voluntarily on the outside as a pariah-self, the latter being a positive necessity of the Jewish self? Is it not extremely eloquent that Abraham, the real father of the nation, had to experience in the course of his long life the double adventure of the ascent to the Promised Land, followed by descent from it and return to Egypt?

In short, no sanctification of land, politics, or society.

And the nation? Even more so!

There is even less sense, if this were possible, in the idea of a Jewish nation that, individually and collectively, would be rooted in holiness!

The idea of a fast track and special access to the holy of holies, the idea that because one is Jewish one is on God's short list and that there is nothing left to do but show up, enjoy it, and congratulate yourself for the good luck that deposited you one fine day at the foot of the little mountain: That may be what some Jews believe; it is most assuredly what the anti-Semites are thinking with their fantasy about the chosen people and its election; but for Moses, faced with Korah and the Korah impulse, it is the worst of errors, the most monstrous of superstitions, and it certainly is not what he understood up there when God spoke to him.

WHO IS JEWISH?

It is not even certain that being Jewish is enough to be a Jew.

It is not at all clear that having a Jewish name fulfills one's vocation as a Jew.

What is certain and clear is that having that name without knowing the secret name that lives within it is the best way of turning one's back and not hearing the outcry of divine intelligence.

It is quite an adventure to be a Jew.

Very beautiful.

But it is also a heavy load.

Yes, heavy: The same word, *kavod*, as I noted at the very outset of this book, denotes both glory and weight, enlightenment and its price, the divine Name that dazzles and its weight in gold, copper, or barley.

Yes, *kavod*, the only word to express election and its burden, the stupendous effort it takes to pull oneself out of the human mass and set out on the path toward the angels and the almost unbearable gravity of the life of the spirit that ensues.

Rare are the Jewish lives, the truly Jewish lives, that experience fully, even if not for their entire lives, the test of being Jewish.

Rashi, without any doubt, of whom it is said that each drop of ink was like a precious stone.

Maimonides, the second Moses, carrying on his shoulders the philosophical and scientific weight of his time—in addition to the Torah.

Kafka, implicitly, but when he repudiated his own books—what a pity.

My friend Benny Lévy in the second phase of his existence, which was so short.

Others, a few others, that history has forgotten but who, through study and knowledge, succeeded in hewing close to the unpronounceable.

Others who—in the poor shtetls of Galicia and the lost ghettos of Kaifeng in China where they had been isolated since the time of King Solomon, cut off from all knowledge, all memory, and, perhaps as a result, from all binds—managed to hear anew the speech of the Sinai and of prophecy.

But still so few.

Grains of sand.

The Talmud says that if the Sabbath were properly observed by ten Jews, the messiah would be here.

So, fewer than ten!

Not even a decury!

Bright spots.

Fleeting Jewish moments of life.

Glimmers of clarity, pinpricks of light, pearlescent shimmers, almost incongruous.

In life we are Jewish intermittently but not, dare I say, essentially.

We are Jews one day, less so the next day, and Jews again the day after that.

We are Jews on the days when the Book is revealed in its perfect harmony, but we are not Jews as a condition that we are able to maintain every day or once and for all.

And I know there are some who are Jews on Yom Kippur, splendid in the happy nudity of renewal; of resetting the clock, counting the days from one; of beginning anew the year, time, and themselves. And I know that many of those Jews will be less Jewish, some much less so, the day after—such are life and its little compromises! Back to the lie and the social comedy! That "have an easy fast" with which New Yorkers greet me the evening before! I am well aware that it translates the Hebrew *tsom qal* and that it really means that the *ve'initem et-nafshotekhem*—that is, the challenge, the hardship, or the self-affliction of the soul—must be done with a certain lightness and without self-conscious martyrdom. But, still, there is in it a nettlesome air of frivolity, and this bothers me. But, on the other hand . . . What would life be like if every day were the eve of Yom Kippur? If the moment of nudity went on forever? Perhaps it would be a life that would never begin and never cease not beginning. Who knows if that would not be the opposite of a Jewish life?

Happy is the one who, like the young *moreh* who is teaching me the little Hebrew I know, has taken the trip.

Happy the one who, in contact with a master, has even glimpsed the light.

They are true to the treasure.

They have been pierced by Judaism.

For that is the secret: a piercing, penetrating force.

That, truly, is the Jewish being: a disposition—brief, unpredictable, perpetual—toward the voyage of intelligence.

To think how long we have been bombarded with this business of the "wandering Jew"!

A Jew, by definition, wanders.

We must accept that he is a spiritual datum that transforms only fleetingly into a destiny.

We must yield to the idea of an ungraspable bounding quality that inhabits certain lives, and not always or necessarily those assumed to be Jewish.

A dybbuk as in Romain Gary, more Jewish than acknowledged.

A passing guest, in the lexicon of André Malraux, a man and a thinker more attuned to the Jewish enigma than his scholars and followers know.

A Jew who wanders within himself, more delicate and more secret than communities and churches would have him be—all churches, including those of the Jews themselves.

A Jew who must remain unknown and unmanifest, so intolerable to society is the care he takes to lighten the human load, to unburden it of the weight of idolatry.

And what is called Judaism is, at the intersection of all these expressions of Judaism, a vaporous outline.

That is what it means to be chosen.

That is the genius of Judaism.

And the Jewish condition, fragile as it is, is the price of the secret and the condition imposed on the treasure.

We are here far from the practitioners of competitive orthopraxy, who, like trained lions, can recite the Talmud by heart but who the Kabbalists say border on knowing too much, because the mass of their knowledge will end up blocking understanding. (Don't they need to free up some space in their minds?)

But we are close to Exodus.

Close to the Maharal of Prague.

And especially close to one of the books of the prophetic corpus that I have always cherished and which I now realize is among those that deliver with a maximum of intensity (obscurity and clarity closely admixed . . .) this idea of hidden intelligence and this concentrate of the secret universal that are the only possible definition of election: the Book of Jonah.

CHAPTER SEVEN

THUS SPAKE JONAH

Jonah is known in the biblical canon as a minor prophet.

But if he is minor in the brevity of his prophecy (forty-eight verses), he is hardly so by birth, belonging through his mother to the tribe of Asher and through his father to that of Zabulon.

Nor is he minor by his legend: It seems that he is the son of the widow who nursed the prophet Elias, and, according to the First Book of Kings, Elias revived him.

And still less by his earlier prophetic path: Some commentaries, notably those of Abravanel, say that he was the prophet who joined Jehu and told him about the Lord's promise to maintain on the throne of Israel four generations of his heirs.

He is a major figure, who shares with Moses the quality of radiating light from the glorious moment that was the day of his birth. This, too, distinguishes him from the eleven other minor prophets.

And to this major, miraculous figure, almost a Moses, the equal of Isaiah and Ezekiel, to this *Yonah* (Hebrew for dove), in whom I cannot help seeing a reincarnation of the dove of the ark, is given an order that is unique in the prophetic literature, as emphasized by the most stimulating of the post-medieval commentators, Meïr Leibush ben Yehiel Michel Wisser, a nineteenth-century Russian rabbi known as the Malbim.

Rarely do the prophets address the *akum,* the "servants of the stars," the pagans.

And when they do, like Abdias addressing Edom, it is certainly not to urge them to do *teshuvah,* to repent of their sins.

And, as for actually going to Edom, going face-to-face with foreigners physically and in person, and sinning foreigners on top of it all, that never happens.

But that is precisely what Jonah is commanded to do.

The Lord tells him explicitly to go to Nineveh, the Assyrian capital.

Amos denounces social injustices on Israeli territory. Hosea thunders against the cults of Baal and Asherah that are starting to take root there. Joel laments the invasions of grasshoppers that are devastating the land of Moses. Haggai and Zechariah plead for reconstruction of the temple. Much later, after the temple has been reconstructed, Malachi bemoans the cold, spiritless formalism that there prevails. Micah announces a messiah. Habakkuk is surprised at the silence of God. Zephaniah invites the kingdom of Judah to acknowledge its faults and expiate them. But Jonah is the only one to whom God mentions none of this but, instead, he speaks to him of Nineveh, a large and supremely sinful foreign city whose defects have recently come to his attention. He asks Jonah to repair them so that he is not forced to punish the city.

A HERO FROM CORNEILLE . . .

Nineveh, the verse tells us, is *the* big city.

It does not say a great city, a foreign city like any other, one capital among many, but "the" great city, "the" city par excellence, one whose origins, according to the commentators, are lost in the night of time, since they date back to Genesis.

Built along the Tigris, not far from present-day Mosul, during the era of Nimrod—that is, three generations after the flood—it is famous for its splendid palaces, its impregnable walls, its parapet atop which three chariots can roll side by side, its artisans and artists, and its library, one of the richest in the ancient world, in which archaeologists of the twentieth century will find tens of thousands of tablets devoted to astronomy, poetry, history, medicine, and agriculture, as well as to the arts of divination and exorcism.

It is, in other words, the most prosperous, shining, civilized city of the time.

But (because these qualities often go together) it is also the most corrupt, depraved, and decadent.

It is a city whose inhabitants the verse describes as like the "beasts in great number," alongside which they live in a deep and shadowy unity, incapable of distinguishing the true from the false, the good from the evil, "their right from their left."

But it is also a city (and this is the strangest part, the heart of the story, which makes the voyage that Jonah is commanded to take so very odd!) whose kings are Israel's hereditary enemies, its fiercest and most fearsome adversaries; it is a city that, according to the Bible, will destroy Israel.

Jonah is aware of all of this.

He is a wise prophet who understands that Assyria (of which, I repeat, Nineveh is the capital) is becoming increasingly aggressive.

He is a well-informed prophet, a contemporary of the cruel Ninevite king Tiglath-Pileser III, who has already occupied a part of Galilee and brought thousands of Hebrews into exile. There is no reason to suppose that he will stop there.

And he knows that this city, whose magnificence is equaled only by its corruption, this Egypt-but-worse, this aggravated Babylon, this place that Nahum, another "minor prophet," would say had more merchants than there were stars in the sky, has one and only one obsession (like so many countries today), which is the annihilation of the two kingdoms, Judah and Israel, whose suicidal rivalry has rendered them vulnerable.

So Jonah's dismay is understandable.

One can imagine his reluctance, if not his repugnance, to make himself—a Hebrew!—an instrument of Nineveh's rescue and thus of the strengthening, in the short to medium term, of the hostile city.

You want me to do what? he wonders.

I, an upstanding Hebrew, should go warn the capital of crime and sin that the Lord has it in his sights and will not hesitate to reduce it to rubble unless it changes its ways?

I, the faithful subject of King Jeroboam, who may not be a very good king but who, good or not, is my king, should go put back in the saddle an arrogant foreign monarch who is full of himself and his misdeeds, one who will have nothing more pressing to do, after hearing my warning and escaping divine punishment, than to recommence his moral and military rearmament? This business of saving Nineveh, of rushing to assist the great power of the day (the Midrash emphasizes, again and again, that there has never been a city greater than Nineveh), this folly of confronting the enemy not to fight him but to save him by calming the wrath of God—would this not be the act of a bad Jew? Would it not be playing with the fire of my *klal,* of my "love of the Jewish people," the very love that, a few millennia later, a sage of Judaism by the name of Gershom Scholem will fault a certain Hannah Arendt for having so cruelly lacked in her account of the trial of a distant relative of Amalek?

Even though Jonah obviously does not see this far into the future (although Micah announced the coming of Christ; Isaiah, Cyrus; and Jeremiah, according to some, the Babylonian captivity), he must be wondering if, in going down the path laid out for him, he is not going to the origin of a geostrategic upheaval that no one wanted but in which the survival of Israel hangs in the balance.

The simple truth is that he is lost.

It cannot be said that, like Job, he does not understand what is happening to him.

On the contrary, he understands it only too well: His worldly intelligence makes him certain that his prophecy, if it comes to pass, will lead to the persecution of what is most dear to him.

He is torn, in other words, between his twin loyalties to the Father and the Son, to God and to Israel.

He is plunged into a debate straight out of Corneille, between two contradictory duties: to heed the voice that summons him to go "speak to the great city" and so to be the instrument of his people's loss, or to think first of his people and disobey the voice.

And that is what gives to this dialogue—which is no longer a dialogue with God but the interior dialogue of Jonah with himself—its edge of tragedy, the engine of which is the clash between two incompatible ideas.

FLIGHT, ONLY FLIGHT! . . .

The more Jonah thinks about it, the less clear God's intentions, and thus his instructions, seem to be.

According to some commentaries, he is expected to look no further than the end of his nose and to be concerned with nothing other than the beautiful, opulent city, which, if he cannot convince it to return to the right path, will suffer catastrophe.

According to others, notably the Malbim, he is supposed to look ahead and understand that God is never reluctant (he often said as much to Jeremiah and Isaiah!) to give Israel a corrective push when merited; but, before doing so, he requires that the agents of that correction, in this case Ashur, king of Nineveh, be worthy of their role and be washed of their sins before being authorized to strike. Absurd, thinks Jonah, incomprehensible and absurd! By what perversion of the spirit can the Almighty set himself the goal of redeeming the executioner before setting him loose on the chosen people? Is that hypothesis not as shocking, and perhaps more so, than the one concocted eight centuries later by that sycophant, that traitor, Flavius Josephus, who writes in *The Jewish War* that Vespasian and Titus are the saviors of the Jewish people and attack Jerusalem only to purify it?

Other commentaries emphasize that the Almighty is less irresponsible than he appears, because the verse also says that Jonah must go "speak to Israel"—in other words, he must hide from Israel nothing of his mission and thus nothing of the calamity that he is reluctantly preparing or of the short time available to Israel (provided it were willing to be a little less blind than the Jews of fifteenth-century Spain or those of Germany in the 1930s would prove to be) to prepare for the shock and put itself in a better position to resist.

It may even have occurred to Jonah (this is *my* hypothesis, but why not?) that all this may be no more than a bad dream, a trick on God's part, a whim, a prank designed to test his faith as well as his intuition and his knowledge of higher plans. Stupid prophet! How could you have fallen into such an obvious trap or believed in that nutty story? How could you forget that I am a God of leniency and love but also of great anger, a God whose chariots fly like a hurricane at the enemies of my beloved people? How could you imagine for even a second that the God who did not hesitate to have Korah swallowed by the mouth of the earth; who did not raise a finger, despite the pleas of Abraham, when the sinful populations of Sodom and Gomorrah were wiped out; how could you imagine that the Father who did not shrink from sending a flood to liquidate most of humanity and the animal world without explanation, warning, or qualm; how could you believe that this God, this YHWH of armies, this blacksmith who judges by iron and fire, could seriously ask you to go save the inexcusable Ninevites?

Or perhaps (a crazy idea; another personal hypothesis—but with God, you never know) Jonah's real mission is, as said in the last words of the prophecy of his colleague Isaiah, to go to Nineveh to make sure that none of his brothers remain there in exile, as they do in Tarshish, Tubal, and Javan, those "to the isles afar off, that have not heard my fame." Perhaps there are in Nineveh the equivalent of *falashas,* lost tribes, and Jonah is assigned to mount a rescue operation to bring them back on horses or camels to the "holy mountain."

In short, he is caught in the revolving door of these contrary views that are and always have been the hallmark of Jewish thought and that can cause it, at any moment, to explode into irreconcilable theses, hypotheses, and conjectures.

He no longer senses within him that inner wall of sapphires and crystals bound with a sturdy colored mortar, a wall built by God himself, which is elsewhere said to protect the just, certainly not from doubt but from disorientation, from the loss of touchstones. Suddenly, with that wall gone, it is Jonah who can no longer tell his right from his left.

In a panic, he chooses not to choose.

Carried away by inner torment, he takes to his heels and departs in the direction opposite to the one God told him to take. Reaching the port of Jaffa, he spies a ship about to sail for Tarshish (the present-day Gibraltar), one of the "isles afar off" that have not yet heard of the glory of YHWH and where there is good work to be had.

Perhaps remembering, finally, that a prophetic order is valid only in the territory of Israel and that, once the border is crossed, it is no longer imperative or, in any case, binding and enforceable, he buys his ticket, as well as all the other tickets available, and embarks.

Some commentators think that if Jonah is not content to buy his own ticket in advance (whereas the custom is to pay for your passage upon arrival) and instead buys up every last place on the boat, it is because he does not have a moment to lose and wants to depart without delay. Others say that he is a good man, a worthy descendant of Zabulon, who, foreseeing a difficult crossing, does not want to imperil others not involved in his dispute with the Holy One and so prefers to privatize the vessel.

In any case, it was the right thing to do.

For prophetic precedent, like legal precedent, is more complicated than it appears.

And the fugitive, in his panic, has forgotten a few things.

That a prophet who "withholds" his prophecy is condemned to death.

That although there have been prophets, like Jeremiah, who believed themselves too young to prophesize or, like Isaiah, too impure (not to mention Moses, who deemed himself "heavy of mouth and heavy of tongue," not up to the task, and "of uncircumcised lips"), all of them managed to fall into line and, with varying degrees of grace, rise to their mission.

That there is just one case of a prophet who thought he could claim the "territorial" precedent that Jonah seems to want to cite as a reason for not obeying. Ezekiel received his message in Israel but, before he could gear up, before he could reflect on what he wanted to say, chew over his words, and spit them out, he found himself sent into exile. But all of the commentaries, beginning with that of Rabbi David ben Zimra, the Talmudist of Safed, are in agreement that exile is not an excuse, because the applicable law is that of the country in which the prophecy was issued. Exile or not, Ezekiel had to fulfill his mission.

Finally, Jonah has forgotten that this particular prophecy, this *vay'hi dvar H'* (literally, "the Word of God"), despite its brevity or perhaps because of it, is the highest form of the Word and thus, as the Malbim says, the most difficult to avoid. Tough luck, Jonah! Plus, he forgets that God "made the sea and the earth dry" and that, if he has mastery over the second, he has no less mastery over the first, making it literally impossible, according to the Radak, to flee from him.

TYPHOON

The result: He had barely set off when God "caused a mighty wind to blow toward the sea." It was a terrible wind, says the Malbim.

A black wind that seems "born from the abyss."

A wind, he observes, that does "not conform to the nature of wind."

Other lessons tell us that it is one of the most terrible winds in the history of humanity.

And it is a typhoon that, while it slaps, buffets, and nearly sinks the ship, does not prevent the other craft around it from sailing quietly on.

Jonah leaves the sailors to busy themselves on the bridge, to panic, to jettison their cargo to lighten the boat, while he descends deep into the hold.

And there, contrary to every expectation, although his previous inner torment had sent him into a terrible panic, he falls into "a mysterious sleep."

Is Jonah the sort of man whose cool cannot be broken by anything and who is capable, when sleepy, of sleeping whenever he needs to, even if he is tormented?

Is he overcome by the events and does he, like any ordinary man confronted with impossible choices, curl up into a ball and return to fetal form?

Or perhaps, having understood that he is the cause of the cataclysm and that said cataclysm will cease only when he perishes, does he take to the hold so as to be certain, given the architecture of the boat, of drowning as soon as the bilge rises high enough to reach him, thereby calming God's rage by removing its object?

This third interpretation is the one that the Malbim embraces.

A peaceful wait for death, a death he probably hopes will be quick and relatively painless, a death unlike that of the sailing Rabbi Akiva, who would be tossed around and smashed on the shore—this might be the hypothesis that seems to square best with what we can guess about the psychology of Jonah, with his wisdom and measured mind and spirit.

Except the storm does not die down.

The mariners pray in vain. In vain they cry out, as the verse says, "each in his own language to his own god." In vain they invoke the pagan gods of the sea, before deciding to draw lots (as one does when one seeks an infallible and precise response) to identify the individual responsible for the typhoon. Meanwhile, the vessel rocks ever more violently and, as the verse so beautifully puts it, "dreams of destruction."

Until the captain, descending into the hold and finding the mysterious passenger snoring like a bell, shakes him, wakes him, and asks why he is not up with the others, praying and bailing. He learns from Jonah (1) that he is *ivri,* descendant of Eber, himself a descendant of Ham and thus of Abraham; (2) that he fears the god not of the sea but of the heavens, whom he inopportunely angered by refusing to go "speak in the city"; and (3) that his companions in misfortune have no other solution to escape from the disaster in which he has ensnared them but to get rid of him by throwing him overboard.

An offended refusal from the sailors, who are good men. (Is it not implied that they who had begun by "praying each to his own god" quickly allowed themselves to be converted to the religion of Jonah's One God?)

Indignation on the part of these men, whom the Talmud repeats are just men, who have risked their lives, men who, like all sailors, dangle above danger and therefore have a noble relation with Providence—indignation from these unnamed men of no particular identity, which I like to think is designed to tell us that they are the best from among the nations, just sorts, like those who protected or hid or saved Jews during the war, and who exclaim, "Who do you take us for? Don't you realize that we base our life on the unshakable prin-

ciple of solidarity among men of the sea? How can you possibly think
that we could sacrifice one of our own?"

But finally, trapped themselves now in the jaws of one of those
contradictory imperatives that seem to be the rule in this story, wanting neither to make themselves "responsible for the death of an innocent" nor to "die because of that man," they conduct a test by
dipping one part of his body, then another and another, each time for
a little longer, into the dark and furious waves.

And when they realize that this works, that the storm calms when
they dip him in and starts up again when they haul him back on the
deck, they come to understand that there is no other solution but to
get rid of him. And seeing that he is insisting, imploring, almost beg-
ging to be allowed to take his leave of them, that in fact he has but one
fixed idea, which is to save them, even at the price of his own life, they
very reluctantly end up throwing all of Jonah into the water.

IN THE BELLY OF THE WHALE

A whale is passing nearby.

The Hebrew text specifies a *tanin,* which means "big fish."

The Greek text, departing, as it often does, from the Hebrew,
speaks of a sea dragon, an octopus.

Whatever it is, while the storm dies down as expected and the
good sailors, like anti-Noahs, escape this recurrence of the flood in
miniature, the animal gobbles up Jonah, just as the mouth of the earth
had swallowed Korah.

So there!

Another dramatic turn of events!

Although the sailors believe that he has drowned, although he believes himself damned and feels the bolts of earth and sea closing over
him, he survives.

Certain Christian teachings speculate that his soul separated from
his body, rose to make a little tour of heaven, took in the throne of
God, and then descended again and re-inhabited his husk lying in the
belly of the whale.

And the fact is that he is going to spend in that belly three very strange days and nights (which the same Christian exegesis obviously does not fail to compare with the three days and nights that Christ spent in his tomb).

These are days of great affliction, during which Jonah believes that he has perished, only to reawaken "in the abode of the dead."

But once he realizes that he is alive, they are also days of happiness, marked by a form of fusion with himself such as he had never before felt.

It is a return to the womb, a regression to primal life, a minimal existence in symbiosis, osmosis, with the most intimate part of himself.

The fish's enormous pupils function as portholes, and the seaweed that clings to its eyes, which appears similar to the rushes of the "sea of reeds" that had opened up before Israel on the day of its birth, give Jonah the impression of reliving, deep in the body of the fish, the greatest miracle humanity has ever known—that of the parting of the sea for the exodus from Egypt. "Surrounded by seaweed," says the verse, in the deepest of the deep, in the abysses of the intimate and elemental, in contact with that pure creaturality, that generative power that defines both animals and plants, he witnesses a recommencement of the world, a surpassing of creation reversing itself to a new rebirth. And for this new miracle of the Red Sea, for this marvel of access to what lies beyond nature and the world, Jonah gives thanks to God.

The canticle of Jonah.

The story of Jonah's life shut up, immobile, in the paunch of the whale.

A thought for the sailors, those gentle men, so noble, so different from the Baudelairean "crewmen" "gliding over bitter depths" and torturing albatrosses, whom he saw with his own eyes renounce their idols and vanities.

Wonderful verses in which he says how, at the bottom of that abyss, in the seawater and seaweed, in the non-place where one might believe that nothing has ever taken place and that the place, as place, has vanished into nothingness, there reappears to him that other place without place, one beyond all places, that is the Temple of Jerusalem.

And as the fish changes from male (*dag*) to female (*daga*) and fills itself suddenly with eggs, which now occupy a cavity that previously had been spacious for Jonah, Jonah sees space shrinking. He feels cramped amid these proliferating possibilities, crowded by the rank and abruptly unchained generative power. The obscurity he loved, in which he felt good and that he had first experienced as introcentrism and perhaps (who knows?) as a proposition to the spirit, becomes pure darkness, entrenched in matter and matrix, absolute and mortal proof of waiting, grounding, loss, murkiness—until God, seeing Jonah suffocating and, this time, dying for real, takes pity on him, guides the whale toward terra firma, and has her spit Jonah up not far from the spot from which he set out.

The Zohar says that the whale, stranded on the shore, dies.

He also says that, like Jonah, the whale revives after three days and returns to the sea.

But Jonah, in any case, is safe.

Did the trial prove his hesitations wrong?

Does he emerge broken from his season in the monster's belly?

Did he have the leisure, during his forcible confinement in that uterus revisited, to reflect more closely on his mission and to understand things that he had not grasped before?

Did he understand that he was trapped and that God, master of the seas as well as of the land, would not let him go and that he had no means of escape?

Did he make the oath, as people often do when confronting great danger, when descending into hell, when obliged to undergo an ordeal from which by all appearances one will emerge alive only by a miracle, that if he did indeed emerge alive, if he did succeed one day in escaping the vast and foul belly, he would do everything that God asked of him?

Or did his passage through becoming a plant or—what amounts to the same thing—becoming dead strip him of the odious shimmer of pride that made him believe that he knew everything better than God did?

The commentaries—and my imagination—diverge.

But he pulls himself together.

He goes finally to Nineveh, the great city, which takes three days to cross.

But without waiting to take it all in, or taking it all in at race pace, he stops and, after just one day, his heart heavy, begins to cry out over and over again, "In forty days Nineveh will be destroyed! In forty days Nineveh will be destroyed!"

Forty . . .

That is the number of years that Moses spent in Egypt.

It is the number of years that he lost wandering in the desert before God decided that the test had gone on long enough.

It is the number of days (and nights) that he spent on Mount Sinai negotiating his alliance with God while the Hebrews down below gave themselves up to idolatry and conspired with Korah.

Forty days is the length of the mission of the twelve explorers that, according to the Book of Numbers, Moses sent into Canaan to size up the enemy and its capacity for resistance.

Not to mention the forty days of which Voltaire made merciless fun, the days during which Ezekiel, in expiation of the sins of Judah, had to sleep on his right side, his bread covered with excrement.

Or the forty-day march, without food or water, of the prophet Elias to Mount Horeb. Or Jesus's forty days and forty nights in the desert.

Forty is an essential number.

It has always been the number of trial. And it restates, on the cusp of the last quarter of the story, the extreme importance of the mission, the highly sensitive nature of the message that has just been delivered and the anxiousness with which we rightfully await the dénouement.

TARTUFFE?

That is where we stand.

Behold the inhabitants of Nineveh, who, "from the greatest to the smallest," take to heart the word of God, declare a fast, and cover themselves in sackcloth.

Behold the king—perhaps Ashur, perhaps Sennacherib, perhaps the reincarnation of Pharaoh—who, seeing the dark cloud gathering above his city, takes off his royal purple and other finery, covers himself with a rag, and sits on a bed of ashes.

And heed the decree in which he orders the entire city, "man and beast, large cattle and small," to eat nothing, to "cry out to the Lord with all their might," to "turn away from their evil conduct and acts of violence," and to purge themselves of the pomposity that he seems to have discovered is the face of idolatry and the opposite of true nobility.

God, seeing this and observing that "each turns from the path of wrong and from the thievery that is in his palms," calms his wrath and retracts the punishment with which he had threatened the city.

Again, it is the opposite of the ark: The story began in the waves, whereas that of the ark ended there. And all's well that ends well, since the Ninevites, like the sailors, having been instructed by a prophet with the name of a dove, "believe in the Lord" and thus are spared.

But Jonah is not happy.

He climbs to the top of a nearby hill east of the city. There he builds himself a hut, though we do not know whether he does this to see how things turn out in the city, to take a well-deserved rest, or, his work done, to return quietly, in the eerie silence that has replaced the agitation of the city, to studying the Torah, as befits a sage of his caliber. (The latter is the view of the Vilna Gaon.)

What we do know, however, is that he is not at all content. The text says very clearly that he "finds the thing bad indeed and becomes angry."

He is convinced, first of all, that the city's repentance is not sincere.

He can see well enough that people are making the right gestures, but, the Malbim says, he does not see them renouncing idolatry or coming to know God.

He sees that they are fasting and wearing sackcloth, thereby showing the outer signs of extreme zeal, but he is experienced, and something tells him that there is more calculation than piety in the show the people are putting on.

And the thought of divine leniency in the face of unrepentant human corruption, the idea that the mere appearance of repentance can get one acquitted of a criminal past, revolts and disgusts him, being so utterly contrary to all that he knows about justice and truth.

And how will this make him look after having predicted the ruin of a city that everyone will now see recovering and prospering?

Now that it will not be destroyed, will he not appear to be a false prophet, a cartoon prophet who, on every street corner, announces that the apocalypse is coming tomorrow?

And the chosen people? They are looking good, the chosen people; they, at least, have the spine to openly disobey God! These hypocritical Ninevites, who do not believe a word they are saying but who are already—already—experts in communication and in the manipulation of public opinion, will they not go on to play the sanctimonious and mealymouthed holy rollers, the children of paradise, hyperobedient, while casting the Hebrews in the thankless role of rebels against the heavenly order? And whatever else you might think about this role reversal, occurring at the very moment of the lifting of divine sanctions, will it not allow Nineveh to rebuild its arsenals? Will it not prove to be a political and military catastrophe for Israel?

That is what bothers Jonah the most. Less than his ruined reputation or wounded patriotism, it is the reversal of all things, the blurring of all the landmarks.

It is the ambiguity, the confusion, the lack of clarity that mortify him: Is the recovery of Nineveh supposed to be taken for an injustice in the service of a higher justice? The ruin of Israel a disaster to pave the way for a more brilliant rebirth? Commentators' words! He does not understand what that means! Or, if he understands it and is able to consent to it from the standpoint of its prophetic reasoning on justice, he still cannot consent to it from the standpoint of the awareness that men will have of it. Alone on his hill, he is overcome with despair.

THE HEIGHTS OF NINEVEH TODAY

That hill exists.

It is one of the high spots that, as I write, look down on the city of Mosul, now in the criminal grip of Daesh, those assassins of man and God. And I am there on an afternoon in August 2015, having accompanied a Peshmerga patrol sent to relieve the handful of advance sentinels who were keeping watch on the barbarians in dried-mud shelters that I cannot help seeing as replicas of Jonah's hut.

It is the same oven.

The same motionless wait.

The same frightful brightness, with specks of dust dancing in the sunlight.

The same days—forty, perhaps—that separate the plain of Nineveh from its new deliverance.

The same scraggly shrub that tries to grow through the rubble in the little piece of ground religiously watered by the fighters between the ammo dump and the sandbags chinked up with quicklime.

And with my head full of the faces of warriors mingled with the possible faces of a prophet who must have been about the age of the oldest of the Kurdish fighters and had the same darkly fiery gaze, the same hermit's leanness, I waver between despair, stoked by the idea of the city at my feet bristling with black flags and for the moment managing to elude (for reasons as unclear to me as they were to Jonah) the judgment of man and heaven, and the scant comfort provided by the presence here with me on the heights—on the edge of two worlds—of this ship of the just, these sailors of the summit looking out from Mount Zartik onto the enemies of humanity.

I am thinking of Jonah.

I am thinking of what he must have been thinking.

I am imagining what he must have imagined in seeing, at his feet, as I see today in the same haze of heat that dissipates when it meets the plain, the Nineveh that is today known as Mosul and that is twice as sinful.

When God, on the first night, causes a shrub called *kikayon*—

sometimes translated as a "castor-oil plant"—to grow over the hut, Jonah begins to hope. Is it a sign? A sign, first of all, of his return to grace and of the precious essence that he is, despite his disobedience and his rebelliousness, in the eyes of the All-Powerful . . . A sign that, in sheltering him from the wind that he has just kicked up, the heat of which Jonah's poor skin (naked or nearly so, because his shabby clothing was in all likelihood eaten away by salt and acids in the belly of the whale) can no longer tolerate, God intends to make him aware, not in the depths but on the heights, not in the abyss but in the canyons of the Most High, not in the reedy sea but on the summits blazing with the work of the world, that there is a place for him, and that place is secure and comfortable . . . A sign, ultimately, that he is still seen as one of the just and that the just are the foundation of the world, or as a wise man and that wisdom is the framework of things . . . Perhaps, too, it is a sign that he has to stay there, in the shade of the protective shrub, alert, focused, undistracted, because something is in the works, and that something will be a huge event, a colossal spectacle, and he who laughs last laughs best. Jonah must sit tight in the front row for just thirty-nine more days to see if Nineveh returns to its evil ways and God punishes it all the more severely for his having believed in its repentance.

Alas, no. That was too good to be true. Jonah's hope will prove short-lived and his disappointment all the more painful when the following night God sends a worm to gnaw at the shrub, drying it up and killing it. When the miserable prophet—exhausted, humiliated, rejected—awakens under the stifling heat of the oppressive sun from which nothing now protects him, when he feels the violence of the east wind blowing just as hard and sapping him just as the worm sapped the tree (the Hebrew *vatakh* is used in both cases), when he grasps that he has lost his shade and that his raw flesh, weakened by his long sojourn in the briny deep amid the reeds and seaweed, will wither and wilt under the white light at its apex, he also understands that all is lost, that he had been too quick to rejoice, and that he has thirty-nine days left, not to laugh last and best but to weep, to drink the chalice to the dregs, and to watch the resurrection of people of whom "not one" could "tell his right from his left. . . ."

Because God has spoken!

And, in the story, God has the last word.

Those are the very last words in the account: the same words—right, left—as the ones just used to describe the immorality of the Ninevites but that now seem to exonerate them from their stubborn sinfulness.

One step further, one more *word,* and the prophet will have to admit that the Ninevites "know not what they do" and that, generally, no one is intentionally bad—the very opposite of the principles that Jonah holds sacred.

What! God says to Jonah. You moan about a castor-oil plant that grew in one day, lasted one night, and cost you no effort! And I should not spend time on Nineveh, a place that is home to a hundred and twenty thousand people and as many animals, that I built with my own hands, and that is precious to me because it is great?

You whine over a tree that is, like your hut, just a thing provided for your use, whereas I am supposed to sacrifice not only all these people but also animals such as Balaam's she-ass, which, as reported in Numbers, saw a *malach*! And these many-colored birds that flit lightly from branch to branch! And this cow that is a mystery of beauty and that even the most extreme anti-paganism does not grant us the right to neglect?

And the Malbim, again: You go on about your shade, but what about mine? What about the shade I derive from that monstrous and obese city with its overelaborate houses, with its share of shadows and crime, with that wind that now and then rises like the spirit of the angry dead, that city from which I can hear the clamor of boots preparing to march against the just, a city that is nevertheless part of my plan—just the way it is?

We have reached the end of the story.

That it remains puzzling in parts is certain.

That we learn nothing about Jonah's ultimate state of mind is equally true.

But one thing is clear: Nineveh was saved; God wanted it that way; he did not want to enshrine for eternity the evil that was in it but instead chose to view that evil as redeemable.

Nineveh as a test.

Nineveh as a thought experiment. Nineveh as the rarest pearl in the world for being the occasion of the most improbable of prophecies.

The occasional sublimity of Nineveh or, maybe better, its *accidental* sublimity: as one might have referred to the occasional and accidental sublimity of the bundle of brambles that was the burning bush.

There is in this tale a portentous action, the consequences of which humanity has not finished assessing, one that strikes me now, suddenly, as a practical, inviting, but also perilous riddle that offers itself up for thought: *Search for the answer, or I will consume you.*

CHAPTER EIGHT

THE NINEVITES OF UKRAINE AND LIBYA

I have been to Nineveh.

I have gone there not just once but many times. And I have spent a non-negligible part of my life and considerable energy working on behalf of people other than my own, people whose fate might have been much less important to me and who were, in some cases, in potential or in fact, the enemies of who I am.

WHERE IS NINEVEH?

For me there have been mini-Ninevehs; Ninevehs without the crime and empire; Ninevehs that it would be unfair to compare too closely with Nineveh but Ninevehs in the broad sense; small ones—very small sometimes; Ninevehs that would make Benny Lévy ask me in irritation how I could devote so much time and thought to them, whereas he estimated, like Jonah, that once saved from their furnace they would be perhaps no worse but probably no better than their persecutors. Such as Angola, on the subject of which he mocked my youthful admiration for another Jonah, or Jonas, this one the son not of Amitai but of Savimbi. Or Eritrea and Ethiopia, where Benny viewed me as engaged in no more than a post-adolescent repetition of Rimbaud's flights. My anguish when Afghanistan's Massoud died. The Bangladeshi friends to whom I remained faithful. A radio station in Burundi. A newspaper in Kabul. Nothing but time diverted, he would rant, from studying the Torah.

There are those quasi-Ninevehs, intermediate Ninevehs, those Ninevehs where Benny was not wrong to remind me that the Jewish name has not always smelled like a rose and where it might become again, once the turmoil has passed, a proscribed or even cursed name. What was I doing, he would fume, with Lech Walesa's Poles? How, he demanded to know the evening after he had presented my book on Daniel Pearl at the Hebrew University of Jerusalem, could a mouth like mine, a Jewish mouth, a mouth eager to honor the name of a Jewish martyr and, in so doing, sanctify my own name and the Jewish name in general, have been able, thirty years earlier, to utter the words, "We are all Polish Catholics," which to Benny sounded like a challenge leveled at the thousands and thousands of Jews shoved into the oven without a peep from the ancestors of those Catholics? And Sarajevo? Yes, he insisted, explain Sarajevo! The bombings, okay. The armed struggle, the new partisans, resisting the stony face of the new fascism: I get it, I've been all over these places, I invented this rhetoric of the leftist priest, so you know I know! But your Izetbegović and his *Islamic declaration*? That Waffen SS division formed in the middle of World War II with the blessing of the Grand Mufti of Jerusalem, who was one of the most prolific killers of Jews not just in the Arab world but in the entire world? I realize that the division lasted only a few months, because the Bosnians you like so much were undisciplined and the Nazis didn't like that. But it existed! Did it never occur to you that you might have been used? Did you never feel, under all the human-righty mumbo-jumbo, that you had lost your way? And Palestine? If Nineveh is to be found somewhere today, is it not in Jenin, in Gaza, those towns overflowing with hate and fury, where people dance in the street when an Israeli soldier is lynched? What do you expect to get from such people? What do you expect from the Geneva plan that you hold so dear? What are you relying on in recognizing this imaginary people's right to a state and in advocating for that state?

There is Nineveh in the strict sense, the real plain of Nineveh, which it really would be wrong to compare to Jonah's Nineveh, since what reigns there is more suffering than sin. There is the specific, concrete Nineveh, with its raped women and girls reduced to slavery and sold; its defenseless people being made to relive, two thousand years after the fact, the same martyrdom as Christ; the houses marked with an "N" for "Nazarean," equivalent to a permit to kill, sack, and pillage. There is the Nineveh of flesh and blood about which I wrote, four long years ago in response to the first wave of assassinations being committed there, that the Christians were becoming the most persecuted people in the world. I claim no special merit or pride at having flagged the problem, having emitted the sickening radar blip that announced genocide. It was the same *nose* I had in Rwanda, in Bosnia, and Cambodia, which I would have been glad not to have had here, given the systematic massacres that were being planned for Qaraqosh, in the Sinjar Mountains, in the villages of Hamadaniya, Bartella, and Tall Kayf.

There is that real Nineveh, otherwise known as Mosul, which I found myself surveying the other day in the company of a handful of Peshmerga fighters, pensive and valiant, who were awaiting the order to attack. There is the Nineveh that I can see a few kilometers away, sometimes less, with the Daesh flag fluttering over villages that have become not just *Judenfrei* but *Christenfrei*, cleared of their Christians after having been cleared of their Jews. And the archbishop of Erbil who, before my departure that morning, described for me the masses of defenseless Chaldeans and Yezidis who were given the choice of conversion, banishment, or death by the sword, and who did so in a French that was, not just perfect, but also refined and reminiscent (was he aware of this?) of Chateaubriand's descriptions of the cohorts of humiliated Jews in his *Journey from Paris to Jerusalem and Back* and his poem "The Martyrs." I will go back. I will enter Nineveh if and when the Peshmerga does. That is another *oath*.

And then there is Nineveh that looks like Nineveh and has all of its bad traits. There is the live Nineveh that is not as powerful as the original but that is no less sinful. There are the two Ninevehs in the sense not of space but of spirit, which, in spirit, never fail to remind me of the real Nineveh of Jonah. There are those two last temptations of Nineveh that Benny did not live long enough to witness and tell me what he thought but about which I am well enough informed to be able, even without him, to see what I was risking in succumbing and how their appeal could be dangerous for a Jew. I am thinking here of two risky adventures that were essential in my eyes but inexplicable in the eyes of some. I am thinking of the two "names" that led me into the two "great cities" of the moment.

Nineveh today?

Its equivalent, for a Jew of the current century?

Here it comes.

Libya, of course.

And, to a lesser extent, Ukraine.

HOSTILE GROUND?

But let's proceed one by one.

Before setting foot in Ukraine, I knew that I was entering one of the theaters in which Nazism, the real article, staged some of its most criminal scenes.

I had read enough of Father Patrick Desbois, and defended him enough, to have had scarcely any doubt about the scope of what he called "the Holocaust by Bullets," the grim vestiges of which he is constantly exhuming.

I knew the history of the SS Galicia Division, which had been formed with the cooperation of Stepan Bandera, the head of OUN, the Organization of Ukrainian Nationalists, who chose to collaborate for a time with Germany, the better to fight the USSR and Poland.

I was familiar with the story of the triumphal arrival, on June 30, 1941, of the first units of the Wehrmacht in the streets of the ancient city of Lviv, capital of the kingdom of the two crowns, bedecked with flags as if for a victory celebration: The first thing residents did, as a sign of welcome, was to pogromize their Jewish neighbors.

And I will never forget the little truth-seeking operation that I carried out in June 2015, on a visit to the same city, where I had just performed my play, *Hôtel Europe,* at the National Academic Opera.

"What do you think of Lviv?" people began asking me the minute I arrived, insistently and anxiously, as people do when they are proud of their city and are welcoming someone visiting for the first time.

I dodged their questions.

Then moved on to muttering polite replies.

Until the day of the performance.

Then, standing before a large crowd composed of very young people who very shortly were going to hear me evoke a sinking and soulless Europe consumed by bureaucracy, a Europe that they were seeking to join, I gave a speech, the essence of which follows.

"A mixed impression, my friends.

"As often in Ukraine, but here more than anywhere else in the country, a very conflicted impression.

"On the one hand, a fully European city, a great capital, the equal of Prague, Budapest, Vienna, or Warsaw, of a Europe that you will tonight hear me urge to wake up and which is the only possible future for the peoples of the continent; an enchanted city full of marvels in which, for three days, I have had the feeling of walking in a novel by Robert Musil or Joseph Roth or a poem by Paul Celan. So, may God grant that you enter our common house! No, not enter it but *reenter* it and, I hope, without delay! For the truth is that you have always been at home in Europe. And who knows? In reentering the house of Europe, you might bring with you a little of the spirit and fire with which the founding fathers of the Union were so richly endowed and that their successors seem to have lost altogether. So, long live Lviv! Long live Ukraine! I am on your side and support you with all my heart.

"But I also have an indefinable malaise that I have not been able to shake since arriving. An anxiety that seizes me at night and prevents me from sleeping. The panic I felt the other day, without apparent cause, in the mirrored gallery of the opera, where you did me the honor of welcoming me, just as you honor me now by coming to my play. The inexplicable terror that gripped me in front of a building on the Place Podval'naya, near the Church of the Assumption. The almost incessant impression of a haunted house. And then the explanation. Having come to visit the ruins of the Janowska concentration camp, where the Jews of your city who had been deemed unable to work were sorted and locked up pending transfer to the Belzec extermination camp, I found a prison, an ordinary prison for ordinary offenders, right in the middle of a poor but ordinary industrial neighborhood: Nothing remains there to indicate that here was the sorting camp for the Jewish cattle hunted and held by the grandparents of some of you. Then, the Lisinitchi Forest, where more than a hundred thousand Jewish men, women, seniors, and children tried to hide but were exterminated with heavy machine guns before being dumped into mass graves under layers of lime that the citizens of your city took the time to spread: It is a beautiful forest, I know; it is sunny and bright; it is a forest where I am sure you like to walk, have picnics, and make love; but it is a forest in which one walks on dead bodies, one that would not be as beautiful and green as it is without the thick layer of human fertilizer decomposing underfoot; and it is a forest where there is no place of reflection, however modest, for the children and grandchildren of those who died without graves and whose descendants are reduced, as Baudelaire would say, to serving as their tombs. And then, again, my visit to the site of the famous golden synagogue that was one of the most beautiful of Europe and certainly of the fifty-odd Jewish houses of prayer in prewar Lviv, all of which, every single one, are gone. I discovered on this day something that I am sure you all know: That something is nothing, nothing to this day but an empty space surrounded by construction-site fencing; nothing, absolutely nothing, on the site of what had been a lofty place of worship, whose glory was sung in the same books that define the European identity of your city but whose destruction is nowhere acknowledged. In short, no memorial. No real stele signifying grief and irretrievable loss. Everywhere, instead of cenotaphs, gigantic holes of memory like this black hole that has replaced the synagogue. And the unbearable presence of badly buried dead, or dead not buried at all, who continue to wander as ghosts among the living of Lviv."

The strange thing is that my audience seemed not to know much about what I was describing.

It was easy to see by their eyes that they were not aware of living surrounded by ghosts—that is, by a population of dead almost as great in number as that of the living but having no tomb and, in many cases, no name.

That ignorance (which parallels the innocence with which Lviv's historians, journalists, and thinkers could continue thinking of Stepan Bandera as a pure national hero without stain or fault) did not wholly surprise me but did fill me with another sort of fear.

Turning now to Libya . . .

I have never doubted the cause that I was defending in Libya.

In no way do I regret, five years later, what I encouraged there.

Nor did I ever have any doubt about the endemic anti-Semitism that raged under the dictatorship, which was not going to disappear just because the dictator fell.

I knew the history of Gaddafi's expulsion of the country's Jews in 1967 and of his closing of the Tripoli synagogue.

I never believed in the fable of an Arab world that, unlike evil Europe that was held to be solely responsible for the Holocaust, would supposedly bring about a thousand years of brotherhood between Abraham's enemy sons, and I had no reason to believe that it would occur in this country more than any other.

I knew about the close links between high-ranking Nazis and Haj Mohammed Amin al-Husseini, the Mufti of Jerusalem, about which Benny Lévy had spoken while teasing me about Bosnia, and I knew that there had been and probably remained go-betweens and apologists for that connection here in Tripoli and even more so in Benghazi.

Neither in my book written during those fearsome months (*La Guerre sans l'aimer*) nor in the film version of that diary, *The Oath of Tobruk,* did I deviate one iota from the position that I had maintained for years on the Nazi connections of the Muslim Brotherhood, which was born in Egypt in the 1920s as an echo of the Hitlerian revolution in Europe, the ideology of which has not changed with time.

The reader, the viewer, will observe that I never underestimated the risk of seeing the Muslim Brotherhood—on which Gaddafi bestowed a halo of suffering, enhanced by their activism in a war of liberation during which I was in a position to know that they often made up the most formidable fighting units—emerge strengthened by the revolutionary turmoil and then by victory.

The same observer will see that I was surprised neither by this or that outbreak of anti-Semitic fever; nor by the tranquil assurance with which President Mustafa Abdul Jalil (the same person whom I had loyally accompanied throughout the insurrection and whose air of making war only reluctantly I much admired), when asked on the last day of the war about the form of government that he wished to see for his country, responded that tomorrow's Libya should be governed by a regime inspired by sharia; not by the eruption of anger and nearly of violence that greeted, on June 2, 2011, the revelation by the blogosphere, followed shortly thereafter by the press, of my "Israeli initiative."

A member of the National Transitional Council visiting me in Paris had seen fit to tell me, supposing it would please me, that his country intended, once victory was assured, to establish normal relations with Israel. He authorized me to make this known.

Having received this message reliably although unofficially—and the messages did indeed please me, because it showed that my Libyan friends were not lying when they would say, in our private conversations, that they were determined eventually to break from the anti-Semitism of the Gaddafi era—I had gone to see the Israeli prime minister, Benjamin Netanyahu. His interest pricked by my news, he took advantage of a visit on that same day from the French minister of foreign affairs to, and I quote, "congratulate France for its action in Libya," to emphasize that that initiative "had made it possible to avoid a massacre of innocent people," and to say that Israel "will certainly not be sorry" to see the departure of a dictator who had had a long history of support for international terrorism and violence against the Libyan people.

For a reason that I have never been able to discover, the news was leaked, and it arrived at Internet speed in Benghazi.

And that is how in a matter of hours the nice "Monsieur Bernard," the man who had been given access to the front lines and to the secrets of the general staff, the ally and even the friend on whom they had counted for several months to serve as liaison between the insurgents and their French and sometimes their American allies, the man they had regarded, I am certain, as "a brother," became a lever of Zionism and Satan, an expert in double-speak who was selling Libya out to its most implacable enemy, and a traitor. Including to the prominent member of the NTC who had given me the message and who called me in the middle of the night, scared out of his wits, to implore me not only to calm the waters but to promise that I would never, ever reveal his identity. And including, as well, the group of women whom I had met with a few days earlier on the Benghazi Corniche in an atmosphere of complete harmony, when they were demonstrating before the NTC: "Our father who art in France . . . please, contact without delay our father who art in France and who favored us with such beautiful words on his last visit to the Corniche . . . he must disclaim . . . he must reassure us . . . we cannot believe that he has committed such an infamy. . . ."

That, too, I disclosed immediately.

I made public the full text of the Israeli communiqué, which, from the point at which we then stood, at least had the virtue of demonstrating that there was no hostility in Jerusalem to the principle of the Arab Spring.

And, although that episode worried me, I was not surprised in this case, either, that a gap might exist between a political elite (of which the friend who delivered the message to me was an honest representative) and the mass of those who, like the Ninevites, obviously still did not know how to tell their right from their left.

That, too, seemed—and still seems—part of the sad order of things.

I lived through that revolution, and not only its last weeks, with the feeling that I was joined in a cause with people who were divided, split, as are all human beings.

They were wrenching themselves free of a relentless tyranny, and that was a noble act.

They were having the unprecedented experience, inconceivable before it began, of sensing that the inner Ninevite to which a bad king had reduced them over his reign of forty-two years was faltering. At no time did I cease believing that that experience deserved support.

But from there to say that it was an unalloyed good, free of base elements and disappointing tomorrows, from there to forget that every good that mankind invents always combines with a new bad, also of their making, from there to ignore that the intelligence they gain also has as a correlate a new opacity, that is a step that no honest and careful reader can say that I took.

LOOKING THE DEVIL IN THE FACE

And so?

So, to those who asked me why I got mixed up in those hot spots; to those who wished me well but feared that I might have gone astray; to those less friendly souls who believed to have found in the Libya experience my big mistake, the fatality that I had been smart enough to avoid up until then but that lurks, it seems, in the life of anyone who takes the risk of thinking and, even more, of acting on what he thinks; and, indeed, to me when I questioned myself along the way—this is how I answered.

Ukraine: Russia, I began my argument, was no less anti-Semitic and no less oblivious of its anti-Semitism. But Russia had the aggravating circumstance of denying it with an aplomb that made possible (frequently!) the surfacing of its repressed notions and resorts to action, which were all the more consequential for having been preceded by denials. By contrast, in Kiev, a process of repentance that was impossible to deny had begun to take hold. With regard to the hundred thousand Jews destroyed in Lviv, that process had not yet led to legislation on the duty to remember. But committees were at work, reporting to President Petro Poroshenko and in liaison with the world's leading Holocaust historians, to observe, among other events, the seventy-fifth anniversary of the Babi Yar massacre.

The Righteous Among the Nations: Their presence is never a bad barometer in moderating this type of debate. In Ukraine there are more than two thousand of the Righteous, fourth in the world after

Poland, France, and the Netherlands and particularly numerous in the regions of Lviv, Ternopil, and Volhynia, where the killers of Jews raged in force, making these areas, in the words of Timothy Snyder, "bloodlands." And these members of the Righteous are recognized alongside other Ukrainian heroes. Obviously, it is not enough. Given the checkered record of some of those other heroes, it is, in a way, to degrade the memory of the Righteous to put them on the same plane. But in the long-term war that is the struggle against anti-Semitism, is this not a point of departure, a prelude, a sign that this history, too, can begin to move again?

The extreme right: The supposed ideological hegemony of Ukraine's extreme right was, and remains, one of the favorite themes of the New Moscowteers. But the reality is that, in every election since the revolution, far-right parties have fared badly, sometimes pathetically so, and in any case ten times worse than, for example, their French counterpart, the National Front (who are financed and supported by the Kremlin).

Still on the subject of Ukraine, I did not fail to point out that, if you want to invoke History with a capital "H," you should be honest enough to do it completely and not to leave things out. Was not Lviv, in those years, also capable of producing Metropolitan Archbishop Andrey Sheptytsky, who was one of the most prominent Christian voices to speak out against persecution of the Jews? And what about his pastoral letter of November 1942, entitled "Thou Shalt Not Kill, Period," in which he forbade his flock, under pain of excommunication, from assisting or supporting the mass murder that was beginning to unfold? Isn't that one of the noble acts of resistance to have emerged from the churches of Europe? Yes, of course, there was Bandera. Of course there were pogroms and a savage holocaust that rivaled the German version. But there was also the courage of an archbishop exhorting the monks and monasteries of the region to hide Jews. There were, in Lviv, the one hundred fifty Jews—most of them children but including ten rabbis—that Sheptytsky hid in the basements of Saint George Cathedral and in his private apartments across from the cathedral.

And finally, in the Maidan, otherwise known as Independence Square, that space for every sort of freedom, that agora where it was forbidden to forbid and where the imagination imagined itself in power, that round-the-clock forum for improvising orators who took full advantage of their right to give free rein to their whims and fancies, there was one fancy that was not welcome, one that was never heard or seen, neither on the rostrum or in the graffiti that covered the walls, and that was the fancy, the folly, of anti-Semitism.

Anti-Semitism was probably there, lying low.

In the manner of a dormant virus.

Or those deactivated microorganisms that can survive for decades in a latent state before rekindling.

Or hibernating moles that wait for the signal to come to the surface—but the signal may never come.

After the Euromaidan, there were, of course, a few outbreaks.

In Uman, notably, midway between Kiev and Odessa, the site of the tomb of Rabbi Nachman of Breslov, where the annual Rosh Hashanah pilgrimage of tens of thousands of Jews from all over the world always produces some minor incidents. In 2013 it was the erection of a cross not far from the river in which pilgrims bathe. In 2014 it was protests from merchants who complained that the kosher-keeping Hasidim who arrive with their own food and do not buy local were not good-enough tourists. And, in 2015, it was a small-scale provocation organized by activists linked to Right Sector, which meant that the entire event took place under police protection.

But the fact remains that during the weeks of the Euromaidan, Ukrainian anti-Semitism was completely muzzled.

As I see the struggle against this form of hatred (my conception is both pessimistic and combative), holding it at bay is half the battle. So, here, too, we did not do so badly. And at least the door was open for some educational work that the Ukrainians may not be equipped to carry out on their own (work that the communist devastators had done everything they could to render impossible) but that they were quite open to seeing done on their behalf and with their cooperation.

I began to do just that, in a modest way, by raising Babi Yar in two speeches in the Maidan before vast crowds of Ukrainians, some of whom were old enough to have been witnesses to that inexpiable crime.

That is what I tried to do in Lviv by proposing to the mayor that he take the initiative to establish a memorial. The ball is in his court. We shall see.

And that is what was at stake when, at the time of the seventieth anniversary of the liberation of Auschwitz and in the midst of the polemic between Russians and Poles over the facts of the event itself, I spent some time researching and establishing the following:

First, the Russian narrative was not completely wrong in saying that the "First Ukrainian Front" that entered the extermination camp on January 27, 1945, had that name not because it was composed entirely of Ukrainians but because the corps "fronts" of the Red Army always bore the name of the territory in which they did the most fighting.

But, second, it was nevertheless true that this corps was one in which Ukrainians were heavily overrepresented (a little more than half of its strength).

Third, in the corps was a battalion commanded by a Jewish Ukrainian officer, Major Anatoly Shapiro, which was the first to enter the perimeter of the camp.

Fourth, at the head of this battalion was a tank unit, and the first tank commander in this unit of tanks—thus the first man to have encountered the gaze of the living skeletons who remained there, the first to have looked on these people with their shaved heads, their shoulders shrouded in thin, moldy canvas, their appearance of being astonished still to be alive, the first to have seen the piles of bodies and shoes, the pictures of which then made their way around the world and have remained, in our collective conscience, the symbol of absolute evil—was another Ukrainian, an officer by the name of Igor Pobirchenko.

And, fifth, although we can and must remind the Ukrainians ceaselessly that they did more than their share in feeding the cadaver

machine, honesty prohibits us from disregarding the no less indubi-
table fact that they also did more than their share in dismantling it
and that, at that moment, like it or not, their redemption began.

Details? No, symbols.

Just as the pilgrimage to the tomb of Rabbi Nachman of Breslov in
Uman is a symbol, *despite everything*. Because finally you can, and I think
you have to, also see the matter from the other way around. That it
was fraught with incidents is one thing. But that it took place and
continues to take place, that the incidents in question do not stop the
pilgrims from coming every year in great numbers—that, it seems to
me, is the real news! You should have seen the tens of thousands of
Hasidim in that little Ukrainian country town, taking up every possible room offered for rent, setting up tents around which, for three
days running, they lived, sang, danced, cried out their *Tzadîk,* tended
fires, spelled each other day and night in reciting psalms in Hebrew,
slept when there were no more rooms, laughed, drank, prayed, and
chanted more psalms. You should have seen—once in your life would
be enough—the beautiful spectacle of these men in their long coats,
heads partly shaved under wide-brimmed hats, accompanied by many
children, visitors from another time arriving from everywhere in the
Jewish world in the hope of touching, just touching, the stone of the
holy tomb. And then you should have seen the puzzled looks, less hostile than perplexed, of most of their Ukrainian hosts, people of anti-
Semitic roots whose ancestors beat and sometimes murdered the
ancestors of today's pilgrims; and you should have seen the police
calmly trying to channel the crowd, to inform a lost visitor, and keeping cars away, even those of the locals. I can't imagine the equivalent
scene in a village deep in rural France, where by now the "threshold of
tolerance" would already have been declared crossed a hundred times
over, allowing the locals to describe themselves as "invaded" and prevented from living and breathing! Even in Troyes, Rashi's hometown,
I have trouble picturing tens of thousands of foreigners flouting noise
ordinances, creating temporary disorder, and leaving behind them a
trail of empty plastic bottles, as would any crowd busy talking to the
sky, the stars, and the ages. Anyone seeing or imagining all that will

understand that, Right Sector or no, fascist cells or no, *something* has changed deep in the new Ukraine.

As for Libya, I have never ceased making the five major political arguments that made nonintervention unthinkable.

The first: No argument, no geopolitical or metaphysical reasoning, no revisiting of history, holds up against the spectacle of columns of tanks speeding toward a city—Benghazi—with the intention of destroying it. My generation has yielded too much to the complacent functionaries of the world, to the friends of death, the servants of disaster; in Libya and elsewhere it has ignored too many gassings of civilians, massacres of innocents, mass machine-gunnings in prison yards; it has cried (or feigned not to hear when others cried) "Long live death!" far too often not to seize the occasion, when for once it was possible, to block the funeral procession.

The second: As bad as war is, there is something worse according to all theoreticians of the "just war," and that is not to make war when (1) the cause is good; (2) the intention is pure; (3) the *auctoritas principis* (in the Libyan case, the collective prince represented by the United Nations) authorizes the process; (4) a successor prince or authority (in this case, the National Transitional Council, most of whose members I knew) seems to stand ready to govern; (5) all other avenues of recourse (discussion, diplomacy, pressure) have been exhausted, all alternatives tried but come to naught; (6) the harm to be caused by the war is clearly less great than that produced by the ongoing destruction; and (7) a will toward truth and truthful discourse animates the response. These conditions, formulated by Saint Augustine, Saint Thomas Aquinas, the School of Salamanca, and, in our time, the American thinker Michael Walzer, were not met at the time of the war in Iraq, which is why I opposed it. By contrast, not since Bosnia had I seen them so clearly fulfilled as in the case of this tyrant who was ready to turn against his own people the weapons of mass terrorism of which he had been not only the great financier but also one of the most bloodthirsty users. For that reason the war

seemed to me then, and seems no less to me now, to have been entirely just.

The third: The tyrant in question was not a rampart against
anything (because that argument, too, is put forward). Not against
terrorism (witness the hyper-crime of Lockerbie). Not against desta-
bilization and war in Africa (it was Gaddafi who had allowed southern Libya to become a hub for contraband weapons destined for the
continent's rebellions). Not, of course, against anti-Semitism (Libya
was one of the world's centers of Holocaust denial, receiving with
honors the herald of anti-Semitism that Roger Garaudy became at
the end of his life and awarding him, during his visit, the Gaddafi
human-rights prize). Not against uncontrolled migration (when the
war broke out, there were between one and two million people hop-
ing to set sail for Italy, people whom the mad dictator had come to use
as an instrument of extortion renegotiated each year at a high price:
five billion euros that year instead of the twenty-five million offered
by the European Union for his "cooperation" in controlling Libya's
maritime borders). And not, finally, against jihad (Europe will have to
lose its collective memory and, in my own country, the Le Pen line
take over completely in order to erase from our minds the speech
Colonel Gaddafi gave in Rome on August 29, 2010, in which he announced* that "Islam would become the religion of the whole of Europe").

The fourth: Jihad for jihad, the real comparison to be made is not
between the new Libyan regime (under which, incidentally, anti-jihad
moderates won all of the three free elections held since the fall of the
dictatorship) and some ideal republic that should have emerged fully
formed from the thigh of Montesquieu to be reincarnated in Tripoli.
No, the only valid comparison is between one country, Libya, in which
the West intervened and another, Syria, located in the same region
and similar in many ways, where no intervention occurred to oppose
the madness of the local Gaddafi. On the one hand, in Libya, indisputable chaos and, in fact, two or perhaps three pockets of jihadists

*L'Unità, August 30, 2010.

(in Derna, Sirte, and Sabratha, near the Tunisian border) against which the revolutionaries of Misrata have declared open war, a war that, as this book is being readied for publication, they are winning. On the other hand, in Syria, the same indisputable chaos around a struggle to the death between communities and tribes; but also, not two or three pockets of jihad but half of the country in the clutches of Daesh, erasing the border with Iraq and forming, indeed, a sort of Islamic State without the tyrant who is supposed to be fighting them, Bashar al-Assad, doing much about it (in fact, he *encouraged* the ascendancy of a form of radicalism that he believed would create a sanctuary for him and oblige the West to negotiate with him). Not to mention the three hundred thousand deaths—yes, three hundred thousand—that his criminal dementia has caused and that could have been prevented if we had intervened, as we did in Libya, when the moderate, secular forces still counted and were calling for our aid, and before the millions of refugees fled a country consumed by flames and awash in blood for Jordan, Lebanon, Turkey, and Europe.

On this I must insist. It is because of the Western intervention that Libya has not become, as of autumn 2016, another Syria. The intervention was justified, because it spared Libya a Syrian fate marked by (1) the flight of an entire people afloat on makeshift rafts (of total migrant arrivals in Europe via the Mediterranean, half are Syrian and, according to the UN High Commissioner for Refugees, a negligible proportion are Libyan); (2) the coming to power of Daesh in the most real and serious sense (not "bastions," "cells," or *katibas* but a quasi-state with weapons, supply lines, territorial continuity, an actual administrative apparatus with a currency and real bureaucrats who manage war and peace with neighboring states); (3) an almost inconceivable bloodbath (I would like the armchair strategists who allow themselves to "regret" the interventions in Benghazi and Tripoli and to ruminate on their "legitimacy" to try to imagine, just to imagine, three hundred thousand cases of a man, a woman, or a child fleeing the rain of fire, trapped, minced or incinerated, their bodies torn apart or mummified, seared by chemical weapons or vitrified, screaming in pain, suffocating, decapitated by a bomb).

And then there is this last argument, which, for me, is not the least among them.

My meetings with tribal leaders in the Green Mountain and elsewhere, which I always opened by saying that I, too, was the descendant of an ancient tribe, and the elders would nod in understanding . . .

That speech in Benghazi's Tahrir Square, at the beginning of the revolution, before a crowd of young people from whom I hid neither my name nor what it meant to me—there, too, I encountered no protest, no clamor of rejection, only cries of *"vive la France,"* which in no way clashed with my reference to the very ancient tribe. . . .

Or that meeting with ultraradical Abdel Hakim al-Asadi, emir of Derna, on the outskirts of Benghazi at the very end of the war, with the emir flanked by two of those fearsome Salafi brothers who, with good reason, passed for representatives of how anti-Western and radical Islam could be . . .

That meeting took place well after the Israeli episode.

Those men knew who they were dealing with, and more besides.

But my feeling was that the picture of this French Jewish intellectual arriving on their turf without protection and in confidence, the idea of this writer sitting across from them that day, who, for months, for no reason other than fidelity to the lessons and commandments given to the very ancient tribe, was using every means at his disposal to support the uprising of their people—my feeling was, and remains, that, thanks to the discussion that went on all night, that picture and that idea caused a slight but real shift in their Islamized heads and shook one of the most solid articles of faith of their jihadism: the almost natural connivance of the West—and, within the West, of the Jews—with those forces in the Arab world most bent on humiliating and trampling the people.

So had I done no more than that, had I merely planted a seed of doubt on this point in the minds of these men and their peers, had I been content simply to jam for an instant their faulty radars and to insert, in that other space-time, that noumenal space and curving time that I have evoked several times already, a place that serves as the repository of good and beautiful ideas, the seed of future reconciliation, then I would not have acted in vain. That is what I thought and that is what I still think today, more than ever.

The time would come, of course, when I would be transformed in the eyes of some of these men into an abominable Zionist who fought as hard as he did only because it was in the interests of Israel to do so.

And, obviously, there remain Libyans who miss the old regime, who believe that it was better to have a sovereign Libya whose sovereign had full power to sovereignly massacre his own people.

But those were not the sentiments that reigned that night in the farmhouse where our long discussion unfolded.

Those were not the dominant ideas prevailing in the broken country without a functioning state, a civil society, or laws that emerged from despotic nothingness.

The Libya infamous and great, bursting with unexpiated crimes but unbowed by its own criminal memory; the Libya whose liberation released, as is always the case but in quantities impossible to gauge in advance, the best and the worst, rays of light and pockets of pestilence; the Libya that sometimes struck me as a heart starting to beat again and sometimes as one of those flowers, autumn crocuses and hemlocks, that, when opening, release their deadly locked-in poisons—I was honored and still feel honored, being alive and free, to have accompanied on its path of emancipation. It was not, of course, the "rose among the thorns" of the Zohar. It was not the rush toward the state of law that the allies of the new Libya should have encouraged, beginning the morning after, as they helped it toward its new freedom. But it was a noble adventure in which life contended with death and the possibility of freedom with the fatality of servitude, one in which I am proud to have cast my lot with life and possibility.

Pride, yes.

And, again, not the slightest regret.

AND NOW, THE WHOLE TRUTH

Those were my public responses.

They were no less true for having been public, of course.

But partial.

Partial *and* true.

Immediate, but faithful to what I had lived, seen, and recounted.

They were geared toward what would be understandable in the kangaroo court of the media, which were asking me for accounts and were not far from laying at my door, in bulk, the development of terrorism, Mali and Daesh, the flow of refugees into Europe, the Syrian tragedy, the Eritrean dictatorship, the 2003 Iraq War, and the death of a child on a Turkish shore.

But, for all that, they were not meaningless.

Still to be done was to travel to the center of the heart of truth.

Still to be said was what I really saw, not in the bodies of Nineveh but in the souls.

Still to be told was what else I recognized about humanity in the faces of Ukrainians brandishing Banderist banners under my nose as I harangued them from the stage in the Maidan and why I held so dear the Libyans, who were no less aware than I was of their tragic balancing act between the sense of the infinite that had seized them from the first moment of their uprising and the destructive temptation that also gripped them.

Still to be explained was how I could think, *simultaneously,* that Ukraine was a fat body reeking of insanity and that, even so, we needed to do everything possible to free it of its ghosts, and why Libya is *simultaneously* a troubling country full of unresolved threats that we can see falling, each day a little further, into chaos and a land of hope that had its moment of greatness, a country pierced by a lightning bolt of high truth, one that demonstrated that a part of itself wished to break with the suicidal loyalty to the generations that had landed it there, and that, for that reason, it was and remains crucial to support it in the next phases of its conversion.

Still to be elucidated, finally, was why the intellectual as well as the Jew in me was thrown into the jaws of the two wolves that might reasonably appear to be the most hostile to that selfsame Jewish intellectual and why he applied himself all the more strenuously to the task because he knew that he had rarely found himself on such fundamentally and ontologically adverse ground.

To clarify that, to go to the secret heart of the truth about myself and these two actions, I had other arguments that I have never really opened up about. Except once, but badly, clumsily. That was on November 20, 2011, during a French Jewish convention. I was asked by a well-meaning attendee to answer for the umpteenth time the question of what led me to wander as I had into the terra incognita of Libya. And I answered as follows:

Everything that I attempted there, I did "as a Frenchman" and because "I was proud to contribute to my country being in the lead" in a fight that would "rid the world of one of its worst tyrannies." To that I added a second, more important reason, having to do with my indestructible belief in the universality of human rights and the sacred task, everywhere and forever, to come to the aid of victims burned on the altar of state machinery. And then a third reason that I said was derived from my unbendable fidelity to my Jewish name: "Like all the world's Jews," I said to the well-meaning questioner, "I was worried," but "nothing of what I did" would I not have done "if I had not been Jewish."

I added some reflections on humanism and universalism that go with my conception of Judaism.

I recalled the very important lesson of Emmanuel Levinas and Franz Rosenzweig, which echoes the Talmud: "He who saves one person, it is as if he saved the entire world."

Shooting wildly, I declared that there lay the deep meaning of the Shema Yisrael and there the ultimate truth of "he created the heaven and the earth."

That was also, I said, what I had gleaned from Isaiah 56, in which the prophet announces a "house" that "will be called a house of prayer for all peoples."

And I insisted repeatedly that a Jew is not a Jew if, in his way, which is never that of a Christian, he does not seek the humanity in his defeat, in his greatest humiliation, at the height of his abasement and degradation, because it is there, in that belittlement, that one finds what is most preciously human.

That statement caused quite a stir.

A lot of conspiracy theories started from there.

But it was the mere truth.

And I can even add, today, the following:

On my trips to Libya, I took with me, as I always do when I venture into unknown territory, a few books that reassure me that I am on familiar ground: my worn copy of *Kaputt* that I had been carrying around since Sarajevo and that I gave to a French-speaking professor of Italian in Misrata; the copy of Trotsky's *Military Writings* that was given to me on the eve of my first trip to Angola and that I lent, several weeks before his assassination, to the commander of the Libyan revolutionary forces, General Abdul Fatah Younis; a copy of *Authors Take Sides*, an anthology assembled by Nancy Cunard during the Spanish Civil War, which we used, my team and I, as the source for the quizzes with which we whiled away nights of waiting and inaction (that book, too, I have lost, probably left behind in a hotel room in Benghazi). But there is one book that I took with me every time and never lost, a book that I have always kept with me since, but one that I realize I never once mentioned.

The book was that part of the Bible devoted to the so-called minor prophets and, among the latter, the Book of Jonah, a text to which, I now realize, I kept coming back without really knowing why.

That is where the essence lies.

The key is there in that book of fire.

Now I will try to explain why.

CHAPTER NINE

THE LESSON OF NINEVEH

For in the end (and for the last time), what does the Book of Jonah say?

What does it say that, from the bottom of my Jewish memory, from the bottom of that memory without memory, from the bottom of that bottomless attachment that I sometimes think is the last word in being a Jew, what does it say that, on the Maidan in Kiev or in the Libyan desert, could bring it to my mind and make me act as I did?

Ultimately, it says five things.

It consists of five lessons that I realize were my true guides in several of my adventures—and, in any event, in those two.

WHEN THEY HEAR THE WORD "CITY" . . .

It says, first of all, "the city."

It says this: "Go into the great city."

As if there were, in that city's existence, in the very greatness of a city, a sufficient reason to stay the arm and check the wrath of God.

As if implying that it is here, in the great city, in the saving of the great city, that Jonah will find his prophetic mission and his responsibility for the world.

That is not obvious.

This concern for the Ninevite masses may appear at first glance to be contrary to Jewish exceptionalism.

And it certainly is not obvious why the fact of being a city, holding sinfulness equal, should make you more precious, dearer to the heart of God, and thus more "redeemable" than if you were anywhere else—desert, remote mountain, jungle, village, cluster of villages, oasis, lowland, countryside, rocky shore.

Nevertheless, that is what is said.

And for me it is of the utmost importance.

For in that opening apostrophe, I could not help but hear the echo of a strain of thought that I have known very well—the thought of Emmanuel Levinas.

From a Jew steeped in Greek and Latin, praise of the city as the locus of urbanity (*urbs*), civic consciousness (*cívitas*), and politics (*polis*).

Praise of the city for itself, with all of the maxims that, for Levinas, flowed from that: serf by birth, free by law; mired in narrow places, with their sacred groves and their mystery, but saved by technical knowledge, Yuri Gagarin, Sputnik, trade, and the spirit of cities; in the Black Forest, perhaps one encounters Being and one's "shepherd," but if you want to encounter others, the real Other, Others in their overwhelming, dazing presence, you must go to the city. . . .

And doesn't this phrase of Jonah necessarily echo my own old musings about Aragon, the self-described "peasant of Paris"? The Baudelaire of the *Fleurs du mal* attempting to escape, in endless walks, in cafés and reading groups, his horde of creditors and his spleen? Or Shelley singing of the teeming, humming city woven from number and music, the most human of human habitats?

Even better. In the idea of the city as pleasant and good, in the notion that in the very idea of making cities there lies something on the order of a blessing, I could not help (again) but hear the echo of another wisdom, one older than that of Levinas, one that I knew less well but that bespoke the nobility of the simple activity that is *Yishuv,* settlement, inhabiting the world—the supreme form of which is the construction of cities.

To inhabit is good, the masters say. There is holiness, they say, in occupying the land and building on it. Any serious attempt to move beyond just being thrown into being, which is the lot of most of humanity, any meaningful effort to construct habitation deserves to be defended. And the raising of cities, the building of great metropolises,

is, of all such efforts, the most respectable, most noble, and most substantial.

The Greeks had this idea as well. They too believed that the city,
as the center of commerce and exchange, was superior to the non-city,
with its worship of roots and its plant-like resistance. The urban in-
dwelling of being was such a high calling for them that it even had a
name, a beautiful name, in the language of the greatest among them,
Aristotle, who compared it to the eternity of the world. But so strongly
is Jewish thought in accord with that, so uncontested its wager, like
the Greeks', on agoras, dungeons, citadels, walls and canals, city halls
and currencies, fairs, markets, and libraries, that Maimonides went so
far as to forget for a moment the contradiction between the eternity
of the world and the rabbinical idea of the created world.

Therein lies the heart of the story. The Jewish truth of the speech
that God required of Jonah. It is only when *Yishuv* is lost, when violence reigns unchecked in the city, or when, as Ibn Ezra says, men
themselves become as beasts in great number, it is only in Sodom or
in the state of the world in Noah's time, that God has no other choice
but to throw his lightning bolts and exterminate the urbanites. We
were not at that point in Tripoli. Even less so in Kiev and Lviv. And
that is why it was a sacred duty to defend those cities and the city
spirit that reigned in them.

Especially as (and this is the most important thing), in God's concern for "the" city, in his command that Jonah go save it at all costs—
in the idea that the city has to be saved from itself and its suicidal
inclinations—it is impossible not to hear the distant premonition of a
perversion that has accompanied human history since its origins but
that seems to have become more serious in recent centuries.

That perversion is what a great Serbian partisan, contemporary of
Tito, and former mayor of Belgrade, Bogdan Bogdanovic, called, during the Bosnian War, the mania of "urbicide." Yes, urbicide, a trait
shared by all forms of barbarism and defined, in his view, as hatred for
the mode of inhabiting the world that we call a city. The idea that
there is in the city as such, in the very fact of being in a city and liking
it, the trace of something that must be eradicated. So, in parallel with
the worst of crimes, genocide, in accompaniment to the murder of the

genos (or perhaps even perfecting it), we have this other crime, the murder of the *urbs,* which, to my knowledge, Bogdanovic was the first to identify and name.

In inventing the word *urbicide* Bogdan Bogdanovic was thinking, of course, of Sarajevo. He had to have been thinking, too, of the Khmer Rouge enterprise, of which the evacuation, sacking, and punishing of Phnom Penh were essential components. I imagine he was thinking of Nero torching Rome; of Scipion Émilien having the ruins of Carthage covered with salt; of Vukovar nearer by; of the sacking of Louvain in summer 1914; of Apollinaire's cry, just before dying, "Listen to Louvain cry, see Reims twisting her arms"; of Warsaw; of Stalingrad; perhaps of Paul Claudel's *The City* and of that miserly character, the "revolutionary," who hopes to live long enough to see extinguished the lights of that city, which he can see only as a thoroughly evil power, a fetid bowel whose inhabitants mingle in hideous confusion "their breath and their excrement" or as a giant slaughterhouse in which people are gathered, not exactly like "beasts in great number" but "in herds," like heads of sheep.

Today, Bogdanovic is dead. But I know that if he were here he would add the Putinists' war against the Ukrainian cities deemed (and here I am quoting loosely from Aleksandr Dugin, a philosopher who seems to have had a strong influence on Vladimir Putin) to have corrupted the Slavic soul and land. And he might add, too, the war of Gaddafi's Bedouins against Libyan cities that appeared to them (here another loose quotation, this time from one of the dictator's sons) the fruit of the devil's seed. There you have it. That's how it is. There are people who, when they see the beauty of cities, reach for their rocket launchers. For my part, when I hear Saif al-Islam Gaddafi baying about drowning a city, Benghazi, in rivers of blood, I reach for the Book of Jonah.

WHO IS THE OTHER?

But the book says a second thing.

And therein lies, you will remember, its rarity and singularity.

Jonah is the prophet who is asked to go speak in a city that *is not* in Israel.

He is not the first Jew, naturally, to speak to Israel's other.

And therein lies, as I have said, the secret of the treasured people: the relation, not to itself, but to the other; not to the Jew, but to the gentile; the rejection of a self-sufficient Judaism closed in on itself in dry and fleshless study.

But, if he is not the first Jew to speak to the other, he is—I want to emphasize this—the first prophet.

And, with regard to the Jewish responsibility for the world, the fullness of Jewish existence that is reached only in dialogue with strangers, the need on the part of the Jew, lest meaning be lost, to look toward the other, absolutely toward the other, and to expose himself to what is outside him—Jonah is the one whom we can thank for having made that part of the prophecy.

Except, look.

There is other and there is other.

And just as the nations could choose, as we saw, among three modes of otherness, and just as Jewish otherness was, for them, the most fruitful of all, so the Jew has a choice among three types of encounter with the other, plus a fourth for which the Jewish being, it seems to me, is most eminently suited and most prominently called.

There is the other who is just barely other, who maintains with his other a link of distant familiarity—but familiarity all the same. Examples are, depending on reigns and periods, Edom, Moab, Tyre, or even Syria. Another example is the relations between the two kingdoms of Israel following the death of King Solomon, relations that were complex and conflictual but also deeply fraternal. And today . . . I don't know. . . . There are many examples today. But one of them has always been particularly important to me and remains so to this day. That is the example of the Kurdish people. And, in particular, that part of the Kurdish people living in Iraq, whose fate as a betrayed and tormented people who are nevertheless incredibly resilient is not dissimilar to that of the Jewish people. An essential but easy alliance. Critical but almost natural. An alliance with a people who, in 1969, soon after Saddam Hussein took power in Baghdad and fifteen years before Operation Moses, which rescued the Ethiopian *falashas,* organized the exfiltration and transfer, first to Iran and then to Israel, of five thousand Iraqi Jews. And the feeling, in my wanderings through the Sinjar Mountains that were the site of the Jews' passage, of being faced with the friendly and reassuring strangeness of a reflection. I have committed myself, and remain committed, to the Peshmerga of Erbil with the same enthusiasm that I felt years ago at the side of another group of enlightened Muslims, who were being bombarded in Sarajevo while the rest of the world, including other Muslims, stood warily by. But there is nothing in that of the paradox, the crisis of conscience, the inner conflict, the drama, that kept Jonah from going to speak in Nineveh.

There is, conversely, the other who is not at all the same. Who certainly does not want to be the same and who maintains with regard to others a relation of radical adversity. The resolutely other other who has violently, totally, and perhaps permanently cut the ties that bound him to the rest of humanity. This is Amalek, from the time when the Hebrews were camping in Rephidim. These are the Amalekites, the sworn enemies of the eternal, the evil ones, toward whom Israel has no other mission than to "erase the memory" from "below the heavens." And today they are those maniacal savages who, between Raqqa and Palmyra, sword in hand, treat people like beasts whose throats are to be cut and, in so doing, become beasts themselves. This, then, is the opposite of the first case. It is nearly impossible to go speak to the decapitators of al-Nusra and Daesh. Fight them, yes. Pray for their eradication, if one is inclined and able to pray—sure, why not? But words, a speech, a dictum, or another verbal act designed, as in the case of the Ninevites, to soften their hearts and open a path into their souls? No, it is too late. Nineveh is not there with them; one might as well stay in the belly of the whale; forget about it.

Pursuing this line of reasoning to its end, there is a third sort of other. This one is not savage or murderous. But absolutely other, still. Of a strangeness as radical, minus the hate, of the savage Adam. The messages that he sends to me, the empire of signs that he emits, though they are not odious to me, are nevertheless indecipherable. These are the lands lying outside the quadrangle of empires drawn in a dream by Daniel, one of the very last prophets, when he saw his four beasts corresponding to the four cardinal points. These are the peoples who are neither Medes, Persian, Babylonian, nor Edomite, in other words Europeans. They are also, to speak today's language, the inhabitants of those lands that Victor Segalen saw as peopled by exotics, notably the lands of Asia. It is permissible to go speak in the land of Confucius. It is fascinating to walk in the footsteps of Victor Segalen or Paul Claudel and to share their "temptation of the Orient." There, one will be listened to politely. One will be welcomed and honorably treated. But the words one speaks will have little effect. They will collide with a wall of amiable strangeness and echo there like the silence of the steppe. There, as another prophet said, one will have spoken to no effect, worked for nothing. It is not in these sorts of places that the world awaits the Jew.

There remains the other Other, the last.

Another in whom there is enough sameness for a speech to stick, but enough difference to make it worth the trouble of delivering.

That Other who is not going to be my friend like the Kurd, but neither will he be my enemy in the sense of Daesh, nor a stranger like the Confucian.

That Other is the Ninevite.

He may be the representative of certain Christian and Muslim nations about which Menachem Meiri said, in the thirteenth century, that although they certainly are not holy, they are not idolators, either, and, because they honor God in their way, they have, with regard to the law, the same status as the treasured people.

Today they are found chiefly in two *situations*. Either they are these Europeans of Ukrainian origin before whom—in the Maidan in Kiev and among the followers of Bandera in Lviv—I went to evoke the memory of the dead of Babi Yar; and the crimes of their parents and grandparents, and the stubborn presence of those forebears who, until stripped of their foul vainglory and redressed in hair shirt and ashes, are like the dead who claim the living. Or they are the Libyan *pere adam* caught between the jihadist temptation and the "interme-

diate Islam" (descended from Averroës and Avicenna) that people
began to describe to me as soon as I set foot in Benghazi and that is
the product of many civilizations, beginning with the Greco-Roman,
as attested by the remains of Leptis Magna. To that Other, too, I went
to say that the time to choose had come, that it was time to leave the
valley of killing, and that the liabilities, the stakes, the importance of
his country were so weighty that on his decision hung not just his own
redemption but, to a degree, that of the world.

All this is to say that I did not really have a choice. Given the available others and accepting that Jewish destiny turns on the relation to
others, there was no better other than these—and thus no better
means, for a Jew, to assume his Jewish destiny.

I could have inhaled, as I did during my investigation of the murder of Daniel Pearl, the scent of other in the form of the most criminal conceivable jihadism. In this case, there is nothing to say to that
other, nothing to be done. One can only narrate the story, plunging
for months into the hell of Islamabad and Karachi, celebrating the
memory of a hero, reconstituting his last acts and those of his tormentors, and pray that they, the Omar Sheikhs and Jihadi Johns, are no
longer in a position to kill.

I could have gone out to gather new impressions of Asia, as I did
thirty years ago in China. But Asia will not be a real participant in the
coming war, the real one, one that we know will not be humane and
that, as we see every day, has already begun to destroy Nineveh again
(this time for good) and, beyond Nineveh, the rest of the region. In
this case it is Asia that does not have much to say to us.

I could have chosen other others, simpler cases, more immediately
likable, others with whom a Jew can relate more readily. I could have
gone back to Bangladesh, which is one of the epicenters (largely un-
appreciated, alas) of enlightened Islam; I could have resumed, in Burundi, the scene of renewed carnage, the path of my forgotten wars
(and I may do that); I could have dwelled longer on the case of that
vast self-pleasuring, self-destructive, pressure cooker of a Nineveh
that Europe is becoming (which was the theme of an earlier work, a
theme that I have no intention of abandoning).

And there is my documentary on the Kurds, the necessity of which became clear as soon as I realized the urgency of fighting Daesh and bearing witness against it. (I began filming *Peshmerga* while I was completing this book.)

But although the military, political, and geopolitical stakes of that project are considerable, the metaphysical paradox does not lie there.

And although there is urgency there, there is *obligation* here.

For example, although giving the Kurds the state that was promised to them and then taken back, or rather denied, a century ago is an imperative for anyone wishing to halt the progress of barbarism with a jihadist face, pitting myself against the descendants of the Ukrainian Nazis or that part of the Umma where the Jewish name is least audible, namely Libya—that, for a man like me, was the most consequential wager, the summons that could not be ignored.

So, no choice, really.

It was Ukraine or the interminable and vain commentary of books closed up as tight as oysters or the bellies of whales.

It was Libya or the innards of the sea monster times two: what I have elsewhere called easy politics (including the Jewish variety) based on identity and reflexive communitarianism.

I took the risk of speaking out in Libya and then in Ukraine because it was the way of what I will call, in tribute to the master whom I cite so often, Levinas, who spoke of "difficult freedom," *difficult Judaism*.

I threw myself headlong into this double jumble because it was my way of remaining faithful to the commandment of universalism that is the heart of Jewish thought and that I found so powerfully expressed in the Book of Jonah.

WHERE THERE IS DANGER, THE IS THE HIGHEST DUTY

What can be said now about Nineveh itself? About the way it receives someone like Jonah, who leaps out of the whale's belly and into the lion's mouth?

What do we know, to put it bluntly, about what the city was really thinking when Jonah showed up?

Are the Ninevites sincere when they don their sackcloth, or did they just understand that their choice was repentance, even if over-acted and faith-free, or fire from the sky?

My Libyan companions in Benghazi—the young member of the Muslim Brotherhood who, as I learned later, probably saved my life on the Ajdabiya front; another, in Misrata, who would say that I was the "treasure" of his company and would be protected "like treasure"—were *they* sincere? Did they know what they were saying? Or did they see me simply as an instrument that they had not chosen but that was ensuring their link with a Western country?

As for the Ukrainians, as for the heirs of Bandera who, in Lviv, discovered while listening to me speak that they were living in a haunted city and were surrounded by tens of thousands of Jews crying for mercy and justice—which of my two arguments stuck? The one that said that a great people cannot live alongside so many restless ghosts? Or the one that reminded them that the Europe to which they were aspiring was built on the "never again" of Auschwitz and that recalibration of their own memory was the first thing they had to do to open the door to the EU?

The answer contained in the Book of Jonah is that it doesn't matter.

The moral to be gleaned from it is that one must never expect to get an answer to such questions before getting involved.

And that is true for three major reasons that were valid for a prophet and even more so for a man who is not even a sage but merely an ordinary Jew who knows what a book is, how to open it, and how to begin to decipher it.

The first reason is that we do not know anything, we will never know anything, and God is not there for the purpose of telling us.

The next is that the principals, the Ninevites themselves, those odd Adam-like creatures halfway between the beast in man and the man striving to be an angel, those alloys of the evil Ashur and, let's say, the good sailors—they know nothing either and fluctuate, depending on the hour, the day, and the position of the stars in the sky, between the temptation of sincerity and a relapse into duplicity.

And finally, Nineveh is not a monolith. In it are found, in uncertain proportions, the cynical and the sincere, Ashurs and sailors, lumps of unrelieved human darkness and kind hearts. Among the second group one finds hearts in which repentance is sincere but partial, others where it is sincere but opaque, still others where it is absolutely sincere but also absolutely indecisive because, in those hearts, the recognition of evil is not accompanied by conceptualization of the lesser evil that might take its place and that could, if so conceived, be counted as a good.

So that, in the presence of doubt, when one is neither here nor there and events are lived at the rhythm of wavering souls and intermittent hearts, when the hearts of men are in the hands of kings and those of kings in the hand of God; when that of God is hesitating and wavering, when debate rages within each man and among men, and between men and God, and between God and the prophet; when history itself fluctuates, seeming to fall this way or that or in between ad infinitum, the best we can do is to adhere to a few simple rules.

First rule: We must save what can be saved and not forget the lesson of Hagar, the servant, cast out in the burning desert, bled dry, near death, food gone, gourd empty, no castor-oil tree for shade, just a stunted shrub under which she places Ishmael, her son, before collapsing. At which point God in his heavens is moved. To the surprise of the angels, who know that the day will come when the child, if he survives, will begin a line that will produce the Islamic peoples and rise up against Israel, He immediately—and unconditionally—opens the eyes of the wretched servant onto a well of water from which her son drinks.

The lesson here is clear. Very clear. A lesson that might be of use to those who, as I proof these pages, are fussing about "the migrants," slamming the door in their faces on the pretext that there are some disguised Amalekites among them, and calculating how much they are going to cost the "native stock." The lesson is that decisions must be made in the moment and based on the circumstances of the moment: Do what must be done today without worrying too much about what may or may not happen tomorrow. And, as is said on the Jewish new year, judge people *ba'asher hu sham*—where they are now, in their current moral and mental state, without worrying excessively about what they really have in their hearts and bellies. Stop the rivers of blood in Benghazi; halt the urbicide in Misrata; jam the machine that kills young Ukrainians whose only crime is to be ready to die clutching the starred flag of Europe!

In the world as it is, inhabited as it is by a human race whose weakness but also whose glory is never to see in a single glance all of time, a good is a transcendental given that builds eternally on itself. The logic of the good is meta-temporal and has no connection with the historical vision of the world, which counts only the durable. So that being a Jew—adhering to the *ba'asher hu sham* and keeping in mind the lesson of God unconditionally saving the servant Hagar and her son— obliges one to consider as inherently just and worthwhile shaking up an order that prevents people from exercising the choice to be human.

Second rule: Because there is debate, uncertainty, changeability, and so on; because nothing is settled and God himself has not uttered the last word in the matter; because he left that last word to man as early as the sixth day and because, from then on, everyone has had his word to add and his part to play in this story; because everyone has his song to sing and his music to be heard, even if it never reaches to the spheres (but who knows?): Because of all this, because this is our situation, our condition, our fate, we must put all our weight on the scale of the good and the bad, we must weigh in with every bit of our meager force, we must lend to it our humblest hand and words.

Words old and new. Words of glory or mistrust. Gratuitous words. Words howled out or whispered. Words boldly pronounced but lacking resonance. Words timorously uttered and echoing long. Spoken words and words that speak. Words conclusive or inconsequential. Interrupted words, punctuated by silence and suspense—but surreptitiously decisive. Meek words; angry words. Words of blame giving way to disgust, as when one executes a fallen dictator. Words of dissociation, almost of rupture, when one feigns not to see the abyss that separated, at the time Babi Yar took place, an anti-Nazi partisan from an anti-communist irregular in an alliance of convenience with Nazism. Words of reconciliation again, of alliance, of rediscovered closeness when the Libyan city that made me an honorary citizen decides to launch an assault on the bastion of the Sirte Islamists or when the mayor of Lviv agrees to a memorial for the country in which, as Celan said, "books and men" live.

These examples are not comparable. But the principle at work is the same in all of them. It is the principle of the thinking that we call messianic, the basis of which is that, once again, one never knows when the messiah will appear, or whether he will appear at all, or whether a sign will announce the arrival or not, or what words might hasten or delay his coming, which words might be lost in the nothingness of words and say nothing or which, by contrast, may appear as so many harbingers or markers. And it is *by association of ideas,* a hypothesis that I am proposing (and one by which I have always lived), that one never knows which words will count and which will count for nothing, which actions will be conclusive and which immediately forgotten, where lies the cemetery of good intentions and where their heaven—and that, when in doubt, one must try, try again, never give up, and tell oneself that just as good people may not always be recognized, there are true words that may not immediately be celebrated as such.

And so—third theorem—concerning all those just acts that have no tomorrow, those tiny sparks that do not erupt into flame, those stars immediately swallowed up in the dark hole of antimatter and nothingness: We must do everything we can to store them up and, in a sense, shelter them. That is because of a final reason explained to us, after Jonah and in the space that he opened up, by Chaim of Volozhin, a master whom I have cited several times already.

Let us imagine, he says in his masterwork, *The Soul of Life,* a world in which no one remained to study the Torah. Imagine the Book, and books, falling into disuse, orphaned, forsaken. Imagine a world in which concern for the good had disappeared, a world in which no prayers, no study, not the smallest word was offered for the good.

That world would be lost. It would be like creation in reverse. Or a decreation. It would fall literally into dust.

But now imagine the opposite. One good person, just one, who somewhere is reading the Torah. A house of prayer at the edge of the earth with a handful of sages who still take the Word seriously. A bit of justice here. A fragment of goodness there. A flash of intelligence like quicksilver. Well, that's enough. Because these are like the beams of the world. They are like its joists, fragile, badly placed but all the more essential, timbers. They are what, when God is nowhere to be found, prevent his creation from collapsing. And even if the beams groan, even if the ridge cap holds only by virtue of precarious and temporary sympathy, there is all the more reason to hold on with redoubled care and effort. We must do everything, absolutely everything, to pull these words and deeds together, to store them up as one would treasure.

Shifting the focus to Nineveh, to Jonah's Nineveh, and to the new Nineveh, Nineveh without Jonah, in its Ukrainian and Libyan forms, we can draw the same conclusion. Even if murkiness were to spread instead of clarity, if the phosphorescences of a race that remembers that there was an Adam were to become ever more rare and nearly imperceptible, if there remained in the country where books and men lived only a handful of man-books, if there were only an infinitesimal minority of Tripolitans to begin to take the measure of their criminal memory and simultaneously to begin to understand that there was a text before their own—that alone would be a beautiful thing, the most precious of remnants. And it would be imperative (such is the truly Jewish gesture, the only way of remaining faithful to the spirit of Jonah and his Jewish teaching) to gather these rare words and acts and to do everything, absolutely everything, so that they are not actions without a trace, foam without water.

Which is better: to be transiently wrong and absolutely right or to be temporarily right and wrong for eternity?

Which is better: to lock Nineveh within its permanent curse or to bet on its possible, even if partial (very partial), redemption?

For me, the answer is clear.

For a simple Jew spurred on, or at least trying to be, by the fraternal word of Jonah, here were three powerful reasons not to stay in the belly of the whale.

At the very bottom of Jewish thought, here were good reasons for a Jew not to dodge the Ukrainian and Libyan rendezvous. That they were uncertain and dangerous made it all the more necessary not to shy away.

PURIFYING THE SWORD

Let us now suppose that the balance should tip markedly in the wrong direction.

Let us suppose that, because the worst is sometimes a sure thing, the pessimists were the ones who had it right.

And let us suppose that, in real time and history, Nineveh and its contemporary offshoots turn out to have pulled the wool over our eyes.

In the case of the actual Ninevites, this is not a supposition but a certitude, because a century of elapsed time allows us to see, through the eyes of the prophets Nahum and Zephaniah, that in 612 B.C. (a century after Jonah's visit) the Ninevites repented of their repentance, fell for good into lies, debauchery, the frantic practice of occultism, generalized corruption, and the "me and only me" of the egoism of power pushed to the extreme. It then fell to Arbaces the Mede to carry out the sentence, to tear down the cedar ornamentation and destroy the accursed city, its possessions trampled under the Babylonian boot.

Now let us suppose that the same is true of Libya and Ukraine.

Suppose that the former succumbs wholly and irrevocably—which, as I write, is far from being the case—to the sirens of total corruption of the soul that is radical Islam.

Suppose that the latter slips—which at the end of 2016 is still further from being the case—down the dark slope of a "Banderism" that produced Ukrainian Nazis while, down another slope, it also gave us Metropolitan Archbishop Andrey Sheptytsky and so many Righteous Among the Nations.

And suppose that, as natural inclinations rush back at breakneck speed, both rediscover the structuring hatred that they have so long had for Israel and that they would thus continue, sotto voce, to feel for the country that exists no less in our heads than it does on the earth.

You may well imagine that I have asked myself that question.

Not so much with respect to Ukraine, which I believe to be firmly committed to the path of real and rigorous democratic reforms and where anti-Semitism seems to have become like a shameful malady, but, yes, with regard to Libya, so loud and strong the voices of regression and hate have become five years after the revolution.

There, too, the answer is in the Book of Jonah.

Or, more accurately, it is in a commentary of the Malbim with which I was not familiar when I arrived in Kiev and even less so when I entered flaming Libya. That commentary says that God's true intention in sending Jonah to Nineveh, what he probably had in the back of his mind when he commanded the whale to deposit Jonah back on the very shore from which he had embarked, was not so much to exact "repentance" from the city as to "purify" the sword that its kind would one day raise against Israel.

That theory is chilling. It lies at the outer limit of the conceivable.

This idea of helping Ashur or his successors to be in the best possible shape, dashing, their military and moral arsenal gleaming new, polished to a high shine, for the day of the final assault against Jerusalem, seems almost unbearable if we take it literally.

But, as is always the case with this type of text, we have to look beyond the literal meaning, and into the burning heart of what the letter expresses.

For what, after all, is the "impurity" that supposedly afflicts Nineveh, the removal of which appears to be the basic requirement of Jonah's mission before it can launch, if indeed it must, its attack on God's treasured people?

We know, according to all the Jewish texts, according to Nahmanides, Rashi, Maimonides, Menachem Meiri, the Malbim, Rabbi Nahman, and Rabbi Chaim, according to the commentators whom I have cited from the outset and all of the others that I know even less well, that the height of impurity, the most abominable of abominations, the ultimate symbol of idolatry, is magical thinking.

We know that in its crude forms, in speculations on the occult influence of the moon and stars on the wisdom of princes, in ramblings on the beneficial or harmful effects of solar eclipses, on the political and military consequences of the appearance on the palace grounds of a yellow dog, a red rooster, a horse with the head of a goat, or a woman with a harelip, such magical thinking filled a good half of the tablets that made up the library of Ashurbanipal.

And we know that magical thinking has forms that are less crude and more modern, forms that, for the most part, survived the first fall of Nineveh and that twenty-six centuries later continue to infect enlightened minds—and even, to hear them tell it, the most sublimely enlightened minds that are to be found (pushing the predilection for enlightenment to the point of claiming the ability to hunt down, reveal, and unravel the mystery of the hidden underside of things). I have in mind, obviously, that barely evolved form of magical thinking, the belief in occult forces that secretly control the world, a belief that goes by various other names in other realms but that is known in the political arena as "conspiracy theory."

And finally we know that one of the world capitals of conspiracy theory, one of the places in the world where it has reached the highest points of idiocy and violence, the contemporary spot that produced the worst replicas of the astrological and numerological treatises of the library of Nineveh, was Libya, the Libya of Colonel Gaddafi and of his nonstop insanity.

Ukraine was another of those capitals.

The Soviet era, and even the years that immediately followed its fall, provided a great fund of plot theory—and thus of magical thinking. Ukraine held its own in this regard.

But few modern regimes have been able to claim to rival that of Muammar Gaddafi. I am thinking now of the 1998 fable surrounding the Bulgarian nurses who were supposed to have inoculated Libyan children with the AIDS virus and, beyond that particularly spectacular episode, of all the ideological constructs assembled by Libya's ersatz learned institutes around Israel's supposed conspiracies aimed at humiliating, oppressing, and devastating the poor "Socialist People's Arab Jamahiriya," which had no other choice, along with its African allies and clients, but to respond with a declaration of total war against the Jewish state.

Which leads me to this hypothesis.

What if the Libyan revolution of February 17, 2011, had the effect of contradicting—and even of breaking and shattering—this conspiratorial view?

What if, by laying bare both the savagery and the real sources of a repression that suddenly had nothing to do with Bulgarian nurses or any Satan great or small but everything to do with a national despot working for himself and his clan, that revolution confronted Libyans with a reality very different from the fairy tales that had been served up to them for forty-two years?

What if, by tearing away the veil of illusions, by dropping the masks behind which the real barbarians had operated for decades, by watching as the fire of revolt and the war it triggered dispelled the fog of absurd lies that the Libyan tyrant had deployed to justify his criminal intrigues; what if, by pulverizing the crazy idea, endlessly recycled in official propaganda, that the Arab peoples faced one sole enemy that was the source of all their ills and that they therefore needed to fight until the end of time, and that the enemy was Israel and, beyond Israel, the West—what if, then, the revolution that I supported served to dissipate some of the cloud of magical thinking that was the glue that held the old dictatorship together, that could easily become that of a new dictatorship, and that, by fomenting extremity and hysteria, was capable of transforming into a mortal struggle any old episode of war or peace with other nations? What if that revolution served in this strict sense to "purify" the Libyan Nineveh?

To see the wide-eyed Libyans entering Gaddafi's deserted palaces (and, for that matter, the Ukrainians discovering those of Yanukovych).

To see them hesitate, still a little afraid, dumbstruck with amazement, as they explored their former leader's reception rooms and bunkers and, in the manner of so many regicidal people before them, made the double discovery of the enormity, first, of the arsenals built up over the years to deal with the sort of event that had just occurred (arsenals that expressed nothing so much as the naked, pure, and calculated brutality of an indigenous despotism born of its own madness) and, second, of the great void beneath the pomp, gilt, and marble of official residences opened up for sacking, places that told no secret except that there had been no secret, no conspiracy except, of course, the conspiracy to make people believe in the existence of a conspiracy.

Perhaps those Libyans continued, deep in their souls, to be enemies of Israel and the West.

Perhaps, with the help of the laws of political inertia, they were not yet done with the old war-like rhetoric against "the Jews and the Crusades."

Forgetfulness being at the heart of the history of nations, I am not surprised when I hear demagogues urging Libyans to hate the very people who went far out of their way to help free them.

And the death of Ambassador Christopher Stevens, a true American hero who believed in Libya, liberty, and the rule of law, attests to the atrocious and imbecilic extremes to which that hate can lead.

But despite the tragedy of Stevens's death, nothing in that hate will be as it was before.

Once torn away, the veil of Maya can never be completely restored.

And, from now on, it will be difficult to make the Libyan people swallow the story of Israel and the West being always and forever guilty of every calamity that ever befell them. It will be very difficult, when the time comes to build a state such as never has existed in Cyrenaica, Tripolitania, or Fezzan, to continue with the same old anti-Semitic and anti-Western saws.

Libya, in other words, may never be a sister nation, but it will never fall entirely by its own will under the sway of Daesh.

It may continue to nurture the same vague hostility toward imaginary enemies, but it will not transform itself easily or lightheartedly into a jihadist state.

And if war there should continue to be, if the sword is not quietly sheathed, that sword will indeed be "purer," yes, for having been cleansed of that aspect of conspiracy thinking that in Libya, as everywhere, had the twin effect of supplying fuel for the threat to civilization that is radical Islam while also lending to the confrontation a fatal, irremediable character in which no exit or solution was conceivable.

That, too, is a good thing.

That, too, is a step in the right direction.

For peoples as for individuals, there is a moment of passage from childhood to adulthood, or, in Kantian terms, from a minor state in which one is happy not to think too much to the more daring state of thinking for oneself and relying on one's own understanding.

And that is what happened when, in the weeks that followed February 17, 2011, the Libyan people discovered that they were not dispossessed of their future and that, for better or for worse, they could exert control over at least a part of that future.

If only for that, if only to help this people and others watching them to return to reason or, more aptly, to move toward awareness of the basic laws of practical reason, if only because of this moment of realism and truth, of responsibility for self and others that, like a ray of light, shone briefly but will stabilize, normalize, and rationalize its relations with its adversaries, if only for these reasons, it was necessary to go to Nineveh.

KOJÈVE, JONAH, FALSE MESSIAHS, THE END OF HISTORY

The book offers a final lesson contained in its closing words.

Those words are, I believe, the most difficult to understand and to translate into today's language.

Jonah has been lamenting the desiccation of the castor-oil plant that had offered him much-needed shade.

And God, it will be remembered, answers as follows: If you feel sorry for this shrub, why would I not feel pity for the "great city" in which, aside from the animals, there are a hundred twenty thousand human beings who still cannot tell "their right from their left"?

One can, if one wishes, read in those words the protest of a merciful God belying the foolish image promoted in the Middle Ages of a cruel and vengeful Almighty.

In them one can read a trailblazing declaration of humanist faith in which ecological concern for the shrub is contrasted with the far more laudable and noble concern for a collection of souls and bodies that came very close to extermination before being saved.

But the most important thing in these concluding words is that although the Ninevites have already donned (four verses previously) the garb of penance and mourning, God continues to describe them as still not being able to tell their right from their left.

The important thing is that, if words mean anything, God does not believe in the reality of their repentance, or, if he believes it, if he indeed noticed them covering themselves with ashes and so on, he also saw them already repenting of their repentance and reverting to their prior proclivities.

The most crucial point is that this state of non-conversion, or of conversion that almost immediately tumbles back into sin, this state of people who have not heard him or, if they heard, turned quickly around and laughed in his face—that is the situation in which God pities them.

More important still is the fact that this pity is presented, if only through the order of the verses, in the choice of words, in the tone and rhetoric of the questions posed, as being strictly symmetrical with Jonah's relation to the castor-oil plant.

Let us reread closely.

Jonah pities the plant, but he also needs it.

And the need he has for it is a very specific form of need. It could have been a need for its pleasing color or harmonious shape or for the quality of its foliage or for the feeling of peace that it gives him. But no! It is its shade that he needs. The castor-oil plant is "precious" to him solely for the shade that it provides.

From which one can and must deduce two things.

That Nineveh, too, is not only "pitiable" but also "precious," and that, if it is precious, if God needs it, he needs it, as Jonah needed the castor-oil plant, as a form of shade. . . .

This symmetrical effect is highly enigmatic and, as I say, difficult to grasp.

First because, God being infinitely perfect and, in principle, lacking nothing, it is hard to see how he might need anything at all, let alone the unconverted and infamous people of Nineveh.

But also and especially because he is light itself. He is the one whose own inner and outer form, according to the Kabbalah, is represented by light. He is the continuous creation of light that, according to Isaiah, must spread "to the end of the earth." So what are we to make of this business of shade, and why would it be shade, literally and truly shade, that all of a sudden he needs?

It is easy to see how the castor-oil plant provides shade.

We see its long branches protecting sensitive skin by filtering the sun's harsh rays.

And we grasp why the survivor from the whale's belly could not do without shelter from the light and the excessive heat that reign above Nineveh.

But God?

Shade against what, and why?

Is he not, to say it again, pure light and pure heat?

Are we to understand that he needs to be shaded from himself? That he might take umbrage at himself? Could he be at once both heat and shade, like the poet's wound and knife? Or the "dark sun from which shines the night" that another poet saw in mourning? And how does Nineveh relate to all this? Why the comparison between a shrub and a city of a hundred twenty thousand people and as many animals?

This story is really very strange.

It is less frightening than that of the purification of the sword but nearly as unsettling.

For one must, if one follows the text, accept simultaneously that God is all light, that if it were up to him alone, his light would flood the world, filter into every crack and crevice, and dispel every shadow, but that that would not be good because God needs, yes, a "shadow" that prevents him, at least for the moment, from spreading his light throughout the universe.

And so?

So what I glean from this is an echo of Jewish distrust, as evidenced in the story of Korah, of those gripped by the desire to rush to the end of time, to hasten the end of days.

What I hear in it is the fear of every sage, every rabbi, every interpreter of tradition with regard to the impatient souls who want there to be light too soon, too fast, and too far.

If there is really a failing, they all insist, if there is a danger greater than magic, it is forgetting that desire for God's light is a desire suitable only for the end of things, when the "world of emanation" finally arrives. But here, for the time being, those tempted to hurry to wrap things up will suffer the fate, if not of Korah's two hundred fifty conspirators, then at least of Nadav and Avihu, the two sons of Aaron, who are themselves imposing figures but who, because they passed body and soul to the side of light, are—in this world, in the dark chamber that is the universe in which we are given to live and where only study, deep and laborious study, allows us to break through the "screens" that the Kabbalah describes as barriers blocking the divine flux—holy but impossible figures and, like Korah's confederates, fated to die by fire.

This failing, announced in the Book of Jonah, has a name in Jewish history: It is the belief in false messiahs.

But does it not have another name in profane history, a name that is a barely disguised version of the original: the Hegelian belief in the end of history?

The proof that it is the same name lies in the signs that, according to Alexandre Kojève, and all modern interpreters of Hegel, attest to our having arrived, once and for all, at the end of history.

The slowdown of events, certainly.

The end of the great tragedies, of course.

But also the flooding of all things by an absolute light that, throughout the world, arrives to dispel pockets of opacity and shadow.

And, above all, a return to the animal state, the "becoming animal" that, for Alexandre Kojève, is the bad correlate of the end of history and that transforms humanity into an immense garden of beasts in great number that cannot tell their right from their left . . .

The words of Jonah and Kojève are identical.

Nearly identical, too, is the fright that one detects in the two cases.

And, from there, nearly identical is the choice that is open to them and that they hold open for us.

It has to be one or the other.

Either Nineveh *in shadow,* with its inhabitants who do not know their right from their left. Or else Nineveh *unshaded,* flooded with light, in which case it is no longer just Nineveh but the rest of the world, as well, that will not know right from left.

Either save Nineveh and accept the fact that it will remain Nineveh, complete with the set of traps that sequester the divine light, or save it on the condition that it be purged of the shadow it was, that it be fully illuminated and fully illuminating—thus taking the risk of the whole world being caught up in Nineveh's destiny.

On the one hand a reluctant, almost rebellious Nineveh, inured to sin and redeemed only by half, a quarter, or even less. On the other a Nineveh, all the Ninevehs, fully bathed in light by virtue of the end of time occurring right now. That should be good, right? But in fact it is less rosy than it might appear, because, as implied both in the biblical verse and in Kojève's commentary on Hegel's *Phenomenology,* Nineveh is everywhere now—Ninevism has been chased out of the city of Nineveh only to Ninevize the rest of the planet. And that is because the becoming animal, the transformation of humanity into beasts in great number no longer recognizing right from left, once purged from Nineveh proper through the window returns to greater Nineveh through the door of the globalized end of history.

In still other terms, we have on the one hand the shadow of Nineveh, which is far from brilliant—indeed extremely disappointing, but history marches on with its moments of greatness and of misery—its victories and defeats, its suspended catastrophes, its small reparations, and the patches of clouds that prevent the holy light, for the time being at least, from penetrating the shells of darkness. On the other we have Nineveh unshadowed, which would appear much better at first glance, the ultimate goal of all good people, starting with the prophets and their followers, but this has the perverse effect of the animalization of humanity and, thus, the Ninevization of the world.

I am not a Kojèvian.

Nor do I believe that the lesson of Jonah must be followed to the letter.

But it does contain, translated into today's language, real wisdom.

That good Ninevites should emerge from it, that acts of repentance should occur in Kiev and Libya, that the authorities in Lviv and Tripoli agree, as I heard them commit to do, to erect a memorial worthy of the name on the spot where the trains left for the extermination camps in the case of the former and in the case of the latter to restore the synagogue vandalized under the dictatorship and kept closed during the revolution—those were obviously the goals. But the idea was not necessarily that Ukraine bring to light completely and immediately the terrible ambiguities of a doctrine, Banderism, that had its season of Nazism and anti-Semitism and even tacitly anti-Ukrainism—as in the famous episode in April 1940, when the bells of thirty-eight churches were handed over to German foundries. Nor was it ever the idea to oblige Libya tomorrow morning to establish diplomatic relations with Israel or to throw off in a day, as if by magic, centuries of anti-Semitic prejudice.

The original Nineveh could remain a sinful city. The important thing was that there should remain in the city—or appear in it—workshops in which were carved the frescoes of Ashurbanipal's palace and tablets celebrating the exploits of the divinities of plague and pestilence, the revolt of the god Zu, and the story of the goddess Ishtar forcing open the gates of hell to rescue her beloved son from the clutches of Allat, the queen of the great gods. The same holds true for today's Ninevehs. The question is not whether or not a massive conversion occurs, with appropriate fanfare, in Lviv or Tripoli. Even if there should be, in Libya, just a few militiamen who decide that it is a sacred duty to save the vine friezes, the winged victories of marble, and the columns and arch of Antoninus Pius in Leptis Magna, and, in Ukraine, just a few great Christians who evoke and revere the memory of Metropolitan Sheptytsky, primate of the Uniate Church of

Ukraine during World War II; even if there should remain just a small community of the faithful who find pride in his interventions with Pope Pius XII on behalf of the Jews of Galicia; even if there should emerge no more than a handful of people willing to speak up for and to exemplify human greatness: Then something would have been accomplished.

Not democratic messianism of the type proposed, for example, by the American neocons in Iraq, but a true Jewish messianism both ambitious and modest, aspiring to the infinite but respectful of the laws of this world and choosing, ultimately, *tikkun* over apocalypse.

Not the alignment of the provinces of the empire (Kojève's book) or unification of the four empires (the Book of Daniel) but, on the borders of the empires (and that is what Ukraine and Libya are, in fact: the borders of two of the four empires), opening breaches and channels through which can pass words that, once accumulated, committed to memory, and more or less aligned, will, at the end of time, add up to redemption.

A true word is rare.

And it is good when one appears.

I think that human history is like a long sentence interspersed with silences that give the human learner time to breathe. To save the world, it is enough to save fragments of true speech, knowing that the intervening jumble was nothing more than breathing space.

Are shade and shadow passing, like clouds? Or is it light that is intermittent and full of holes? I am searching for passages.

CHAPTER TEN

DOES GOD ARRIVE AS AN IDEA
OR THROUGH FAITH?

This book is nearing its end.

I have the feeling of having returned to a meeting, postponed five years ago in Libya, ten in Pakistan, twenty in Afghanistan, forty in Bangladesh.

I feel I am keeping a promise I made to myself after reading Emmanuel Levinas's commentary on my *Testament de Dieu.* At the time, I promised to return, once I was better equipped, to the "hard Law," to the "people of the just Law," to the "miracle of the Name," which I had described as being the finest attribute of the Jews.

But I feel as if I have answered another call, as well, this one much older, dating from childhood, from well before my time at the École Normale, before I even knew what a book was or what books are made of, a call I heard upon seeing (without really understanding what was happening, let alone knowing which side I was to take) my father embarrassed by his own father and the sort of Jew he was: a handsome man, like my father; proud, like him; as ascetic, too, and with the same thick, white head of hair; but, in my father, an embarrassment, yes, an awkwardness the meaning of which I sometimes half-understood in hearing him whisper to my mother, as if they were discussing a black mass, that his father was *observing Shabbat.*

His face rushes back to me now.

Along with that of another ancestor, my mother's grandfather, a rabbi, whose face I know only from a century-old photo and about whom I know nothing more than that he was both very pious and very learned.

And another, his son-in-law, my mother's father, a shepherd in the Spanish Sahara. By what misalliance, I have always wondered, had he come into the family of a rabbi? He was pious, as well, extremely so, but illiterate, as pious Jews seldom are, to the extent that he used his last words to say that the great regret of his life was to have died so young, without having had time to learn enough even to begin to approach the holy books.

With those, too, I feel that I have an appointment to keep.

They, too, are here, surrounding me, so different from myself and yet so similar, posing the same basic questions that I do.

DON'T SHOOT THOSE WHO STUDY

Beginning right here.

The question of the books, of their holiness, and of the time that one devotes to them.

That of Shabbat, which so embarrassed my father and which was not observed in our house.

That of this old man, of this Lévy who observed the Sabbath, who was described within the family as "orthodox," the possible meaning of which I never succeeded in learning, despite the fact that his was the only one of the three faces that I actually knew.

To hear my parents tell it, it was his overall vision of the world, of raising children, of a woman's place in the home, of the books one should read or not read, his practice of going everywhere on foot on Saturday and of bringing his own dishes and utensils when he visited for lunch, that was hidebound and blinkered.

In my memories of him, from his dry, smooth face, his close-cropped white hair covered by neither hat nor yarmulke, his jacquard-patterned sweaters, the plain gray jacket that he wore in all seasons without a coat, he was a simple, meditative man who expressed himself by allusion and in what he chose not to say, a relative stranger to worldly affairs to the extent that I never heard him offer the slightest comment on current events—but he certainly was not a religious fanatic.

But what difference does this make?

If I can draw a conclusion from this anecdote, it is that the business of orthodoxy, the division between those who are supposedly orthodox and those who are not, may be less important than we think.

There are Jews who inhabit their name, as he did, as did my other grandfather, my great-grandfather the rabbi, and, for that matter, my father, whose willingness to distance himself from his religion stopped short of a bright line: that of insults to our name, to the playground calls of "dirty Jew," which my father taught me never to let pass unanswered, supporting that teaching with lessons in martial arts. And there are others who do not inhabit it, like my uncle Armand, my father's older brother, whom my family ridiculed for his grotesque efforts to de-Judaize his life, his name, and even, like Proust's character Bloch, his appearance.

There are Jews who expose themselves to the shadow of the outside world, the shadow of the Other, even the radically other, as I have tried to do all my life, just as my father did, a practice that I have repeatedly described here in this book as the first commandment, the one in the absence of which all the others shrivel and become dead letters. And there are Jews who are careful not to do this, who refrain from such exposure and the unlimited responsibility to the world that it implies, and who, from Mascara to Paris or New York, prefer the empty light of easy and low-stakes community life to the shadows of Nineveh.

In another division or disjunction, there are Jews who study a little or a lot, or even enough to drive themselves crazy, as I imagine my rabbi great-grandfather might have done or like the Jews of Bnei Brak, the town founded by the ancestor of Daniel Pearl, whose name he spoke in the video shot a few minutes before his beheading. And others who do so only by rote or sparingly or, like my parents, do not do it at all, their deep feeling being that Auschwitz marked the end (and the beginning) of something but that what ended there, what became impossible, was not, for example, poetry but study, Jewish knowledge, the Talmud.

But "orthodox"?

What exactly is an "orthodox" Jew?

The word "orthodoxy"—as Althusser said of certain concepts that could not be found anywhere in Marxist theory—is absent from Jewish thought.

And if, by this word, one means the familiar men in black who wear the sidelocks that neither my grandfather Lévy, with his white hair, nor the shepherd wore but that my rabbi great-grandfather probably did wear; if one means the people in present-day Jerusalem who devote most of their life to study and who live in neighborhoods, like Mea Shearim, set aside for their use, is this not a very strange misinterpretation and a faulty manner of distinguishing people?

Because ultimately, if orthodoxy means thinking that is frozen or petrified in its dogma and supposedly correct, well-rehearsed forms, then there is one place that, by definition, is antithetical to orthodoxy: the houses of study in which scholars devote all of their time to endless dissection of individual verses of the Torah, to commentary on each verse, and to commentary on the existing commentary and so on, ad infinitum.

If an orthodox person is one who takes refuge in a forever-settled idea and spouts it obstinately without ever reconsidering it, there are certain people, again by definition, who are almost naturally immunized against the closing off of thought: the rabbis who never cease turning an idea over in their heads, spending hours, days, years, and many pages spinning out interminable paradoxes on the subject of the thousand and one ways of acting in the face of the tangle of contradictions posed by the slightest political, moral, metaphysical, or practical thought or decision—such as the appearance of a red heifer, an offering of flour, the sadness of a widowed sister-in-law with no children, a drop of milk on a piece of meat, or the story of the death of Rabbi Akiva who was mauled with metal brushes while reciting the Shema Yisrael.

I am not such a person, of course. I can barely read Hebrew. I do not say daily prayers. I do not follow the dietary laws.

I am, moreover, a lay Jew who seldom visits synagogues and has not devoted so much time or energy to study.

But I remember a preface I wrote thirty years ago, well before I reconnected with Benny Lévy, for a book of photographs devoted to the men in black of Mea Shearim.

In that text, now lost, I expressed my wonder and amazement at these tenuous beings, suspended between heaven and earth and so different from the standardized, globalized beings that were beginning to clone and spread from one end of the world to the other.

I was moved at the grace of their existence, plainly abstemious yet so very light and, I surmised, studious and in dialogue with the beyond.

I had agreed to write that text, I suppose, because a part of me believed them to be depositories of the secret that I attribute today to the treasured people and because another part liked thinking that they were there, committed to their misfit status and their paradox, as if I were telling myself that one day I might have to defer to them as one might defer to a bum after learning that he was the messiah hidden among the beggars of Rome.

Well, I have not changed my mind.

And I do not mind repeating here, in today's words, though hardly less ignorant than I was then, the distant respect that they inspire in me.

I am even less reluctant after reading the papers and being troubled by the witchcraft trial to which they have been subjected since a man with sidelocks who obviously came from their world joined the ranks of the murderers—terrorists, fascists—by stabbing to death a young homosexual during Jerusalem's Gay Pride event while others from a nationalist religious group firebombed a Palestinian house in Duma, burning a baby alive and killing his parents.

I watch the Jerusalem man on television in the hideous pose of ugly self-righteousness that all assassins seem to adopt when arrested.

Looking at the mask (it is hard to call it a face) of this somber Jew with the long beard who I imagine passed through one of those houses of study whose innocence intrigued me at the time I wrote the preface for the book of photos of Mea Shearim, I see the finger extended for the world's cameras, but it is not toward the Sefer Torah that is held up three times each week in the houses where he studied; he holds a ghastly pale dagger that contrasts with the black in which he is clad.

Over and over, I see the image of this Jew pinned to the ground, handcuffed by Israeli police officers who—this should go without saying, but is better said, given the wave of hatred that was immediately unleashed on the theme of the cancer-eating-at-Israeli-society and the growing-danger-of-ultraorthodoxy—do their work well.

And suspended, no longer between heaven and earth but between texts and sewers, I tell myself that justice will have to be severe; I want to see clearly displayed the theological reasoning (and that reasoning exists, alas—it is explicitly laid out as far back as Rashi's commentary) that these sorts of bastards rely on, which always turns, as it did in the 1995 assassination of Yitzhak Rabin, around the figure of Phineas, son of Eleazar, son of Aaron, of whom Rashi says that he became *kohen*—in other words, that he acceded to the priesthood, only after he had killed Zimri, Prince of Israel, because Zimri had slept with a Madianite princess and threatened to lead the treasured people into the debauchery sought by Moab's people. I also tell myself that, while waiting for the other murderers, the ones who murdered the baby and his parents in Duma, to be put out of harm's way, it is necessary to outlaw from society the very few rabbis—perhaps it was just one, but that is one too many—who, like Rabbi Ginsburg, uttered words that might be construed as justifying the appalling act. But I would also like it if a fraction, even a small fraction, of the legitimate concern that we have not to lump things together each time a Muslim kills in the name of Islam and, in so doing, disfigures and disgraces it, I would like it if the reflexive warning against guilt by association that is rightly broadcast each time a follower of Daesh takes the message of the Koran hostage and claims to act not only in his own name but in the name of the entire Umma, I would like it if a fraction of that restraint could also be applied here so that the crimes in Jerusalem and Duma are not used to exaggerate the danger of ultraorthodoxy in Israeli yeshivas.

There.

I said it.

It has now been said (and by a secular Jew) that the line intoned by the media, who were just waiting for this to happen, about "all those with beards, the intolerant ones, the obscurantist, they're all the same, all equally horrible," is simply intolerable.

It has now been said (yes, by a secular Jew!) that we must resist the reductionism of the ubiquitous form of reporting that forswears all nuance and, just as it ignores any differences there may be between ultra-anti-Zionists who see in Israel's existence an obstacle to the coming of the messiah, the ultra-Zionist crazies of the "hilltop youth" responsible for the Duma murder, and the Zionist state that both of the previous groups hate with equal fervor but for opposing reasons, jumps on an event in order to settle its score with the "backward men in black" who are supposed to be the fertile womb from which the foul beast will forever give birth to its theological-political monstrosities.

It has now been said that reasoning like that leads straight to an auto-da-fé. But this time the burning will not stop with the Talmud: Thanks to Facebook and Twitter and in the climate of hate for the exceptional that underpins the spirit of the moment, it will carry away writers who are too good at writing, painters who are too good at painting, and thinkers who have not yet grasped that we are entering a world in which there must be no more Jews (but rather anti-globalists) and no more ancient Greeks (but professors of philosophy), and no more slaves (but ultraorthodoxies), and no more free people (but a free pass to post and tweet and lurk).

And it has been said that the genius of Judaism that I am seeking most certainly resides in the effort of going to Nineveh, in the relationship with the other and with the outside world that is the meaning of the lives of so many Jews and definitely of mine. But it lies also—no, it lies first and foremost—in the profusion of intelligence that flows from reading the Talmud, a practice that some would have you believe is the invisible church of ultraorthodoxy.

THE BOOK AND BOOKS IN GENERAL

But that is not quite it.

In fact, things are just a little bit more complicated.

Orthodoxy can be found among those who are called orthodox.

There are criminals among them, as I have just said.

There are bad apples who would be the shame of the Jewish world if, each time they appeared, Jews had not denounced them with near unanimity.

But, yes, there are also orthodox Jews who are orthodox in the sense that their thinking is fixed, narrow, and fossilized.

That said, however, two observations are in order.

If such people become orthodox in their thinking, it is not because they read the Talmud too much but rather because they do not read it enough.

It is not because they remain faithful, too narrowly faithful, to the old masters, who, before they were born, questioned the crusty old texts to the point of torture, causing them, literally, to give up the ghost (those old texts that Levinas said were like the folded wings of the spirit that had to be redeployed either gently or forcibly). On the contrary, it is because they have broken with that world of interpretive superintelligence and dissemination of meaning; it is because they have given up the hard work of negating, forsworn this methodical and joyous deconstruction, relinquished these paradoxes wrapped around other paradoxes and leading to new and often almost aberrant conclusions that others will then elaborate, complicate, contradict, and turn inside out; in short, it is because they have abandoned the idea of multiple meanings that has always been the beating heart of Talmudic scholarship and because, by hypostatizing the text, just as others hypostatize the state, the community, or the temple, by falling prey to the mistake of mass thinking, which is always ready-made thinking, they have walked away from patience and confident, even violent, interpretation, the two best defenses against the temptation of orthodoxy. In so doing, they have entered a world of routine in which the creativity of the mind and spirit are lost, a world in which, as the commentators on the history of Korah and his allies observed, one dons clothes already worn by others.

In other words, if they are orthodox, if they fall into orthodoxy, it is because, having tired of thinking, believing themselves excused from their duty of piety because they wear sidelocks and caftans that protect them, they suppose, from time's ravages, they have given up on that infinite flexibility of mind, on the exhausting practice of leaping like trapeze artists from line to line; it is because they have lost their taste for those arguments with twenty-six steps and nineteen different speakers that had to be learned by heart on pain of failure, that were the routine (I was going to say the choreography) of the curriculum in the yeshivas of Vilnius in the era of the Vilna Gaon, or of Volozhin in the time of Rabbi Chaim, and have found themselves holding in their hands predigested verses ready to be thought and spoken, godforsaken, like sloughed-off skins.

But here comes the second observation.

If that is true—if orthodoxy is what I say it is, if it is this cessation of thought, this triumph of routine, of recycling and repeating what has already been thought, and, above all, not thinking new thoughts, if it is the icing over of minds that have become incapable of invention and renewal—I hope my secular friends will forgive me for saying this: but thinking of that sort, prefab thinking, thinking that no longer takes the trouble to think for fear of bringing on a headache, one finds plenty of it in the lay world, plenty among the worldly, those at home in their time, among the prominent and famous, the Sadducees of Judaism who never even began to think. Such "secular orthodox" are like new arrivals in the Holy Land, happy with a ready-to-use kit of ideas or, like the French Jews of days past, and even of today, settling for a reluctant, minimal, somnolent Judaism not accompanied by the flares of complexity and controversy that were the perfect vaccine against convention and cliché. Yes, one finds plenty of that prefabricated and repetitive thinking in the word mills of our profane Judaism as it stammers out its protests of "anti-Semitism will not pass," its "when a Jew is killed, mankind dies," or its "the law of one's country is the law" (usually removed from its Talmudic context).

I am not preparing to put the "orthodoxy" of the two groups side by side.

The more so because, although both groups are opposed to true Jewish values, the second deserves credit for not having produced any killers.

What I mean is that the real cleavage is not found here.

The important debate is not, despite what the papers say and what many Jews seem to believe, between secular and religious members of the faith but between Jews who think and those who do not.

What I mean, to take an example, is that the Jewish world is not divided between those who wear a yarmulke and those who do not—because in the obligation to cover one's head there may not be much more than a moment of the immense intellectual teaching of Moses and Adam: the real question is whether an individual is ready, yarmulke or no, to accept that teaching and make it the point of departure for a new hope.

I mean that the genius of Judaism, its main genius, resides in the ability—whether or not one prays, whether or not one observes holidays, whether or not one follows the proscriptions of Leviticus or Deuteronomy—to produce a little of the intelligence that will offer people, all people, a little of the teaching that they need to be different from others, to stand out from the crowd to which they are never fated to belong, and from themselves to the extent they cede to the crowd and the mass.

That, I believe, is what Benny Lévy, Alain Finkielkraut, and I understood when, in June 2000, we founded the Institute of Levinassian Studies in Jerusalem.

It is what was most essential when our improbable trio appeared together in the huge amphitheater, the hall full to bursting and crackling with the metaphysical uproar that Benny had hoped for.

We differed in the way we dressed and ate.

We diverged in most of our political and philosophical positions.

But there were one or two points on which we did agree.

First, Alain Finkielkraut and I.

Both of us were weaned on literature and classical philosophy.

But we were also aware of the importance of Jewish philosophy.

We knew, though we were infinitely less knowledgeable than our friend, that somewhere there exists an immense foundational book known as the Talmud that, unlike all the other immense foundational books in the history of humanity, is neither authorless (like the Vedas, the Mahabharata, the thirteen books of the *Heike monogatari* chanted by the blind monks of ancient Japan) nor of uncertain authorship (*The Iliad, The Odyssey*) nor supposedly dictated by God (the Pentateuch, the Koran) but rather a real signed book, a book about which the reader can know, to the line, what comes from where, an encyclopedia of a hundred voices discussing and arguing over the truth, a polyphony of word and chant in which the authors are identified very specifically (Shammai and Hillel, Eliezer and Yehoshua, Abaye and Rava, Nehorai and Hiyya bar Abba, Ben Zoma, and many others).

Above all we were aware, albeit in different ways, of two essential properties of this Book.

Its dialogue, a dialogue that is sometimes mute, sometimes resounding, with many great modern minds that we revered: what the book said to Proust; what it whispered to Sartre; what it gave to Hermann Cohen when he decided, in the last years of his life, to break with the Kantian views of his beginnings to produce his admirable *Écrits juifs*; or what it said to Moses Mendelssohn, the inventor of the Jewish enlightenment, one of whose great causes was the struggle against Karaism, that is, against the very ancient heresy according to which the Talmud is not essential to Jewish thought—that the Torah alone suffices.

And finally the fact that, in that teeming book that I somewhat neglected after publishing *Le Testament de Dieu,* but to which I was gradually returning under the influence of Benny Lévy, in that book of science and music that I was just beginning to truly decipher, in its tides of black letters punctuated with flashes of light that helped me grasp for the first time, if dimly, what the Kabbalah meant when it said that those letters have as many faces as the Jews who have read them, in that book were posed, no less than in the words of Dante, Shakespeare, Virgil, or Homer, the great questions that have stirred humanity since the dawn of time, as well as pieces of possible answers, provided one still knows how to read those letters as did those who wrote them.

Next, Benny Lévy.

His awareness of the danger that awaits Jews who study—the danger of parroting or "psittacism."

A devitalized form of language closed in upon itself, lacking verve and spark, no longer knowing what it is saying or why, which is a possible outcome of the life that Benny, unlike Alain and I, chose.

And the need to counter the fatigue that can sap Talmudic intelligence and that leads many observant Jews, wading in the mush of a language forged in the shtetls of Poland and Lithuania, to become terrified by Western intellectualism and cut off from the real life that challenged Rashi and the Tossafists of France's Champagne region.

I know that Benny would occasionally say that a Jew's purpose is not to produce literature but to study.

But I also know that he was aware of the trap inherent in that position.

And I know that he knew that a remedy lay in offering a strong and confident reception to the best that Western culture offers, which would lend to one's study added intensity, energy, and power.

He knew better than anyone the passage from the Midrash announcing that, in messianic times, the nations "will serve" Israel, which signifies that the cultures of said nations, even if "idolatrous," will achieve ultimate knowledge of things and contain, there and then, seeds of intelligence that the Jews would be wrong to pass up.

A part of him continued to think that, just as Moses's companions set out carrying with them the worldly goods and treasures they acquired during their enslavement, so, too, had he begun his return without casting off the profane treasures represented by Western literature and philosophy that he had come to love during his time at the École Normale Supérieure in Paris.

And I do not believe that I am overstepping the bounds either of friendship or of the respect owed to the suspended voice of a great figure now gone by stating that he was aware that, in order to afford the rabbis of the Talmud their full measure of modernity and youthfulness, it was necessary to do what they had done in their time—to bring them and their language into close contact with other treasures of thought embedded in the languages of the present day. Benny pretended to have grown out of those treasures and to have forgotten them, but he knew very well that the *teshuvah,* the return to God, though it is believed to change a man's past as much as his future, never erases anything. And profane knowledge—the sciences of language and structure, the metaphysics studded with anti-Judaism and often written in its ink—Benny continued to master them as well as Alain Finkielkraut and myself.

The genius of Judaism is the Book and books. And it is when one chooses to close those books—that is, to comment on them no further, to challenge and oppose them no more—that the genius dies.

Those are the views that the three of us shared that day under the merciless sun of Jerusalem, where often one must choose between madness and the will to truth.

And that, in my own eyes and with hindsight, was the meaning of that moment when three voices spoke in the first-person singular but joined in common combat against dull-wittedness and leaden thinking.

TO BELIEVE OR NOT TO BELIEVE

I asked my children to read some of these pages. One, expressing surprise at my way of evoking as well as avoiding, without ever actually invoking, the name of the divine, asked me a question that may have occurred to some readers of this book: Do you believe in God?

As directly as the question was posed, I responded that the problem lies elsewhere and, in any case, does not present itself in those terms.

For in the end, if everything I have written to this point is, if not true, then at least cogent, if the genius of Rashi, Maimonides, and Jonah is as I have proposed, if the Talmud is indeed the shower of sparks that continue to glow among those who have retained a taste for contending with the language of Moses as recorded and reactivated through repeated enigmas and paradoxes, through words both limpid and tricky, through meanings constructed and deconstructed, through utterances well articulated or brusquely aberrant—then that means that the Jews have come into the world less to believe than to study, not to adore but to understand; and that, in turn, means that the loftiest task to which the holy books call us is not to burn with love or to swoon before the infinite but to know and to teach.

I recall the passages from Levinas that guided my first steps toward this book, which emphasized the deep hostility of Jewish thought to mystery, sacrament, mystical presence, and religiosity.

I recall his cautionary words, echoed by Maurice Blanchot, about what a mistake it would be to place our duty to God over our obligations to others, our "optic" over our "ethics"; our offenses to God over care for our neighbor.

I think of Franz Rosenzweig, Levinas's true master, and mine, and the master of Benny Lévy, who told me one day that he had cried like a baby when entertaining this thought, the harshest of all, the hardest to tame, the cruelest; I think of Rosenzweig and of the lines that were the motto of his small yeshiva, which was short-lived and as fragile as the initiatives of the Jewish intellect sometimes are; I think of those words, addressed to Rudolf Hallo, which, he said, summarized his task: *unreligiös sein*.

My task, our task, the task of the Jews as Jews, is to be "irreligious," he meant. Not blasphematory, of course, and certainly not indifferent. Not even atheistic, which is another way of saying the opposite: a theologian of Nothing. No, irreligious. Refusing simply and stubbornly the easy ways of effusiveness and expansiveness that eventually give way to sentimentality. And holding fast, with equal stubbornness, to the intellectualism for which Judaism has been so roundly criticized but that Rosenzweig retained from his Hegelian youth and believed to be congruent with the science on which he was embarking.

I think of the Vilna Gaon, throughout his long life, battling by example and argument but also by excommunication and anathema against those who saw study solely as a first or second order of knowledge leading to a third order, the sublime or mystical. No to mysticism, he said! *Torah li-shma*. The goal of study is study. And between a lazy person who reclines in purported communion experienced as a foretaste of future worlds and a studious one who has said goodbye to apparition and miracle but still labors over the text, I will take the studious one!

I think of the third great generation of Kabbalists, haunted, as all their contemporaries were, by the ghosts of Sabbatai Zevi and Jacob Frank. I think in particular of the Ramhal, who came two centuries after Isaac Luria and argued, in response to Luria, that allegory, or *mashal,* must remain, of course, the basic principle of Kabbalah (How, without it, to capture knowledge, to reserve it? How, above all, to make of its appropriation the long and rugged path that it must be if each of us is to find his face in it?) but adding that this *mashal* must absolutely be translated within its *nimshal,* the allegory within its idea, the symbol within the concept of which it has become the coded sign. Temporary mysteries! Images stripped of images! Enigmas, of course, because there is no other way to get closer to the concatenation of beings! But the ultimate goal remains clarity!

I reflect on the long tradition that, around the Kabbalah and particularly Chaim of Volozhin, interpreted God's withdrawal not as a dialectical moment, a game with the devil or the world, a ruse, an eclipse, a hide-and-seek with evil, but as a normal and stable state of his presence—a true *tzimtsum* this time; a contraction and concentration of God into himself; and, in fact, a great void that is the precondition for the existence of the world but which may resemble a disappearance, a fall into nonexistence.

And, of course, Maimonides; the first section of the first chapter of the first book of the Mishneh Torah, which he intended to make the summation of Jewish law, the true substance that must be comprehended by a member of the treasured people who lacked the time or the energy to venture into the library of the Talmud. That first book is called the Sefer Hamada, or the "book of knowledge." And the first law requires that one "know" that there is a "first being" that "brings into being all that has come into being" and that this first being must be conceived as the peak of a "column of intelligences" that depend, from end to end, on the "truth of his being."

Maimonides speaks of truth, not belief.

He says, or rather implies, that knowledge of that first being, and knowledge alone, is the first commandment.

Without rhetoric, without a magical, mystical, or incantational word, he insists that the foundation of all the world rests on a first knowledge, a thought, a *da'at*—never on an initial faith.

And he waits until section 4 of the chapter—while reinforcing his column, consolidating his spiral of knowledge and science but never deviating from the clear Greek of the Stagirites intermingled with Hebrew that was the language best suited to the *hokhmah,* the wisdom, that he believed to be the ultimate meaning of the prophecy—he waits until section 4 before finally, after rounding the bend from a statement about the word *emet* (truth), he writes "God." After which he waits again before, in section 6, saying that what this "God" requires is "knowledge" rather than "intuition" or "belief."

So, the Name is there, of course.

It did not evaporate in the great spiral of fine distinctions.

And it is even omnipresent in the Torah, which is all about his names and surnames, his speeches to Israel, the traps that he sets for Jonah, the wheel on which he breaks him, and, elsewhere, in the books of the other prophets, major and minor, his thundering rages and no less sudden leniency.

But his name is, as we know, unpronounceable. Moses himself, as we also know, saw him only from behind, which, in the language of Maimonides's negative theology, signifies that he did not see him at all and that no visible face corresponds to this inaudible name.

And all of the Jewish texts of which I am aware say and repeat: Man cannot both see and live. To occupy this space at this time precludes one from seeing the One who is outside this space and time. Were one to see him, if he were to reveal himself fully and truly, I would cease to exist in this space and time. I warned you . . . so long!

But never, ever, is there any question of believing in him.

The *credo in unum deum* that is expected from those who are asked if they "believe in God" never appears—anywhere.

The truth is that this business about belief arises from another story, one of equal beauty, one deeply lodged in hearts and feelings: that is the Pauline story of "saving faith"; but it is not the story of those who call themselves Jews.

The *credo quia absurdum,* for example, the choice not to explore the mystery of the tomb opened on Easter, that constitutes the beauty of the blind faith of Augustine and Claudel: Nothing could be more contrary to the no less great beauty of the will to understand that is at the core of Judaism.

The idea of the wager, the sublime leap into the unknown of a Pascal who, tired of flitting between the computation of probabilities, pleasant diversions, and the silence of infinite space, decides to scale the wall toward the sound of the voices that he hears sighing in the shadows, to go faster than the music of the spheres though he is resigned to never knowing their ultimate secret, and even to travel beyond the light of the most powerful human understanding (his own) that the century had produced but that, despite its power, understood nothing: his wager took him beyond all that and, in a single bound, propelled him to the summit of creation and its end. But what could be more different from a Talmudic effort that never offers itself freebies, that skips no steps or rungs on the ladder, that forgoes no audacity of thought and will be satisfied with itself only once it has arrived at the end of the end of what it can think (not believe, but *think*)? And even then, suppose that another, sharper intellect appears, takes hold of what was elucidated, and begins to probe more deeply. It is enough for the process to take off in another direction, toward that sea of perpetual nontranquility that is the Talmud. . . .

And as for discovering in the phrase "we will do and we will understand" the equivalent of the *credo* or the wager, as for seeing in the Hebrews' promise some sort of investment or advance against earnings—or even, while we are at it, one of those leaps into the void that one makes because the house is burning and jumping is the only way out—that would be the epitome of misapprehension. . . . The phrase, in reality, signifies the exact opposite: We will understand, yes; we will understand, of course; but this "understanding" is "to be done"; and, while waiting to understand one must tirelessly *do*—one must *do* without seeing, *do* without believing, *do* without making an act of faith, *do* without that doing depending to the slightest degree on what one has not yet understood; one must do without ever committing the error of relying on belief or escaping into faith. . . .

Maybe I'm laying it on too thick.

But to think about the name of God, to reflect on its immanence and transcendence, on its presence and its absence, to ponder this outside what resides within language, to conceive of this spiral and, at its center but overhanging it slightly, this name that is pronounced only by the high priest in the holy of holies on Yom Kippur, to think about the Temple that must not be entered, not because it is magic and sacred, as Titus believed, but because it is a place apart where one muses on the oddity of a Time that is interrupted each week by the appearance of the same sequence of days and by the works of the men and women who inhabit the world—to think about all that requires other categories or, at least, other images than the one offered by the Christian language, of which the Jews have too often been the prisoners.

I will propose one.

The scene is Moses receiving the law and passing it on to Joshua, who then passes it on to all the others.

And this fact is noted many times in commentary: that Moses is the only human being who saw through a bright glass (*aspaclariameira*), in contrast to the other prophets, who would see what they eventually saw through a glass that functioned as a screen, to dim somewhat the brilliance of the divine message.

The unrivaled perfection of Moses, say the commentaries.

The sublime humility, in the words of the Maharal of Prague, of this man who could be so self-effacing that he no longer formed a screen.

The wonder—say all of the texts that dwell on the inevitable degeneration of the transmission after Moses's moment—of that extraordinarily bright vision of the divine message.

Indeed, most commentators see in that image of the bright glass another way of saying that the divine had never been and would never again be experienced with as much clarity and brilliance.

Except for Rabbeinu Tam, a Frenchman, the disciple and grandson of Rashi, who, it is said, went on hunts with the Count of Champagne accompanied by hawks with silver-sheathed talons.

Yes, Rabbeinu Tam, in the great tradition of the Talmud, raises an apparently trivial objection that will turn everything upside down.

Place yourself, he says, with the finesse of a great analyst, before a bright window.

The light coming through the glass will dazzle and blind you.

It is a glass through which one can see precisely nothing.

The prophets coming after Moses will perhaps see dimly or dreamily, because, between their eyes and their vision will be the substance of the glass acting as a screen; but Moses, because he has no screen, because his window is perfectly clear, sees nothing at all.

The greater the prophecy, the less one sees.

The closer one is to perfection, to wisdom, to sanctity, the less all this has to do with seeing or believing.

That is what Rabbeinu Tam is saying: The greatest, most powerful, and most essential prophetic experience is not that of the existence of God but that of his absence and near nonexistence.

I who write this am infinitely removed from any such perfection.

I am far indeed from living up to the Jewish name or even to my own name.

But I do know one thing, which I will repeat one last time: No Jew, from the most learned to the most ignorant, from the grandest (who is also the smallest) to the smallest (who is also the grandest), is required to "believe in God."

To have a relationship with God through belief is the point of departure, the birth certificate, of Christianity—but, for the Jew, it can be a failing; this surrender to the heart, this recourse to naïve faith on the grounds that it is impossible to know, is a way of deferring intellection, which is the reason the Jews were put here.

And it need not offend Christians, any of them, those who focus on communion and confession or those who, following their hearts, serve the poor, to be reminded that their theology, born out of a relationship both inspired and tragic with the Jewish text and its applications, is not the point of departure for all human stances. There remains one stance, the Jewish, that stubbornly insists: What one knows, one knows; when one knows something, there is no need for belief; and if one believes it, that is because one has stopped trying to know it, one has chosen to save time, to roll the dice to abolish not chance but the need to keep thinking; and this throw of the dice, this leap to which Pascal gave the greatest existential, emotional, and intellectual charge that one can possibly imagine, this leap that was his prodigious and unhappy genius—it is demanded of the Jew above all else not to make it.

EPILOGUE

One last word.

And one last return to Nineveh.

I must admit that I sometimes get tired of Nineveh.

It is not a question of time.

Nor of what changes and what remains.

The lassitude was already occurring, very early on, when my Mukti Bahini companions in the resistance cells of Jessore and Khulna, in Bangladesh, would test me by quoting anti-Semitic verses from the Koran.

No, I am weary of the night that hangs over Nineveh.

Weary of the darkness of the executioners and, sometimes, of the executed.

Tired of telling myself, over and over, that this time we have the real thing, the real Edom, the real Ishmael, the one that Maimonides himself recognized in the enlightenment of Averroës, Avicenna, and Al-Fârâbî.

And always it is the same tale of sound and fury, told by an idiot, signifying nothing.

Sometimes, though, I tell myself that I have understood.

Yes, sometimes I have the feeling of knowing everything that it is humanly possible to know about the lesson of death and life taught by the burned bodies of the Jews of Auschwitz.

Everything that it is humanly possible to understand from the voices of the unnamed, unburied, unnumbered dead of Lviv or Libya—I tell myself that the day will come when I will have understood it.

And, as for the duty of moving toward the other, as for the obligation of the Jew toward the non-Jew, that responsibility-for-the-nations that is so essential to the Jewish person and that we do not always embrace firmly enough, haven't I done my share and more? Haven't I paid my dues? Can't I call myself even?

I have done the tour of Nineveh not once, not twice, but forty times—enough!

On days like that, I tell myself that Jonah was right about not going to preach in the great city.

I tell myself that I understand his resistance, his strange way of balking, of staying in Jaffa, of leaving for Tarshish to hide among the sailors—anything but Nineveh!

And I tell myself that, if you have to remain in the dark, you might as well stay in the wet but (at least initially) agreeable shade of the belly of the whale.

He did not have it too bad there.

It was large enough, spacious enough, for him to be happy there.

Was that not where, after all, he composed his most beautiful song?

"This room isn't so bad," one of his distant descendants will say from a room in Sarajevo where he prefers to keep his own company rather than go out, to play the prophet in Nineveh for the umpteenth time rather than sing.

There is nothing wrong with wanting to be yourself.

A man is more than his deeds, contrary to what the young Sartre and the old Sartre believed.

Once he has done and risked much, is it not time for that other encounter, the last one, which is not necessarily death (or at least not the death that men fear, where their work is halted)?

That is what a great French writer, Michel Leiris, a toreador of sorts, was saying when he confided to me in his last years that, essentially, there is no bull's horn more menacing than a face-to-face encounter with oneself.

That was the thinking, according to the old dame of Torcello in Venice who was one of the last people to speak with him (and who reported it to me), of the great American writer and matador Ernest Hemingway when he said that it was the only appointment one must not miss. Hemingway missed it, alas, several weeks later in Ketchum, Idaho.

And perhaps it was Jonah's last thought as well, the one not reported in the Book because God himself breathed back the answer, not in a whisper but in a spiriting away.

In such moments, I hear the voice of my father, which is the one thing of his that for me has remained alive.

I hear the voice of his own father as well, nearly as alive—I had forgotten it, but now suddenly it has come back to me.

Is he speaking to me or to his son?

Disciplining me or pursuing the endless argument in which father and son engaged?

I hear them calling me by the name they gave me, which is another name for Cistercian solitude.

I hear the angel of that given name and of that family name who, further away in me than I will ever be able to go, whispers that all detours are permitted, because detours are minor matters that take little time, after which we all regain the humble beyond the chimeras of splendor. Ultimately, the last word comes back to the secret name that awaits each of us beyond ourselves and that, one day, must be allowed to speak.

It is indeed to me that they both are speaking.

What are they saying, exactly?

"You have wanted to rescue many people. Now we want you to rescue yourself. We want you, just this once, to leap to the very bot-

tom of the sea into the belly of the whale that you have been out-
smarting by pushing yourself ever closer toward the lands of Nineveh.
We do not want you to visit a dangerous land but to sojourn in (and
not detour from) a dangerous *you,* a vegetative you, a fallen, lost you, a
you severed from the fleeting successes that pose a great danger for
you. There, in that you, we want you to learn from Jonah the art of
singing in the night."

And there is more: "You put your head into the lion's jaws, you
went toe-to-toe with the worst, you entered the labyrinths of terror
and evil? We are here to tell you this: No Maidan, no Tahrir Square,
no forum or gathering place in Burundi or Bosnia was a real lion's
mouth—the real lion's mouth was and will always be your own. You
can't save Nineveh unless you are part Nineveh; you can't preach to
Nineveh if you are incapable of putting yourself in the position of
having forty days to wait, to hang on, and to hope—before being destroyed; Nineveh will be no more than a word or an image unless you
decide one day to go down into the belly of the whale in some manner
and there face yourself, trapped, immobile as time passes, like a plant
half-alive and half-dead, like a lost animal, like a man without reason
or goal, like a wayward question without the answers provided by culture, words, and love—then, alone, with no way out, you will encounter the Jew in you."

And they continue: "On that day, when you are relieved of the fortunes and favors of this world, you will have to resolve to honor your
name, not because it is yours or ours, but because it is the name of one
of the sons of Jacob who did not worship the golden calf, who commanded that another name, that of Dinah, that of his sister and also
of your mother, not be dishonored."

In such moments I think again of Solal's two glories. The vain and
illusory glory of the prince among princes, lord of Samaria, of which
he will be deprived at the appointed time as one snatches a paper
crown from a carnival king. And the other, hidden glory, but true
glory, that of the Jew among Jews, "strangers in their exile" but "firm
in their strangeness," which he regains at the end of the story.

I think of Abraham, alone in the oven of Ur Kasdim, so alone, so fragile on the land that his vision offered him. "I am a stranger and reside with you," he says to the children of Heth in order to purchase the cave of Machpelah in which to bury his wife. And they: "Yes, of course, you are a prince among us; you are a prince of God and here can feel at home." Well they know, these hypocrites, these kings of doublespeak, that a prince of God does not consume much bread. He's not such a big deal and, in any case, he won't cost much. He'll be quiet—until the other glory, the living one, which shines from his pores, becomes too burdensome for those around him; and then they abuse him, spurn him, and the wheel of human anger and violence reengages; and how they are torn apart, the little princes of God, put to death, like Rabbi Akiva, for the sanctification of the Name!

And then I think of Benny Lévy and the trap he set for me (set in the sense of holding up a mirror) on the day when he urged me to go deeper into the joy of study and, in the same breath, extolled what he called my "lordship." It was indeed a mirror. For, obviously, it had been I who had set the trap at the outset. Vanity. Pride. Idolatry of the great and the loud. Relationships with powerful people, carried on without illusions but cultivated all the same: Are they not useful when it comes to obtaining for those who have little as much space as the vast metropolises can offer them? But, still, they will be an obstacle for me— this, I have always known—if I want to go further, to push beyond the bounds of this book and leave for good the path of arrogant men.

I also know that I will have to convene Datan and Aviram one last time, the accomplices of Korah, the anti-Moses conspirators, those servants of nothingness, consumed by use of the wrong language, the sociopolitical language spoken in the palaces where the fate of the world is decided but on which the true salvation of humanity does not depend.

Will I have the strength, one day, to separate myself from them?

The strength to understand that the true glory of the Jews, the glory that is like the light that turns a blade of grass, wet with dew, into the true scepter of the splendor of things, has but one real obstacle:

the false language, the wooden language that, when it burns, produces an acrid fire with sickly flames and a smoke so heavy with soot that it leaves a bitter taste and poisons even the most beautiful of books?

Will my ear be keen enough, against the din of the Sicarites, to hear the voice of Moses?

His law and his voice?

Not only the hard and inflexible law brought from heaven to give wings to ordinary people who know how to use it, but the music of his true voice?

A part of me hopes so.

When exactly, I could not say, because in such matters one cannot prejudge or swear before committing oneself.

But one day, yes, this is my hope.

Even though I well know that I have work yet to do (a little? a lot?) before I, too, will be able to say that my other journey, the present journey, is over.

Even though the world, with its marvels and misery, with its petrified people yearning to live, continues to call to me in a voice that I have never been able to ignore.

And even if I am well aware that, with all that I still need to learn, understand, absorb, and pass on, I am for the time being worth about as much as the little Jew who, in Leonard Cohen's song, thought he had written the Bible.

Other battles await.

Other Ninevehs to which I shall have to report.

But I have all the time in the world.

We always have time, until we are one hundred twenty, to finish learning that a life of mind and spirit is an astounding exception, wrested, not only from the order of death, but also from that of the most noble tasks.

The trip has only just begun.

INDEX

Jerusalem, Grand Mufti of. *See* Husseini, Haj
    Mohammed Amin al-
Jessore, 225
Jesus Christ, 14, 103, 141, 148
Jésus et Israël (Isaac), 30
"Jewish Question—Again, The" (Bernanos), 7
Jewish War, The (Josephus), 142
jihadism, 16, 172–74, 185, 186, 197
Joan of Arc, 81
Job, 141
Joel, 139
John Paul II, Pope, 6, 55
Jonah, 137–56, 157, 158, 217, 226, 227
    lessons of, 178–183, 187–204
Jordan, 173
Josephus, Flavius, 78, 105, 142
Jose the Galilean, 92
Joshua, 79, 222
Journal du voleur (Genet), 15
Journey from Paris to Jerusalem and Back
    (Chateaubriand), 159
Journey to the End of Night (Céline), 90
Joyce, James, 93, 106–7
Judah, kingdom of, 139, 140
Judah, tribe of, 81, 82, 106
Judaic Academy of Saint-Guilhem-le-
    Désert, 82
Judaism. *See also* Torah; Talmud *and specific*
    individuals and biblical figures
    affirmative, 57, 64–68
    beauty in living, 3
    idea of revolution abolished by, 95–111
Judas of Galilee, 80
Judeo-Christianity, 55–58
just war theory, 171

Kabbalah, 89, 92, 106, 123, 128, 130, 131, 136,
    200, 201, 215, 218–19
Kafka, Franz, 93, 106, 126, 134
Kaifeng ghettos, 134
Kant, Immanuel, 64, 96, 126–28, 198, 215
Kantorowicz, Ernst, 48
Kaputt (Malaparte), 178
Karachi, xiii, 186
Karaism, 215
Khmer Rouge, 33, 38, 96, 97, 99, 182
Khulna, 225
Kiev, 168, 179, 181, 185, 203
King, Martin Luther, Jr., 18
Kings, Book of, 80, 138
Klarsfeld, Serge, 38
Koestler, Arthur, 110
Kohath, 129
Kojève, Alexandre, 108, 198, 201–4
Korah, 129–33, 143, 147, 150, 201, 212, 229
Koran, 16, 121, 124–25, 210, 215
Korea, 96
Kriegel, Blandine, 78
Ku Klux Klan, 19, 42
Kurdish people, 17, 39–40, 125, 153, 183–85,
    187

Lacan, Jacques, 95, 101, 120
Lamartine, Alphonse de, 85
Lancelot (de Troyes), 126
Languet, Hubert, 79
Lanzmann, Claude, 24
Lardreau, Guy, 99
Latin language, 71, 73–74, 79, 106, 180
Lautréamont, Comte de, 86, 94
Lavisse, Ernest, 77
Lazare, Bernard, 59
Lebanon, 44, 173
Leipzig Mahzor, 105
Leiris, Michel, 226–27
Lemkin, Raphael, 33
Le Pen, Jean-Marie, 172
Leptis Magna, 186, 203
Levi, Primo, 34–35
Leviathan (Hobbes), 78
Levinas, Emmanuel, x, xiii, 27, 64, 65, 91, 102,
    103, 120, 122, 123, 177, 180, 187, 205, 212,
    217–18
Leviticus, 214
Lévy, André (father), 24, 29, 30, 205–7, 227
Lévy, Armand (uncle), 207
Lévy, Benny, xiii, 100–105, 109–11, 134, 157–
    59, 163, 209, 214–18, 229
Lévy, Chalom, 29
Lévy, grandfather, 205–8, 227
Lévy, Hyamine (uncle), 29
Lévy, Joseph, 29
Lévy, Maklouf (uncle), 29
Lévy, Messaoud (uncle), 29
Libre Parole, La (Drumont), 87
Libya, 18, 41, 160, 163–66, 171–79, 181, 182,
    185–88, 191–98, 203–5, 225
Libyan Jews, 41
Libyan National Transitional Council (NTC),
    164, 165, 171
Ligne, Prince de, 92
Lin Biao, 99
Lindet, Robert, 80
Linhart, Robert, 101
Lippmann family, 92
Lisinitchi Forest massacre, 162
Lithuania, 216
Lives (Plutarch), 77
Lockerbie bombing, 172
Logos, 64
Louis the Pious, King of the Franks, 82
Louis VII, King of France, 81
Louis XVI, King of France, 80, 81
Louvain, sacking of, 182
Luke, Saint, 106
Luria, Isaac, 89, 219
Luther, Martin, 54
Lviv, 160–63, 166–69, 181, 185, 188, 191,
    196–98, 203, 225
Lydda massacre, 14

Macron, Emmanuel, 7
magical thinking, 195–97

ABOUT THE AUTHOR

BERNARD-HENRI LÉVY is a philosopher, journalist, activist, and filmmaker. Among his dozens of books are *American Vertigo, Barbarism with a Human Face,* and *Who Killed Daniel Pearl?* His writing has appeared in a wide range of publications throughout Europe and the United States. His films include the documentaries *Bosna!* and *A Day in the Death of Sarajevo.* Lévy is co-founder of the antiracist group SOS Racisme and has served on diplomatic missions for the French government.